Every increase in elevation brings a decrease in air pressure, which results in a lower boiling point. At 7,000 feet, for example—the altitude of many towns in the Southwest—water boils at 199°F. This means slower cooking times (and makes a pressure cooker a more desirable appliance). Families who have been living in the mountains for years have already discovered, though trial and error, the best ways to adjust.

Newcomers to high altitudes must be patient and experiment to discover what works best. But here are some general rules for high-altitude cooking:

1. For stove-top cooking, use higher heat when practical; extend cooking times as necessary. Beans and grains will require significantly more time than at sea level.

2. Assume that batters and doughs will rise faster than at sea level.

3. Over 3,000 feet, increase baking temperatures by twenty-five degrees.

4. Over 3,000 feet, reduce baking powder (or other leavening) measurements by about ten percent; increase liquid in baked goods by the same percentage. You may want to reduce the amount of sugar slightly as well.

5. For every 2,000 foot increase in altitude above 3,000 feet, reduce leavening even further.

Imperial Measurements

Theoretically, both the United Kingdom and Canada use the metric system, but older recipes rely on the "imperial" measurement system, which differs from standard U.S. measurements in its liquid ("fluid") measurements:

$1/4$ cup = 2.5 ounces
$1/2$ cup ("gill") = 5 ounces
1 cup = 10 ounces
1 pint = 20 ounces
1 quart = 40 ounces

Some Useful Substitutions

1 cup cake flour = $7/8$ cup all-purpose flour + $1/8$ cup cornstarch
1 tablespoon baking powder = 2 teaspoons baking soda + 1 teaspoon cream of tartar
1 cup buttermilk = 1 scant cup milk at room temperature + 1 tablespoon white vinegar
1 cup brown sugar = 1 cup white sugar + 2 tablespoons molasses
1 cup sour cream = 1 cup yogurt (preferably full fat)

Measurement Conversions

Note that volume (i.e., cup) measures and weight (i.e., ounce) measures convert perfectly for liquids only. Solids are a different story; 1 cup of flour weighs only 4 or 5 ounces.

Dash or pinch = less than $1/4$ teaspoon
3 teaspoons = 1 tablespoon
2 tablespoons = 1 fluid ounce
4 tablespoons = $1/4$ cup = 2 fluid ounces
16 tablespoons = 1 cup = 8 fluid ounces
2 cups = 1 pint
2 pints = 1 quart
4 quarts = 1 gallon

Imperial vs. Metric

These are approximate, but are fine for all uses.

1 ounce = 28 grams
1 pound = 500 grams or $1/2$ kilo
2.2 pounds = 1 kilo
1 teaspoon = 5 milliliters (ml)
1 tablespoon = 15 milliliters
1 cup = $1/4$ liter
1 quart = 1 liter

How to Cook *Everything*™

the **basics**

simple recipes anyone can cook

Mark Bittman

Illustrations by Alan Witschonke

Wiley Publishing, Inc.

Published by Wiley Publishing, Inc., New York, NY

For general information on our other products and services or to obtain technical support please contact our Customer Care Department within the U.S. at 800-762-2974, outside the U.S. at 317-572-3993 or fax 317-572-4002.

Wiley also publishes its books in a variety of electronic formats. Some content that appears in print may not be available in electronic books.

Library of Congress Cataloging-in-Publication Data:

Bittman, Mark.
   How to cook everything : the basics : simple recipes anyone can cook /
Mark Bittman ; illustrations by Alan Witschonke.
       p. cm.
Includes index.
   ISBN 0-7645-6756-X (alk. paper)
  1. Cookery. I. Title.
   TX714 .B57322 2003
   641.5—dc21

2002153467

WILEY PUBLISHING, INC.

Publisher: Jennifer Feldman
Executive Editor: Anne Ficklen
Senior Editor: Linda Ingroia
Production Editor: Donna Wright
Cover design: Edwin Kuo and Jeff Faust
Book design: Edwin Kuo, Holly Wittenberg, and Nick Anderson
Manufacturing Buyer: Kevin Watt

Manufactured in the United States of America
10 9 8 7 6 5 4 3 2 1

Table of Contents

ACKNOWLEDGMENTS   iv

WHAT TO KNOW BEFORE YOU BEGIN COOKING   v

1   SALADS AND SOUPS   1

2   PASTA   19

3   FISH   35

4   POULTRY   57

5   MEAT   79

6   GRAINS AND BEANS   101

7   VEGETABLES   117

8   FRUIT DESSERTS AND PIES   139

9   COOKIES AND CAKES   157

10   BREADS AND BREAKFAST   169

GLOSSARY   193

INDEX   203

Acknowledgments

The original *How to Cook Everything* has a lengthy acknowledgments section, so I will keep this brief.

Chief among the people supporting me, in many ways, while I was working on *How to Cook Everything*, were Karen Baar, John Willoughby, Angela Miller, and Jack Bishop. I'd also like to thank (once again!) Pam Anderson, Linda Giuca, Rick Flaste, Trish Hall, Jean-Georges Vongerichten, Jennifer Griffin, Pam Hoenig, Justin Schwartz, Chris Kimball, and my parents, Murray and Gertrude Bittman.

This book owes a huge debt of thanks to Linda Ingroia. Jennifer Feldman, Edwin Kuo, Jeff Faust, Holly Wittenberg, Donna Wright, Helen Chin, and Kevin Watt also played large roles in seeing it produced.

Personally, thanks and love to Doc, John Ringwald, Alisa X. Smith, and especially Emma and Kate.

Mark Bittman
Summer 2002

Dedicated to beginning cooks everywhere

What to Know Before You Begin Cooking

When I first wrote *How to Cook Everything,* I began with this statement: "Anyone can cook, and most everyone should." I no longer believe that "most everyone 'should'" cook, but it's clear that in recent years more people want to learn how. Including you, or you would not have read this far.

Good. Home-cooked food can be easy and fast, and is almost always better for you than anything you buy prepared. We are blessed with supermarket food of reasonably high quality, and an incomparable variety—including imports that were once found only at the swankest shops—at prices so low that visitors from other countries are frequently shocked. Even as a novice home cook, you have the opportunity to create, simply and with minimal effort, a variety of food unparalleled in the history of the world. Really.

And, contrary to what many beginners believe, there are no "secrets" to cooking—only good guidance combined with experience. To begin, you must consider five distinct elements. These are time, ingredients, recipes, equipment, and technique. To take each in turn:

Time

There are few better ways to spend your time than by preparing high-quality food for yourself and those you love. And, as often as not, "convenience" food takes as long to get to the table as real food. For example, it takes no more time to cook many meals than it does to call for a pizza and pick it up, or even wait for it to be delivered. Grilling a piece of meat or fish and steaming a vegetable or preparing a salad is a 20-minute operation; so is making a simple pasta dish. A little forethought makes things go even more smoothly.

Ingredients

It's easy to have the makings of many meals on hand just by maintaining the right mix of staples. Stock your pantry and refrigerator with pasta, rice, and other grains; canned beans and other vegetables, especially tomatoes; spices, and dried herbs when fresh are unavailable; liquid seasonings such as olive oil, vinegar, and soy sauce; eggs, butter, and milk; flour, cornmeal, and the like; onions, potatoes, garlic, and other long-keeping vegetables; and canned stock.

With just these essentials you will be equipped to make dozens of different dishes, from pancakes to pasta. When you throw in the fresh ingredients that you're likely to have in the refrigerator as a result of weekly shopping jaunts—vegetables, herbs, fruit, meat, fish, cheese, and other perishables—you'll be able to prepare entire meals without going out to search for special ingredients.

In general, better ingredients make for simpler cooking. Combining the best ingredients is the easiest way to make great food. An omelet made with farm-fresh eggs, a local chicken roasted with extra virgin olive oil, sliced tomatoes straight from the garden—these are dishes that require almost no skills at all to be delicious.

Recipes

The most important factor in determining whether a cookbook is useful lies in its selection of recipes. This book is the most basic collection of simple, straightforward recipes I could devise, selected from among the 1,500 in *How to Cook Everything*, for their appeal to the beginning cook.

You'll find my top 100 core recipes such as Simple Roast Chicken, plus "Good To Know" recipes such as Black Bean Soup or Baked Sweet Potatoes—simple personal favorites that anyone can make. "Best From Scratch" recipes such as Vinaigrette or Easy Tomato Sauce are basic ingredients, condiments, or sauces used with other recipes. They can be store bought, but in my opinion are always better if homemade.

An important note is that every recipe, regardless of the source, is a series of guidelines. The timing, for example, is always approximate. The rate at which food cooks is dependent on the moisture content and temperature of the food itself; measurements (which are rarely perfectly accurate); heat level (everyone's medium-high heat is not the same, and most ovens are off by 25 degrees in one direction or another); the kind of equipment (some pans conduct heat better than others); even the air temperature. Part of learning how to cook is judging doneness. As you're learning, poke at the food, peek inside it, taste it, and learn what each ingredient looks and feels like when it's done; experienced cooks use time as a rough guideline, but judge doneness by sight, touch, and taste.

Equipment

You can spend tens of thousands of dollars on kitchen equipment, or you can spend a couple of hundred bucks. In any case, try cooking for a while with minimal equipment so that you can discover your preferences and priorities. Perhaps you need three or four skillets, a huge stockpot, and a pie plate, but have no use for cookie cutters or a pizza peel; it depends on what it is you want to eat. Here, then, is a list—with highly personal comments—about what you ought to start with and what you might want to wait for. Items that I consider essential are in red.

Knives

Buy those with high carbon-steel alloy blades, which are easily sharpened and will last a lifetime. Plastic handles are somewhat more durable than wood, and are dishwasher-safe. A good **8-inch chef's knife,** essentially an all-purpose blade, should set you back no more than $30, although you can spend many times that if you like. Buy one that feels good in your hand.

You also need a couple of **paring knives**—3 or 4 inches long—for peeling, trimming, and other precise tasks. Again, buy those that feel good in your hand, and don't spend more than $5 or $6 on each. Serrated blades are best for cutting bread—unless you eat only presliced bread, buy a long, sturdy **bread knife;** this is a good place to economize, since even the $10 models work fine.

Remember this about all knives: Dull ones are dangerous. They slip off the food you're cutting and right onto the closest surface, which may be your finger. Although you must be extremely careful with sharp knives—casual contact will lead to a real cut—at least they go where you want them to.

Skillets and Sauté Pans

No matter what you call them, you need a couple of flat-bottomed pans, with sides that angle out to give you easy access to the food. Copper is undeniably the best material (it conducts heat evenly), but it's expensive and difficult to maintain. Cast iron is very good and quite inexpensive, but it's heavy.

Generally, I prefer heavy-duty aluminum skillets with a non-stick coating. They're lighter and cheaper than anything else, and they do a good job. Non-stick coatings, while not perfect, are extremely forgiving, a real bonus for less experienced cooks.

If aluminum pans are not good-looking enough for you (a real possibility), you can go with stainless steel, which is more expensive but attractive. Be aware, though, that you'll probably be spending a lot more money for it. Do not be tempted by inexpensive stainless steel, which is a poor conductor of heat; all good stainless steel pans have a layer of copper or aluminum on their bottom and sides or sandwiched between two layers of steel. Stainless steel with a non-stick coating is a good, if fairly expensive, option.

Buy skillets as you need them, rather than in sets with saucepans. Start with two **skillets:** one **10 inches** in diameter ("medium") and one **12 inches** in diameter ("large"). When you're ready to make omelets, or fry a single egg, you'll want an 8-inch pan ("small" to "medium") as well. Pay attention to the handles: They should be riveted on and feel comfortable and sturdy. Although you can't judge this in the store, they should remain fairly cool when cooking on the stove top. Also, you want handles that are ovenproof—you should be able to put any skillet in the oven, and you frequently will. This means no plastic.

Lids for skillets are essential; the advantage of aluminum is that they are inexpensive. Many are interchangeable; you need not buy a new lid for every pan you own.

Saucepans and Pots

Here you have more leeway, because the non-stick issue is less important. (Because you cook mostly liquids in saucepans, preventing sticking is simply a matter of paying attention and making sure that all the liquid doesn't evaporate.) Stainless steel is a good choice, as are aluminum or cast iron with a baked-on porcelain coating. You can also use aluminum pans with non-stick coatings. (Uncoated aluminum is generally not a good idea, because the metal will react with acidic ingredients.)

You need at least one pot large enough to cook pasta; an **8-quart pot** is big enough for this and most tasks other than making stock. If you're going to make stock, get a 16-quart stockpot. Then get two or three **smaller saucepans** to start with—a small one (2 or 3 cups), a medium one (1 to 1½ quarts), and a large one (around 4 quarts). Build from there—a large meal will use up all of your pots, so if you're going to cook regularly you'll eventually need at least six or eight.

Baking Dishes, Roasting Pans, and Pastry Pans

Begin with a simple **8 × 12-inch** or **9 × 13-inch metal roasting pan** and an **8-inch square** or **9-inch square metal baking pan.** They will meet most of your initial needs—you can roast a chicken, broil meat, bake quick breads or brownies, make macaroni and cheese, and more—and you can always add to your collection. Any metal except uncoated aluminum is fine; aluminum with a non-stick coating is also good.

Baking sheets, pie plates, bread (loaf) pans, muffin tins, cake pans, tart pans, and the like are all for special uses; none is likely to be essential in your daily cooking, but all are critical when you need them. The sole exception is probably the baking sheet—it's great for broiling, especially if it has a small lip. Go with aluminum; for most purposes, uncoated will be okay here, but non-stick coating never hurts.

As for the others:

- **Pie plates:** Start with one, 9 inches across; ovenproof glass is very nice. Add an 8-inch and a 10-inch when you need them.
- **Loaf pans:** You need two, 9 × 5 inches or thereabouts. Non-stick aluminum is best.
- **Muffin tins:** Cheap aluminum ones, with non-stick coating, are fine. Antiques of cast iron are much more attractive.
- **Cake pans:** For layer cakes, 9 inches across. You need two or three.
- **Tart pans:** May be metal (removable rims are good) or ceramic; the latter is preferable because it will not interact with acidic tart ingredients, as will most made of metal.

And more . . .

Bowls

Start with **small, medium,** and **large bowls.** Stainless steel bowls are cheap and extremely useful. If you want attractive serving bowls, buy them, but don't use them for mixing, because you will inevitably chip them.

Cutting Boards

Whether it's of plastic or wood is your choice. Plastic can go in the dishwasher, wood is more attractive.

To keep your cutting board from sliding around on the counter, place a damp towel under it; it took me 20 years of cooking to learn this trick, so if you start now you're way ahead of the game.

Spoons, Spatulas, and Other Utensils

Wooden spoons have a pleasant feel and do not absorb much heat; they're best for stove-top use. **Large stainless steel spoons** are best for serving and transferring wet food from one container to another. **A slotted spoon** is essential, as is a **ladle**. Rubber spatulas are handy—especially the spoon-shaped ones. You need **two metal spatulas:** one narrow (for loosening all around the rim of cakes) and one wide (for turning pancakes). A pair of large metal tongs (get the spring-loaded, rather than tension-driven, variety) is very useful for turning foods.

A set of **measuring spoons** is essential; two are even better, because one is always dirty at just the wrong moment. Same with measuring cups: two sets are better than one. Start with a **2-cup glass or plastic cup for liquids,** and a **set of** $^1/_4$- **to 1-cup dry measures** (they're not the same thing).

Anything with holes in it to drain liquid or force through pureed food is a **strainer**. A colander is the first order of business, and you probably need it right away, because it's hard to drain pasta without one. Soon, though, if not immediately, you'll also want a fine-meshed strainer as well, and probably two—one large, one small.

A scale is not essential, but as you progress in your cooking you will find it useful.

Beyond a can opener, you also may need:

- **Cheese grater:** A sturdy box grater is best.
- **Instant-read thermometer:** The most accurate way to determine whether food is done, especially for inexperienced cooks.
- **Timer:** May be manual or electronic; some electronic types allow you to time several things at once, a definite plus if you can figure out how the things work.
- **Vegetable peeler:** The new U-shaped ones are best. Absolutely essential.
- **Whisks:** Start with a medium-sized, stiff whisk, and build from there.
- **Brushes:** Great for spreading oil, melted butter, marinades, etc. Start with a 1-inch brush, and buy it at the paint store, where it'll be much cheaper.
- **Rolling pin:** Buy a straight rolling pin without ball bearings; it's lighter, more easily maneuvered, and unbreakable.
- **Salad spinner:** Nice item, and not only for drying salad greens. It's excellent for dunking anything that you want to rinse and drain repeatedly. Not essential but close.

A time-saver you use once a year is probably not worth having. Because there are few kitchen tasks that cannot be accomplished with what you already have on hand, it doesn't really pay to make a fetish of gadgets. I say it again: Buy things as you need them.

Appliances and Electric Gadgets

Now we're on to the big-ticket items. There are several that everyone should have, and several that no one should have, but most are judgment calls determined by what you cook. Here's a list of appliances in my order of priority.

- **Food processor:** Hands down the most important electric tool in the kitchen. It can grate massive amounts of almost anything in seconds; it can make bread dough, pie dough, even some cookie batters, in a minute; it can grind meat, puree vegetables, slice potatoes. If you have one, use it (I rely on it heavily, although not exclusively, in my recipes). If you don't, make the investment as soon as you can; there are very good ones available for less than $200, and if you cook a lot you will use it daily. Get a large one, a model that can handle at least 6 cups of batter or dough.

- **Electric mixer:** If you bake a lot, you will want both a powerful standing mixer and a small, handheld mixer. If you bake occasionally, you will want either. If you never bake, you still could use a hand mixer or an eggbeater for the occasional egg white or whipped cream.

- **Blender:** Perhaps not for everyone, but if you make a lot of soups and want to make some of them creamy, this is the tool. Also great for any blended drink (most food processors leak if loaded up with liquid). Immersion blenders are handy, too, but not as powerful.

- **Pressure cooker:** For people in a hurry. Pressure cookers don't make anything better than regular cookware, they just make it faster. If you are short on time and big on stews, soups, stocks, or beans, it's a worthwhile investment. If you can take time to cook, or don't like slow-simmered foods, don't bother.

- **Coffee/spice grinder:** If you drink coffee, you probably have one of these. But even if you don't, consider it a wise $10 investment. Freshly ground spices are a real joy, and this takes the work out of them.

- **Microwave:** This is a useful but hardly indispensable tool, for warming, melting, and defrosting.

Technique

Correct technique comes with good instruction combined with practice. Sometimes good technique is everything. A skillet, for example, must be hot before butter is added in order for the butter to sizzle without burning, so that it can sear and crisp the food that is in turn added to it. This cannot be learned in an instant; you must get used to preheating the pan before adding the butter, you must judge the correct level of heat on your particular stove, you must learn to be ready at the right moment. If you haven't done this before, there's no reason to expect to be good at it right away.

On the other hand, there are some techniques you can ignore altogether. Most people who learned to cook from their parents, or from cookbooks, never learned the "correct" way to slice or dice an onion. Chefs tease me all the time about my own technique. Yet although this may mean that it takes me ten seconds longer to do it than it would otherwise, and that my pieces are not exactly uniform, it does not affect the flavor (or in most cases even the appearance) of my finished dishes. That's what counts.

In fact, there are only a few basic, master techniques in cooking, and most have been the cornerstones of cuisine for centuries.

The Basics of Heat

Most beginning cooks fail to get sauté pans and ovens hot enough; but they make grills too hot. When you're pan-grilling or sautéing, you should get used to preheating your skillet for a minute or two before you start to cook. Likewise with an oven. Yes, preheating ovens is a common practice, and a good one. But 350°F is not hot enough to brown most meats in an oven; you need high heat, 450°F and higher, if you want to put a nice crust on the food you're cooking, whether it's bread or chicken.

If you have an electric range, you've probably been told that it's impossible to cook well with it. But heat is heat. The disadvantage of an electric range is that its elements take time to respond—they're slow to heat up, and equally slow to cool down. All this means is that you have to plan ahead. If you want to start cooking over high heat, turn a burner to high a few minutes before you're ready to cook. If you know that you're going to want to transfer that skillet to low heat after an initial searing, have another burner ready at low, or medium-low heat, and simply move

the skillet. It's as if you're cooking on a stove top that has hot and cold spots, rather than on an infinitely flexible burner.

The Basics of Grilling and Broiling

Grilling (and broiling) are the only methods that use direct heat—nothing but a thin layer of air separates the heat source from the food. This virtually guarantees a crisp crust quickly.

The main idea behind both of these techniques is to get a slightly charred crust on the food's exterior while cooking the interior to the desired degree of doneness. Generally, the best foods to grill or broil are less than an inch thick; thicker foods tend to burn on the outside before they are fully cooked inside.

But you can also grill or broil thicker cuts. In the broiler, just move the food farther from the heat source so it browns a little more slowly, turning occasionally and giving it time to cook through.

On the grill, start thicker cuts close to the flame and move them a few inches away after the initial browning. If you can raise the rack to 4 inches, you have effectively lowered the heat below 400°F, a good place to cook bone-in chicken, for example. If you can't raise the rack, move the food to a cooler part of the grill.

Or, on many grills, you can use indirect heat to finish cooking larger pieces of meat. After an initial searing, bank the coals to one side (on a gas grill, lower the heat, or turn one of the burners off) and move the food to the cool side of the grill; then cover the grill. To try grilling, see Grilled Steak, American-Style, page 80.

A couple of notes about the broiler:

- Always preheat it. If your electric broiler requires the oven door to remain open in order to stay on, preheat the oven to 500°F, then preheat the broiler, and broil with the door open.

- Generally, you will broil 2 to 6 inches away from the heat source, the closer distance for thin, quickly cooked foods, the greater distance for thick, slowly cooked foods.

The Basics of Roasting

Like grilling and broiling, roasting uses dry heat; the difference is that it does so in a closed environment, and the heat is indirect. Most roasting should be done at high heat—450°F or higher—and, at its best, crisps up the exterior of foods without much danger of burning, while cooking the interior relatively slowly.

Electric ovens tend to be more accurate than gas ovens, but both are unreliable. A difference of 25 degree doesn't matter much when you're roasting a large piece of meat (although it will affect your timing), but it can be a killer when you're making a delicate dessert. Buy an oven thermometer, and use it. To try roasting, see Roasted Root Vegetables, page 138.

The Basics of Sautéing

Sauté is French for "jump," and simply refers to food that is cooked in a hot pan with some amount of fat. Whether that fat is $1/2$ cup of butter or 1 tablespoon of olive oil, naturally, has an effect on the finished product.

Traditionally, the fat used in sautéing served two purposes: to crisp the coating, and to prevent the food from sticking to the pan. Thanks to non-stick pans, however, you can use just enough fat to provide some sizzle. But regardless of the amount or type of fat you use, sautéing can put a crust on food. The simplest, most straightforward sauté begins by dredging thin slices of meat or fish in flour, bread crumbs, or other seasonings; the food is then cooked over high heat, in hot fat, for 10 minutes or less. To try it, see Sautéed Chicken Cutlets, page 60. Sautéing has a couple of advantages: Properly done, sautéing does not dry food out, and it gives you a base on which you can easily build a sauce (see Reduction Sauce or Pan Gravy, page 62).

Pan-grilling: Non-stick pans have led to an increase in what is often called "pan-grilling"—cooking over high heat, in a skillet, with no added fat. (It is not truly grilling because the food is not cooked by direct heat.) For some very sturdy foods with even surfaces, such as steaks, pan-grilling can be done in a heavy cast-iron skillet as well. You should only try pan-grilling with thin, quickly cooked foods (not, for example, with bone-in chicken), and you should only try it if you have a good exhaust fan.

The Basics of Stir-Frying

Stir-frying is similar to sautéing in that food is cooked over high heat in a small amount of fat, but food to be stir-fried is cut up before cooking, which further minimizes cooking time. Liquid is added during the cooking; and stir-fries are most often associated with Asian flavorings, while sautés are European. The design of a wok is not well suited to most home ranges; a large, deep-sided skillet, with sloping sides is best.

To stir-fry successfully, you must have all your ingredients ready and at hand; once you begin cooking, there will be virtually no time to dig things out of the cabinet or refrigerator and begin measuring them. In addition, you must use very high heat; set your burner on "high" and leave it there. (If, however, at any point during the cooking you feel that things have gotten out of control, turn off the heat and think for a minute. You will not ruin anything by doing so.) To try stir-frying, see Stir-Fried Chinese Noodles with Vegetables, page 32.

The Basics of Deep-Frying

Deep-frying is the most challenging cooking method for home cooks, not because it is difficult—it's actually quite straightforward, given a few simple rules—but because it is invariably messy (and usually smelly).

The rules of deep-frying are simple: The oil must reach a good temperature to brown the exterior of the food quickly, while cooking it. That temperature is almost always between 350°F and 375°F—365°F is a good all-purpose compromise—and is most easily measured by using a frying thermometer. You can use small amounts of oil in narrow pots to deep-fry—for example, it only takes a couple of cups of oil to gain a height of 2 or 3 inches in a small saucepan. But the disadvantage of this is that you can only cook small bits of food, and not very many of them at once.

It's essential to avoid crowding when deep-frying. The food must be surrounded by bubbling oil, and you must keep the temperature from falling too much. So the basic recommendations are: use plenty of oil (although, to prevent the oil from bubbling over, never fill the pot more than halfway); dry the food well with paper towels before adding it to the pot, in order to reduce spattering; and add the food in small increments to keep the temperature from plummeting. To try it, see Fried Chicken, page 64.

The Basics of Cooking in Liquid: Braising, Stewing, Poaching, Steaming, and Parboiling

Cooking in liquid is useful and easy, and no other technique is as efficient at tenderizing. There are several different ways to use liquid in cooking:

- **Braising:** Begins like sautéing—you brown the food in a bit of fat. But it continues when you add liquid to the pan, cover it, and finish the cooking over moist, low heat. It's the ideal way to cook larger cuts of meat, or big chunks, especially those that need tenderizing, such as certain lean cuts of beef or veal, or those that might dry out if cooked otherwise, such as chicken parts.
- **Stewing:** Like braising, but usually with no initial browning (although this is not an iron-clad rule) and with more liquid. To try it, see Classic Beef Stew, page 82.

- **Poaching/Simmering/Boiling:** Cooking food through in water (or lightly flavored water or even stock) to cover. Usually the temperature is moderated so that the water just bubbles during cooking; you want to start it at the boiling point, or a little below, but moderate it. Temperatures can be controlled not only by raising and lowering the heat of the burner, but also by partially covering the pot. See Pears Poached in Red Wine, page 142.

- **Steaming:** Cooking over—not in—liquid; the liquid is usually water, and is usually not used in the finished dish. You can use a bamboo steamer, or a collapsible steamer insert, or simply elevate the food above the simmering water by building a little platform for it, using metal chopsticks or a couple of upside-down cups. In any case, keep the water simmering, not rapidly boiling, and make sure it does not boil away—add boiling water to the pot if necessary. See Steamed Corn, page 125.

- **Parboiling/Blanching:** Here, you partially cook food, usually vegetables, in boiling water to cover. This is an excellent technique for keeping vegetables bright and partially tenderizing them, detailed in the Vegetables chapter (page 117).

1 | Salads and Soups

Salads and soups are natural starters for any meal, but can also be satisfying enough for a main course.

Salads, in particular, are among the quickest dishes to prepare, especially if you take advantage of three basic facts:

- Because most salads are cold, many of the ingredients can be prepared in advance, and leftovers can readily be thrown into the mix.
- Most salad dressings—especially vinaigrettes, which contain little more than oil and vinegar—keep for at least a few days, and often longer, as long as they're refrigerated.
- Anything you want to call a salad is a salad, from canned tuna mixed with bottled mayonnaise to a variety of exotic greens tossed with oil and vinegar.

To make salad, you need good-tasting extra-virgin olive oil, and decent vinegar—like sherry vinegar, balsamic vinegar, or well-made wine vinegar. You usually need good greens, too, and now, even in winter you can find more than a dozen greens for sale, from the standards—iceberg, green leaf, red leaf, romaine, and Boston lettuces—to radicchio, arugula, chard, watercress, endive, chicory, escarole, frisée, mesclun, and a slew of prepacked salad mixes.

Salads can be as simple as a combination of these greens (they can be a single green, for that matter), or they can contain a variety of other vegetables. Generally, all ingredients should be really at their peak, as they will be featured raw and only lightly seasoned. (There are exceptions, though: Canned chickpeas or roasted peppers are usually quite good in salads, though not quite as good as those you prepare yourself.)

Making soup is among the most satisfying of kitchen tasks. In many instances, it is also the least precise, which makes it the easiest and most fun. It's almost impossible to make "bad" soup: At its most basic, you start with water, add some means of making it taste better—usually meat, poultry, fish, or aromatic vegetables, along with seasonings—and finish with a few (or a slew of) vegetables and/or grains.

There are some basic techniques that make soup better. But the point is that although soup-making may conjure up an image of huge pots containing hundreds of ingredients simmering all day long, that need not be the case. You can make a batch of soup in the same amount of time it takes to make many other dinner dishes; the process need not be elaborate or especially time-consuming.

The Best and Simplest Green Salad

Makes 4 servings • **Time:** 10 minutes

Almost any combination of greens can make a salad, and you don't have to get fussy about dressings, either. Many are simply dressed with freshly squeezed lemon juice or vinegar, olive oil, and salt and fresh pepper, all to taste. Substitute any vinaigrette or other dressing you like for the oil and vinegar.

For flavor and texture, try adding any of the following: nuts or seeds, crumbled or chopped if necessary; fresh herbs, torn into pieces; sliced pears, apples, or other fruit; cooked beans; thinly sliced celery or fennel; very thinly sliced Parmesan (use a vegetable peeler to produce thin curls) or other hard cheese.

> 4 to 6 cups torn assorted salad greens (trimmed, washed, and dried)
>
> 1/4 to 1/3 cup extra-virgin olive oil or walnut oil
>
> 1 or 2 tablespoons balsamic vinegar or sherry vinegar
>
> Pinch salt, plus more to taste
>
> Freshly ground black pepper to taste (optional)

Place the greens in a bowl and drizzle them with oil, vinegar, and a pinch of salt. Toss and taste. Correct seasoning, add pepper if desired, and serve.

Shopping Tip: Iceberg lettuce keeps brilliantly, romaine only slightly less so, because the outer leaves keep the inner ones moist. Loose leaf lettuces should be used more quickly. Store all greens in plastic, loosely wrapped, in the refrigerator. Use them as soon as you can, though all but the most delicate will keep well for several days.

Preparation Tip: To wash and dry greens, place them in a colander set in a bowl (or, better still, a salad spinner). Fill with water and lift the colander out; repeat until the water contains no traces of dirt. Dry with the salad spinner or let drip and then dry with towels. You don't have to get obsessive about drying, but the dressing won't stick to really wet greens—it'll just sink to the bottom of the bowl. Though some greens are "pre-washed," I'd wash them, too.

Simple Greek Salad: A bright-tasting salad. Toss together 4 to 6 cups torn mixed greens (at least some should be strong-tasting) with 1/4 cup cleaned and chopped radish; 1/4 cup minced fresh mint leaves or mint mixed with parsley; 1/4 cup chopped feta cheese, or more to taste; and 1/4 cup pitted and chopped black olives. Drizzle with olive oil and freshly squeezed lemon juice to taste.

Vinaigrette

Makes 1 cup • **Time:** 5 minutes

Traditionally, vinaigrettes are an emulsion of vinegar and oil. When emulsified (thoroughly blended) the dressing has a creamier texture, but this is not essential. I often just toss everything in a bowl and whisk it for thirty seconds or so.

> $^1/_4$ cup good vinegar, such as sherry, balsamic, or high-quality red or white wine, plus more to taste
>
> $^1/_2$ teaspoon salt, plus more if needed
>
> $^1/_2$ teaspoon Dijon mustard (optional)
>
> $^3/_4$ cup extra-virgin olive oil, plus more if needed
>
> 2 teaspoons minced shallots (optional)
>
> Freshly ground black pepper to taste

1 Briefly mix the vinegar, salt, and optional mustard with an immersion blender, food processor or blender, or with a fork or wire whisk.

2 Slowly add the oil in a stream (drop by drop if whisking) until an emulsion forms; or just whisk everything together briefly. Add the remaining oil faster, but still in a stream.

3 Taste to adjust salt and add more oil or vinegar if needed. Add the shallots and pepper. This is best made fresh but will keep, refrigerated, for a few days; bring back to room temperature before using.

The Basics of Vinaigrette

The most common dressing for salad is vinaigrette. A vinaigrette is acid and oil, combined. The acid may be freshly squeezed citrus juice, usually lemon or lime, or vinegar—the best you can find.

The oil, most often olive, also may be a nut oil or a neutral vegetable oil. Rancid oils, no matter what their origin, can ruin vinaigrette. Smell oil before adding it to avoid this; you'll know when its taste will be negative rather than positive. Store all oil, except for that you will be using within a week or two, in the refrigerator.

I recommend starting with a ratio of two parts oil to one part vinegar or other acid. You may end up with three or even four to one; you may end up at one to one, especially when you replace the vinegar with lemon juice. It's a matter of taste.

Emulsified vinaigrettes are creamier, and marginally more pleasing texturally, than vinegar and oil separately. Food processors and blenders make perfectly emulsified vinaigrettes. These emulsions are stable for hours and sometimes longer, so they're especially nice for buffets.

Caesar Salad

Makes 4 servings • **Time:** 20 minutes

The essentials in a great Caesar salad are garlic, egg, lemon juice, anchovies, and real Parmesan. Compromise on any of these and you'll still have a good salad, but you won't have a great Caesar.

1 clove garlic, cut in half

2 eggs, or substitute $1/2$ cup pasteurized egg product

2 tablespoons freshly squeezed lemon juice

6 tablespoons extra-virgin olive oil

2 tablespoons minced anchovies, or to taste

Dash Worcestershire sauce

Salt and freshly ground black pepper to taste

1 large head romaine lettuce, trimmed, washed, dried, and torn into bits

Baked Croutons (page 13)

$1/2$ to 1 cup freshly grated Parmesan cheese

1 Rub the inside of your salad bowl with the garlic clove; discard the clove.

2 Bring a small pot of water to a boil. Pierce a tiny hole in the broad end of each egg with a pin or a needle and boil them for 60 to 90 seconds; they will just begin to firm up. Crack them into the salad bowl, making sure to scoop out the white that clings to the shell.

3 Beat the eggs with a fork, gradually adding the lemon juice and then the olive oil, beating all the while.

4 Stir in the anchovies and the Worcestershire. Taste and add salt if needed and plenty of pepper. Toss well with the lettuce; top with the croutons and Parmesan, then bring to the table and toss again. Serve immediately.

Shopping Tip: Anchovies keep forever, so feel free to buy a big jar or can if they're higher in quality or lower in price; once opened, refrigerate it. Be sure to buy anchovies packed in olive (not other) oil. Or buy salted anchovies; these must be rinsed and de-boned before using.

Tomato, Mozzarella, and Basil Salad

Makes 4 servings • **Time: 5 to 15 minutes**

This salad is barely more than the three ingredients listed in the title, so all three must be of excellent quality. I like to salt the tomatoes a little bit before assembling the salad—it removes a little of their excess liquid—but it isn't strictly necessary.

> 4 medium perfectly ripe tomatoes
>
> Salt to taste
>
> 8 ($^1/_4$-inch-thick) slices fresh mozzarella, plus more if desired
>
> 8 basil leaves, washed and dried
>
> Freshly ground black pepper to taste
>
> Extra-virgin olive oil for drizzling

1 Core and cut the tomatoes into about $^1/_4$-inch-thick slices. If you like, lay them on a board and sprinkle them lightly with salt. Set the board at an angle so the liquid can drain into the sink (or a bowl; it makes a refreshing drink).

2 Layer tomatoes, mozzarella, and basil on a platter or four individual plates. Sprinkle with salt and pepper, drizzle with olive oil, and serve.

The Basics of Vegetable Salads

We first think of salads as green, but other vegetables cooked in advance, lightly dressed and served cold or at room temperature, can be wonderful, easy, and even impressive in salads. It doesn't take much to turn the everyday carrot into a salad course that may become the star of the meal. Many of the simple recipes in the Vegetables chapter such as Steamed Corn (page 125) or Sautéed Summer Squash or Zucchini (page 136) can be chilled and dressed with any vinaigrette.

Classic American Potato Salad

Makes 4 servings
Time: 30 minutes, plus cooling time

Especially good with homemade mayonnaise (see next page), which can be made in 10 minutes.

1¹/₂ pounds waxy potatoes,
such as red new potatoes

¹/₂ cup minced fresh parsley leaves

¹/₄ cup minced onion

Mayonnaise to taste (start with ¹/₂ cup)

Salt and freshly ground black pepper
to taste

1 Bring a medium pot of water to a boil; salt it. Peel the potatoes if you like (or wash and scrub them well), then cut them into bite-size pieces; cook them in the water until tender but still firm and not at all mushy, 15 minutes or so. Drain, rinse in cold water for a minute, then drain again.

2 Toss the still-warm potatoes with the parsley and onion. Add mayonnaise until the mixture is as creamy as you like. Season with salt and pepper and refrigerate until ready to serve. (You may prepare the salad in advance up to this point; cover and refrigerate for up to 1 day, then bring to room temperature before serving.)

Shopping Tip: A "new" potato is a waxy potato; it's not necessarily red-skinned, but it is necessarily lower in starch, so it will hold together well during boiling. Starchy potatoes (see page 130) are best for baking.

Five Simple Additions to Classic American Potato Salad

1. Minced fresh herbs especially chives, to taste.

2. Minced red pepper, fresh or roasted (or used canned pimentos).

3. Cooked fresh peas.

4. Crumbled crisp bacon.

5. Minced Hard-Boiled Egg (page 181).

Mayonnaise

Makes 1 cup • Time: 10 minutes

You may wonder "Why make mayonnaise when I can buy it?" but when you taste home-made, you'll know. And with simple additions, it's the base of delicious dressings and dips.

With the food processor or blender you can make perfect mayonnaise in 10 minutes the first time you try it. Remember, however, you need a total of 2 tablespoons of liquid for the emulsion to work. If you don't have lemon juice, which is the perfect liquid, use half vinegar and half water; if you use all vinegar its flavor will dominate.

    1 egg or egg yolk
    Dash cayenne
    $1/2$ teaspoon dry mustard
    Salt and freshly ground black pepper
    to taste
    2 tablespoons freshly squeezed lemon
    juice, or white wine, or Champagne
    or other vinegar mixed half and half
    with water
    1 cup extra-virgin olive oil, or canola
    or other neutral oil, or a combination,
    or more if needed

1 Combine the egg, cayenne, mustard, salt, pepper, lemon juice, and $1/4$ cup of the oil in the container of a blender or food processor; turn on the machine and, with the machine running, add the oil in a thin, steady stream.

2 After you've added about half of the oil, the mixture will thicken; you can then begin adding the oil a bit faster. You can add up to $1^1/2$ cups of oil and still have a pleasant, yellow (or pale yellow, if you included the egg white) mayonnaise. If the mixture is thicker than you'd like, add a little warm water, with the machine still running, or stir in a little cream or sour cream by hand. Check the seasoning and serve or store in the refrigerator for up to a week.

Garlic Mayonnaise (Aioli): Serve with fish, or as a dip for vegetables, or as a sauce for any simple cooked food. Add 1 to 4 whole peeled cloves of garlic at the beginning. If you like, add a small (no larger than 1 inch thick in any direction) boiled and peeled potato to the mixture at the start for extra body. Thin as necessary with cream, stock, or water.

Real Tartar Sauce: Stir $1/4$ cup of minced sour pickles (preferably cornichons) and 1 table-spoon minced shallots or scallions into fin-ished mayonnaise. Add prepared horseradish to taste.

Spicy Coleslaw

Makes about 2 quarts • **Time:** 20 minutes

More interesting, more flavorful, and far less fat-laden than traditional coleslaw, which is mayonnaise based. Dijon is the mustard of choice here, though you can substitute whole-grain mustard if you like it; steer clear of ordinary yellow or brown mustards.

2 tablespoons Dijon mustard

2 tablespoons sherry or balsamic vinegar

1/2 cup olive, peanut, or vegetable oil

1 tablespoon sugar

6 cups cored and shredded Napa, Savoy, green, and/or red cabbage

2 red bell peppers, stemmed, peeled if desired, seeded, and diced

1 cup diced scallions

Salt and freshly ground black pepper to taste

1/4 cup minced fresh parsley leaves

1 Whisk together the mustard and vinegar in a small bowl; add the oil a little at a time, whisking all the while.

2 Add sugar and whisk to dissolve.

3 Combine the cabbage, peppers, and scallions, and toss with the dressing. Season with salt and pepper and refrigerate until ready to serve (it's best to let this rest for an hour or so before serving to allow the flavors to mellow; you can let it sit longer, up to 24 hours, if you like). Just before serving, toss with parsley.

Shopping Tip: The best head cabbage is Savoy, the light green variety with crinkled leaves; if you can't find it, the standard tight, smooth, light green cabbage will do. Napa (also spelled Nappa) cabbage, a kind of "Chinese" cabbage, is a good romaine-like variety, terrific for raw salads and coleslaw. Reject any cabbages with yellow leaves, loose leaves, or those which are soft or not tightly packed.

Cooking Tip: If you're not using cabbage fresh for coleslaw, you can also braise, stir-fry, or sauté it. Simmering is also fine, but not for hours in the old "corned-beef-and-cabbage" style. Rather, separate the cabbage into leaves and plunge it into lots of boiling salted water until tender, 3 to 5 minutes. Then drain and serve, simply salted, or drain and reheat according to Precooked Vegetables in Butter or Oil (page 118). It's done when crisp-tender to soft, but not mushy.

CORING AND SHREDDING CABBAGE

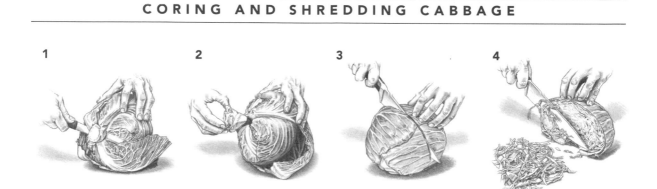

(Steps 1–2) The easiest way to core a head of cabbage is to cut a small cone-shaped section from the bottom, then remove it. **(Step 3)** To shred head cabbage, first cut it into manageable pieces. **(Step 4)** Cut thin sections across the head; they'll naturally fall into shreds. If the shreds are too long, just cut across them.

Minestrone

Makes 4 servings • Time: 45 minutes to 1 hour

Essentially vegetable soup, best made with a little bit of prosciutto. Consider this recipe a series of suggestions, rather than something ironclad; you can make minestrone with any vegetables you have on hand.

4 tablespoons extra-virgin olive oil

1 medium onion, minced

1 carrot, peeled and diced

1/2 cup minced prosciutto or other ham (optional)

4 cups assorted mixed vegetables, cut into small cubes if necessary: potatoes, carrots, corn, peas, string beans, cooked dried beans (cranberry beans, or borlotti, are traditional), celery, zucchini or summer squash, pumpkin or winter squash, leeks, parsnips, turnips, etc.

Salt and freshly ground black pepper to taste

5 cups Quickest Chicken Stock (page 17) or store-bought chicken, beef, or vegetable broth, or water, preferably warmed

10 sprigs fresh parsley, more or less

1 cup cored, peeled, seeded, and chopped tomatoes (canned are fine; include their juice)

Freshly grated Parmesan cheese

1 Place 3 tablespoons of the oil in a large, deep saucepan or casserole and turn the heat to medium. A minute later, add the onion and carrot. Cook, stirring, until the onion softens, about 5 minutes. Add the ham if you're using it and cook, stirring, another 3 minutes.

2 Add the remaining vegetables, season with salt and pepper (go easy on the salt if you've included ham), and cook, stirring, for 1 minute. Add the stock or water, parsley, and tomatoes and turn the heat to medium-low. Cook, stirring every now and then, until the vegetables are very soft, about 30 minutes. (You may prepare the soup in advance up to this point. Cover, refrigerate for up to 2 days, and reheat before proceeding.)

3 Sprinkle with the remaining olive oil and serve, passing the cheese at the table.

Shopping Tip: Homemade chicken stock is always preferable to canned, but you may not have homemade whenever needed. Canned broth is fine in most instances, and, unfortunately, there is no superior brand at this writing; they're all just a little bit better than using water, which is another option.

Beef and Vegetable Soup: Replace the ham with 1/2 pound minced beef (leftover beef stew is not only okay but preferable). Use beef stock if possible.

Five Simple Additions to Vegetable Soups

1. Small pieces of rind from Parmesan cheese, or grated cheese.

2. Any leftover bits of cooked meat.

3. Freshly chopped herbs or quick-cooking greens.

4. Any spice you like, from jalapeños or other chiles to lots of black pepper to curry powder or other spice mixtures.

5. Baked Croutons (page 13).

PREPARING ONIONS

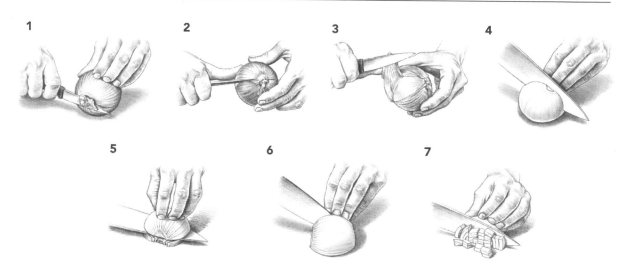

(Step 1) Cut off both ends of the onion. **(Steps 2–3)** Then make a small slit in the skin, just one layer down. The peel will come off easily. **(Step 4)** Cut the onion in half. **(Step 5)** Make two or three cuts parallel to the cutting board into the vegetable; don't cut all the way through. **(Step 6)** Now make several cuts down through the top of the vegetable. Again leave the vegetable intact at one end. **(Step 7)** Cut across the vegetable to create dice. Chop the dice even smaller to mince.

Cream of Broccoli (or Any Vegetable) Soup

Makes 4 servings • **Time:** 30 minutes

There are thousands of recipes for true cream of vegetable soups, but the differences among them are subtle at best. Basically, you cook the vegetable you want with good flavorings until it's done. Then you puree it and reheat it with cream. The addition of rice or potatoes makes the soup smooth and creamy without outrageous amounts of cream. One-quarter cup is enough to lighten the color and smooth the texture; 1 full cup lends an incomparable richness.

The options:

- The original cooking liquid may be water or milk, but it's best if it is stock.
- The cream may be replaced by milk or yogurt—but again, it's best if it is cream.
- The seasonings can be varied infinitely: Use whatever fresh herbs appeal to you, and take advantage of spices as well—garlic, of course, but also chiles and Indian and Asian spices.

About 1 pound broccoli, trimmed and cut up (page 123), to yield about 4 loosely packed cups broccoli, or the equivalent amount of cauliflower, carrots, turnips, celery, or other vegetable

$1/2$ cup rice or 1 medium baking potato, peeled and cut into quarters

4 cups Quickest Chicken Stock (page 17), or store-bought chicken, beef, or vegetable broth, or water

Salt and freshly ground black pepper to taste

$1/4$ to 1 cup heavy or light cream or half-and-half

Minced fresh parsley leaves or chives for garnish

1 Combine the broccoli, rice or potato, and stock or water in a large, deep saucepan or casserole and turn the heat to medium-high. Bring to a boil, then lower the heat to medium and cook until the vegetables are very tender, about 15 minutes.

2 Cool slightly, then puree in a food mill or in a blender. (You may prepare the soup in advance up to this point. Cover, refrigerate for up to 2 days, and reheat before proceeding.)

3 Return to the pot and reheat over medium-low heat. Season with salt and pepper, then add the cream; heat through again, garnish, and serve.

Baked Croutons

Makes about 2 cups cubes • Time: 20 to 40 minutes

Croutons are nothing more than crisped bits or whole slices of bread. They may be dried in the oven with no seasonings at all, as in this recipe, or cooked in oil or butter, with or without garlic and/or herbs. This recipe is the simplest, healthiest method. If you like, rub the whole slices of bread with a cut clove of garlic before cooking.

4 to 6 slices any bread, preferably slightly stale

1 Preheat the oven to 300°F. Cut the bread into cubes of any size, or leave the slices whole. Place them on a baking sheet.

2 Bake, shaking the pan occasionally if you used cubes, or turning the slices every 10 minutes or so if you left the slices whole. The croutons are done when they are lightly browned and thoroughly dried. Store in a covered container at room temperature for up to a week.

White Bean Soup

Makes 4 servings • **Time:** At least 1¹/₂ hours

This makes the transition from simple to complex quite readily. At its most basic, it tastes of beans and little else; when you start adding bacon or ham and vegetables, it becomes more flavorful—and more filling.

1¹/₂ cups navy, pea, or other dried white beans, washed and picked over (see The Basics of Buying and Preparing Beans, page 109)

About 6 cups Quickest Chicken Stock (page 17) or store-bought chicken, beef, or vegetable broth, or water, plus more if necessary

1 medium onion, quartered

2 tablespoons butter or extra-virgin olive oil (optional)

Salt and freshly ground black pepper to taste

Minced fresh parsley leaves for garnish

1 Place the beans, stock or water, and onion in a large, deep saucepan or casserole; turn the heat to medium-high. When it boils, turn the heat down to medium-low and cover partially. Cook, stirring occasionally, until the beans are very soft, at least 1 hour.

2 Put the mixture through a food mill or strainer, or puree it in a blender. (You may prepare the soup in advance up to this point. Cover, refrigerate for up to 2 days, and reheat before proceeding.) Reheat, adding more stock or water if necessary to achieve the consistency you like. Stir in the butter or oil, season with salt and pepper, garnish, and serve.

Five Simple Additions to Bean Soups

1. Scraps of smoked meats, such as ham or bacon.

2. Precooked vegetables of any type, as long as the flavor does not conflict with that of the soup. Onions, carrots, and celery are almost always appropriate.

3. A teaspoon or more of minced garlic or scallions, added about 2 minutes before the end of the cooking time.

4. Any spice you like, from jalapeños or other chiles to lots of black pepper to curry powder or other spice mixtures.

5. Diced fresh tomatoes as a garnish.

Black Bean Soup

Makes 4 to 6 servings
Time: 30 minutes with precooked beans

The best way to serve this satisfying soup is to puree about half of it, then pour it back into the pot. But you can also just mash the contents of the pot with a potato masher or large fork to get a similar smooth-chunky effect.

2 tablespoons canola or other neutral oil

2 medium onions, chopped

1 tablespoon minced garlic

1 tablespoon chile powder, or to taste

3 cups drained cooked or canned black beans

4 cups Quickest Chicken Stock (page 17) or store-bought chicken, beef, or vegetable broth, or water, preferably warmed

Salt and freshly ground black pepper to taste

2 teaspoons freshly squeezed lime juice, or to taste

Sour cream or plain yogurt for garnish

Minced cilantro leaves for garnish

1 Place the oil in a large, deep saucepan or casserole and turn the heat to medium. A minute later, add the onions and cook, stirring, until softened, about 5 minutes. Stir in the garlic and chile powder and cook, stirring, another minute.

2 Add the beans and stock or water and season with salt and pepper. Turn the heat to medium-high and bring the soup just about to a boil. Turn the heat to medium-low, and cook, stirring occasionally, for about 10 minutes. Turn off the heat.

3 Force half the contents of the pot through a food mill or carefully puree it in a food processor or blender; or just mash the contents with a potato masher or large fork. (You may prepare the soup in advance up to this point. Cover, refrigerate for up to 2 days, and reheat before proceeding.)

4 Add the lime juice and stir; taste and adjust seasonings as necessary. Serve, garnished with sour cream or yogurt and minced cilantro.

Chicken Soup with Rice or Noodles

Makes 4 servings • **Time: 30 minutes**

This is a thin chicken soup—a warming but not super-filling first course—with the rice, meat, and vegetables acting as a garnish rather than a major player; see the variation if you want something more substantial. Use orzo or other tiny pasta, angel hair or other thin noodles, ribbons or other egg noodles, or other cooked grains in place of the rice.

You could use canned stock here, but because the liquid itself is showcased, it's the ideal place for homemade stock.

> 5 to 6 cups Quickest Chicken Stock (page 17)
>
> 1/2 cup long-grain rice or pasta
>
> 1 carrot, peeled and cut into thin slices
>
> 1 celery stalk, minced (optional)
>
> 1 cup raw or cooked chopped boneless skinless chicken, or more
>
> Salt and freshly ground black pepper to taste
>
> Minced fresh parsley or dill leaves for garnish

① Place the stock in a large, deep saucepan or casserole and turn the heat to medium-high. When it is just about boiling, turn the heat down to medium so that it bubbles but not too vigorously. Stir in the rice, carrot, and celery and cook, stirring occasionally, until they are all tender, about 20 minutes.

② Stir in the chicken. If it is raw, cook another 5 to 8 minutes, until it is cooked. If it is cooked, cook 2 or 3 minutes, until it is hot. Season with salt and pepper, garnish, and serve.

Thick Chicken Soup with Rice or Noodles:
Increase the amount of rice or pasta to 1 cup; use 2 carrots and 2 celery stalks. Use as much chicken as you like. If you plan to store this soup, cook the rice separately and stir it in during the last stage of cooking or it will absorb too much liquid during storage.

Five Simple Additions to Chicken Soups

1. Herbs, especially dill, parsley, or chervil, but almost anything else.

2. Spices, especially ginger, chiles, garlic, or other strong spices.

3. Any starch you like—croutons, rice, noodles, and more.

4. Leftover chicken, grilled fresh chicken, small cubes of raw boneless chicken (which will cook in 2 minutes), or any other poultry.

5. Precooked vegetables of any type, as long as the flavor does not conflict with that of the soup. Onions, carrots, and celery are almost always appropriate.

Quickest Chicken Stock

Makes 3 quarts • Time: 40 minutes to 1 hour

This stock has three distinct advantages: One, it takes less than an hour to make. Two, it has clear, clean flavor—not especially complex, but very good. And three, it gives you a whole cooked—but not overcooked—chicken, for salad or any other use.

> 1 whole (3- to 4-pound) chicken, rinsed and patted dry with paper towels
>
> 1 cup roughly chopped onion (don't bother to peel it)
>
> 1 cup chopped carrot
>
> ½ cup roughly chopped celery
>
> 1 sprig fresh thyme or pinch dried thyme
>
> ½ bay leaf
>
> Several sprigs fresh parsley
>
> 1 teaspoon salt, plus more if necessary
>
> About 3½ quarts (14 cups) water

1 Cut the chicken into pieces if you like; it will speed cooking.

2 Combine all ingredients except the water in a stockpot; add the water.

3 Bring just about to a boil, then partially cover and adjust the heat so the mixture sends up a few bubbles at a time. Cook just until the chicken is done, 30 to 60 minutes.

4 Strain, pressing on the vegetables and meat to extract as much juice as possible. Taste and add salt if necessary.

5 Refrigerate, then skim any hardened fat from the surface. Refrigerate for 4 to 5 days (longer if you boil it every third day, which will prevent spoiling), or freeze.

Red Gazpacho

Makes 6 servings

Time: 20 minutes, plus time to chill

There is no "genuine" gazpacho; basically, the term can be applied to any cold vegetable soup that contains vinegar. This one, however, is not only conventional, it's also fast and fresh-tasting.

About 3 pounds ripe tomatoes, cored, peeled, seeded, and roughly chopped

1 red or yellow bell pepper, stemmed, peeled if desired, seeded, and roughly chopped

2 pickling ("Kirby") cucumbers, peeled and roughly chopped

4 slices good stale white bread (about 4 ounces), crusts removed

6 cups cold water

1 large or 2 small cloves garlic, peeled

1/4 cup sherry or good wine vinegar, or to taste

1/2 cup extra-virgin olive oil

Salt and freshly ground black pepper to taste

Baked Croutons (page 13) for garnish (optional)

1 Mince a bit of the tomato, pepper, and cucumber for garnish and set aside. Soak the bread in 1 cup of the water for 5 minutes, then squeeze out the excess water.

2 Place the bread in the container of a blender or food processor with the remaining tomato, pepper, cucumber, and water, as well as the garlic and vinegar; process until smooth, then add the olive oil slowly, with the machine running.

3 Season with salt and pepper and refrigerate until ready to serve; the flavor will improve over a few hours. Before serving, check seasoning again. Garnish with reserved tomato, pepper, and cucumber and, if desired, croutons.

2 | Pasta

We associate pasta primarily with Italy, but noodles are important in much of Asia, and have become a staple in the United States, where they are seen as the perfect food for people cutting down on meat and with little time to cook.

And pasta is simple: A good sauce might contain nothing more than olive oil and garlic; olive oil, fresh tomatoes, and basil; or chicken stock, soy sauce, garlic, and ginger. All of these are traditional, legitimate, and unsurpassable, for both simplicity and flavor. Nor is there anything wrong with "new" pasta combinations, in which you vary ingredients according to what's on hand.

Here are some basic rules for best results:

- Buy good pasta. The best pasta is 100 percent durum wheat. It may come from the United States, or from Italy; given that they're usually about the same in price, the Italian brands are preferable.
- Use enough water. A gallon per pound is about right; more than that is fine, but will take longer to come to a boil.
- Salt the water (unless you have a medical reason not to). Use a very heaping tablespoon per pound, then adjust to taste as you gain experience.
- Boil the water, and keep it boiling. It's okay to cover the pot after you add the pasta to bring the water back to a boil quickly. Just keep an eye on the pot and remove the cover before the water boils over. Lower the heat if the water boils too furiously.
- Stir the pasta. It will stick if you don't. Add the pasta, stir, cover the pot if necessary, then uncover it no more than a minute later and stir again.
- Don't undercook or overcook. There's an easy way to cook pasta correctly: Taste it. When it's just about done—when it retains a little bite but is no longer chalky—drain the pasta. It will cook a little more between pot and table—perfect. And don't trust anyone's pasta cooking times. Cook by taste and you'll never go wrong.
- Have a hot bowl ready. Pasta cools quickly; you want to eat it hot. (Warm bowl in hot water, then before serving, wipe dry.)
- Don't overdrain, don't oversauce. Throw the pasta in a colander, then put it in the bowl. Some water should cling to the noodles and thin the sauce slightly.

Linguine with Garlic and Oil

Makes about 4 servings • **Time:** 20 minutes

Not only is this Roman standard one of the world's quickest and simplest pasta dishes, it is among the most delicious. For variety, add a dried hot chile or two to the oil at the beginning, or add a handful of chopped parsley to the oil just before pouring it over the pasta. Gardeners should be sure to try the mixed herb variation.

> 2 tablespoons finely chopped garlic
>
> 1/2 cup extra-virgin olive oil
>
> Salt to taste
>
> 1 pound linguine, spaghetti, or other long, thin pasta
>
> Minced fresh parsley leaves (optional)

1 Bring a large pot of water to a boil.

2 In a small skillet or saucepan over medium-low heat, combine the garlic, oil, and salt. Allow the garlic to simmer, shaking the pan occasionally, until it turns golden; do not allow it to become dark brown or it will be bitter rather than sweet.

3 Salt the boiling water and cook the pasta until it is tender but firm. When it is done, drain it, reserving a bit of the cooking water. Reheat the garlic and oil mixture briefly if necessary. Dress the pasta with the sauce, adding a little more oil or some of the cooking water if it seems dry. Garnish with parsley if you like.

Linguine with Fresh Herbs: In Step 2, when the garlic is done, toss in a mixture of 1 cup or more fresh herbs, whatever you have on hand. Try, for example, 1/4 cup minced parsley leaves, 1/4 cup minced basil or chervil leaves, 1 sprig tarragon, minced, several sprigs of dill, minced, a sprig or two of thyme, leaves stripped from the stem and minced, and 1 tablespoon or more of minced chives. Garnish with more fresh herbs, finely minced.

Shopping Tip: As oil is one of the primary flavors in this and many sauces, you should always use the best extra-virgin oil you have to make them. The bottle label should say "extra virgin." Although simple "olive oil" won't ruin the sauce, it won't have the intense flavor of extra-virgin. There are different flavor variations of extra-virgin olive oil—fruity, olive-y are two—so experiment to find your favorites.

Cooking Tip: There are times when an oil-based sauce is not thin enough to adequately coat your pasta. In this case you have two options: Add more olive oil, or add a bit of pasta cooking water, which adds fewer calories but less flavor. Either option is perfectly fine.

The Basics of Cooking Pasta

There is no rule about how much pasta to cook. In Italy, where pasta is served as a small first course, a pound will easily feed six to eight people. In many homes, where pasta, bread, and a vegetable is often called dinner, a pound usually serves four, as long as none of the four is a starving teen. The kind of sauce and the shape of the pasta also affect how much you will eat; spaghetti with garlic and oil or a simple tomato sauce goes much faster than rigatoni with eggplant and mozzarella. Generally, I believe the recipes here serve three to four people.

If there are leftovers, by all means refrigerate them. You can reheat pasta in a microwave, oven, or non-stick skillet, without additional fat (you can eat it cold, too). Some people frown on this (though they probably do it themselves).

Pasta with Pesto

Makes about 4 servings • **Time:** 20 minutes

Once exotic—at least in the United States—pesto is now sold in supermarkets and offered on fast-food pizza. But you can put it together in minutes in a food processor or blender, and it is one of the great pasta sauces, especially in late summer when basil is plentiful.

These proportions will work for any amount of basil; you're only limited by your supply of basil and patience. You can make pesto thick or thin, according to your taste. Keep adding oil until you like the texture.

2 loosely packed cups fresh basil leaves, big stems discarded, rinsed, and dried

Salt to taste

$1/2$ to 2 cloves garlic, crushed

2 tablespoons pine nuts or walnuts, lightly toasted in a dry skillet

$1/2$ cup extra-virgin olive oil, or more

1 pound linguine, spaghetti, or other long, thin pasta

$1/2$ cup freshly grated Parmesan or other hard cheese (optional)

1 Bring a large pot of water to a boil. Meanwhile, combine the basil, salt, garlic, nuts, and about half the oil in a food processor or blender.

2 Process, stopping to scrape down the sides of the container occasionally, and adding the rest of the oil gradually. Add additional oil if you prefer a thinner mixture. Reserve until pasta is done or if made ahead, store in the refrigerator or in the freezer (see Preparation Tip).

3 Salt the boiling water and cook the pasta until it is tender but firm. When it is done, drain it, reserving a bit of the cooking water. Dress the pasta with the pesto, adding a little more oil or some of the cooking water if it seems dry. Stir in the Parmesan, if you like.

Preparation Tips: To toast pine nuts or walnuts (or any nuts), put them in a dry skillet over medium heat. Cook, shaking the pan occasionally, until light brown and fragrant, about 5 minutes.

Pesto refrigerates well, as long as it is tightly covered, for up to a week; you can also freeze it. In either case, do not add cheese until you are ready to serve. And to help the pesto retain its bright green color, drizzle a layer of olive oil over the top once you have put it in the container.

Pasta with Pesto with Butter: For really special pesto, stir in 2 tablespoons softened butter just before tossing with lean foods such as pasta.

Pasta with Minimalist Pesto: Combine basil, garlic, salt, and $1/4$ cup oil and process. Use warm water for thinning.

The Basics of Pesto

A traditional method of preserving herbs (especially basil) in oil, pesto has become a staple, and pre-made pesto is widely available. But homemade pesto is incomparable, and you can put it together simply in a food processor or blender. I like to keep the ingredients few and the process quick.

The Basil The fresher the better, of course. There are different varieties of basil, with slightly different flavors, but the ordinary large-leafed green kind is perfectly suitable. Use leaves and the smallest of stems only; large stems will not puree, and furthermore tend to be bitter. Flowers may be included. Wash the basil well; dry it in a salad spinner. Other herbs may be substituted. In every case, discard stems and wash leaves.

The Oil Extra-virgin olive oil is best but if you're making a large batch and wish to economize, mix extra-virgin oil with pure olive oil, or with a neutral oil such as canola or grapeseed.

The Nuts Traditionally pine nuts, which are expensive but delicious, especially if you toast them first. Walnuts lend a distinctive bitterness that is not at all unpleasant, and which many people prefer.

The Cheese Genuine Parmigiano-Reggiano is best, of course, but you may substitute other hard cheeses if you like—for example, Grana Padano, asiago, or Pecorino Romano. Cheese should be considered optional in pesto, and is completely inappropriate in pesto-like blends made with herbs such as cilantro.

The Garlic To taste, please. Recipes that call unconditionally for two to four cloves of raw garlic do not take into account that many dishes are completely overwhelmed by the flavor, and that many people find large quantities of raw garlic offensive.

Pasta with Butter, Sage, and Parmesan

Makes about 4 servings • Time: 30 minutes

Without sage, kids love this; grown-ups prefer the sharper edge of sage.

6 tablespoons (³/₄ stick) butter

20 or 30 fresh sage leaves or about 1 tablespoon dried whole sage leaves

Salt and freshly ground black pepper to taste

1 pound cut pasta, like ziti or penne, or long pasta, like linguine or spaghetti

1 cup freshly grated Parmesan cheese

1 Bring a large pot of water to a boil. Melt the butter in a small saucepan over low heat. Add the sage, salt, and pepper. Cook until the butter turns light brown, about 10 minutes.

2 Salt the water and cook the pasta until it is tender. Spoon 2 or 3 tablespoons of the pasta cooking water into a warm serving bowl. Drain the pasta and toss in the serving bowl with the butter, more pepper, and half the Parmesan. Pass the remaining Parmesan at the table.

Fettuccine "Alfredo": Reduce the butter to 2 tablespoons and melt it gently; eliminate the sage. In Step 3, while the pasta cooks, warm a large bowl; when it's warm, add 2 eggs, ¹/₂ cup heavy cream, and 1 cup of grated Parmesan; beat briefly. Add pepper. When the pasta is cooked, toss it with the cheese-egg-cream mixture, adding a little cooking water if needed to keep the mixture moist. Drizzle with the butter, toss well, and serve.

The Basics of Pasta and Cheese

When used right, cheese adds incomparable richness and flavor to pasta. Most commonly used is Parmesan, which should be freshly grated and authentic (look for a brown rind with "Parmigiano-Reggiano" stenciled on it). Hard cheeses made from sheep's milk, like Pecorino Romano, are best for grating on very strong-flavored dishes.

Semi-soft cheeses, when cooked, make good sauces. Gorgonzola (or another creamy blue cheese) makes a smooth, strong-flavored pasta sauce; ricotta—especially creamy fresh ricotta, which is moister and more flavorful than supermarkets options—makes a sweet, rich sauce, whether blended with tomato sauce or simply thinned with pasta-cooking water; and other strong-tasting cheeses, like fontina, combine beautifully with butter, milk, cream, or, again, pasta-cooking water to make a simple sauce.

Baked Macaroni and Cheese

Makes 4 to 6 servings • **Time:** About 45 minutes

This is macaroni and cheese for grown-ups; not that kids won't like it, but it's far from sweet and gooey. Rather, it is fragrant and almost sharp, thanks to the bay leaves and Parmesan.

> 2$^1/_2$ cups milk (low-fat is fine)
>
> 2 bay leaves
>
> 1 pound elbow, shell, ziti, or other cut pasta
>
> 4 tablespoons ($^1/_2$ stick) butter
>
> 3 tablespoons flour
>
> 1$^1/_2$ cups grated cheese, such as sharp Cheddar or Emmenthal
>
> $^1/_2$ cup freshly grated Parmesan cheese
>
> Salt and freshly ground black pepper to taste
>
> $^1/_2$ cup or more plain bread crumbs, preferably fresh

1 Preheat the oven to 400°F. Bring a large pot of water to a boil.

2 Cook the milk with the bay leaves in a small saucepan over medium-low heat. When small bubbles appear along the sides, about 5 minutes later, turn off the heat and let stand. Salt the boiling water and cook the pasta to the point where it still needs another minute or two to become tender. Drain it, rinse it quickly to stop cooking, and place it in a large bowl.

3 In a small saucepan over medium-low heat, melt 3 tablespoons of the butter; when it is foamy, add the flour and cook, stirring, until the mixture browns, about 5 minutes. Remove the bay leaves from the milk and add about $^1/_4$ cup of the milk to the hot flour mixture, stirring with a wire whisk all the while. As soon as the mixture becomes smooth, add a little more milk, and continue to do so until all the milk is used up and the mixture is thick and smooth. Add the Cheddar or Emmenthal and stir.

4 Pour the sauce over the pasta, toss in the Parmesan, and season with salt and pepper. Use the remaining butter to grease a 9 × 13-inch or like-sized baking pan and turn the noodle mixture into it. Top liberally with bread crumbs and bake until the crumbs turn brown, about 15 minutes. Serve hot.

Linguine with Fresh Tomato Sauce and Parmesan

Makes about 4 servings • **Time:** 20 minutes

A seasonal dish, best made with plum tomatoes—the best tomatoes for sauce because they have a higher proportion of meat to liquid than round tomatoes. This takes no time at all and is almost perfect, as long as you don't mind tomato skins. If you prefer not to include skins, follow the illustration (at right). A couple of teaspoons of minced garlic, cooked with the butter or oil, is a good addition.

> 5 tablespoons butter or olive oil
>
> 3 or 4 medium-to-large tomatoes, about 1 pound total, cored and roughly chopped
>
> 1/2 cup shredded fresh basil leaves (optional)
>
> 1 pound linguine
>
> Salt and freshly ground black pepper to taste
>
> Lots of freshly grated Parmesan cheese

1 Bring a large pot of water to a boil.

2 Melt 4 tablespoons of the butter in a medium-to-large skillet over medium heat. When the foam subsides, add the tomatoes.

3 Cook, stirring occasionally, until the tomatoes break up, about 10 minutes; fish the tomato skins from the sauce as they separate from the pulp (or leave them in). Add most of the basil.

4 Meanwhile, salt the boiling water and cook the pasta until it is tender but firm. Season the sauce with salt and pepper; if it is thick—which it may be if you used meaty plum tomatoes or cooked out some of the liquid—thin it with some of the pasta cooking water. Drain the pasta and toss it with the sauce and remaining 1 tablespoon butter. Garnish with the reserved basil and serve with the Parmesan.

PREPARING TOMATOES

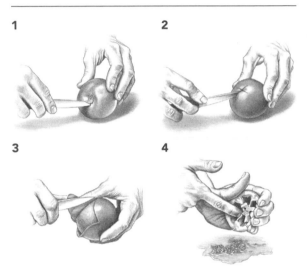

(Step 1) First, core the tomato. Cut a wedge right around the core and remove it. **(Step 2)** Then peel the tomato. Cut a small "x" in the flower (non-stem) end. Drop it into boiling water until the skin begins to loosen, usually less than thirty seconds. **(Step 3)** Remove the peels with a paring knife. **(Step 4)** Finish by seeding the tomato. The easiest way to remove seeds is to simply cut the tomato in half through its equator, then squeeze and shake out the seeds. Do this over a bowl if you wish to strain and reserve the juice.

Easy Tomato Sauce

Makes enough for at least 1 pound of pasta, about 4 servings
Time: 20 minutes

If you keep canned tomatoes on hand, you'll always be able to make fresh, delicious sauce in about the time it takes to bring water to a boil and cook the pasta. Pass freshly grated Parmesan (or Pecorino Romano) cheese with this, if you like.

>3 tablespoons olive oil
>
>3 cloves garlic, lightly smashed,
>or 1 small onion, minced
>
>1 (28-ounce) can whole plum tomatoes
>
>Salt and freshly ground black pepper, to taste

1 Warm 2 tablespoons of the oil with the garlic or onion in a medium skillet over medium-low heat. Cook, stirring occasionally, until the garlic is lightly golden or the onion is translucent.

2 Drain the tomatoes and remove their seeds if you choose to do so. Crush them with a fork or your hands and add them to the skillet, along with salt and pepper. Raise the heat to medium-high and cook, stirring occasionally, until the tomatoes break down and the mixture becomes "saucy," about 10 minutes. Remove the garlic if you like. Stir in the remaining tablespoon of oil, taste for salt, and add more if necessary. (This sauce may be covered and refrigerated for a day or two, or, in a closed container, frozen for several weeks.) Serve over any long pasta.

Preparation Tip: The best way to crush canned tomatoes for sauce is to first drain out the liquid in the can (save it in case your sauce becomes too thick). Then, while the tomatoes are still in the can, swish a sharp knife through them a few times—they'll be cut into pieces in seconds.

Three Ways to Vary Easy Tomato Sauce

1. **Tomato Sauce with Herbs:** Stir in 2 or 3 tablespoons of minced fresh basil leaves, or 1 teaspoon finely chopped fresh oregano or marjoram leaves (or $1/2$ teaspoon dried), while the tomatoes are cooking. If you're using basil, add more as a garnish. Or simply garnish with plenty of fresh minced parsley, basil, or mint leaves.

2. **Pink Tomato Sauce:** Thin about 1 cup of ricotta cheese with about 2 tablespoons of the pasta cooking water and stir into the sauce just before serving. Kids love this pink sauce.

3. **Puttanesca Sauce:** Stir 2 tablespoons of capers (drained), some crushed red pepper flakes if you like, and/or $1/2$ cup pitted black olives (the wrinkled, oil-cured type are best here) into the sauce after adding the tomatoes.

Spaghetti and Meatballs

Makes at least 4 servings • **Time:** About 1 hour

This is the one pasta dish that all non-Italians knew how to make when I was growing up in the fifties. It is as filling a pasta dish as exists and is still a favorite for many people, particularly kids.

3/4 to 1 pound ground meat—
beef, pork, veal, or a combination

1 egg

1 cup freshly grated Parmesan cheese

1/4 cup minced fresh parsley leaves

1 teaspoon minced garlic

1/2 cup plain bread crumbs,
preferably fresh

Salt to taste

2 tablespoons olive oil

1 medium onion, minced

1 (28- or 35-ounce) can whole
plum tomatoes, with their juice

1 pound spaghetti, or more

1   Lightly combine the meat, egg, half the Parmesan, parsley, garlic, bread crumbs, and salt in a bowl. Form into small or large balls, as you like (I prefer walnut-sized meatballs).

2   Heat the olive oil for about 3 minutes in a broad, deep skillet over medium heat. Add the meatballs (do not crowd—cook in batches if necessary) and cook, shaking the pan every minute or so to prevent sticking, then turn the meatballs. When the meatballs are nicely browned all over— this will take about 15 minutes—remove them to a plate and turn off the heat.

3   Pour off all but a film of the fat that has accumulated in the pan. Turn the heat back to medium and cook the onion in the fat, stirring, until it begins to brown. Crush the tomatoes with a fork or your hands and add them, along with their juice, to the pan. Cook, stirring occasionally, until the tomatoes begin to break up, 5 to 10 minutes.

4   Bring a large pot of water to a boil. Meanwhile, add the meatballs and salt to taste to the sauce and cook about 15 minutes more, until the meatballs are cooked through.

5   Salt the boiling water and cook the pasta until it is tender but firm. Put it in a large, warm bowl and toss it with some of the sauce (you may not need it all, depending on how much pasta you've cooked). Top with meatballs and serve, passing the remaining Parmesan at the table.

Leaner Meatballs: Omit bread crumbs, and egg; increase onion and parsley to 1 cup each. Grill, broil, or bake at 400°F until done, 15 minutes or less. Serve without sauce.

Pasta with Meat Sauce

Makes a little more than 1 quart,
enough for about 3 pounds of pasta
Time: Several hours, largely unattended

Pasta with meat sauce (*ragu*), is the ideal sauce for fresh pasta, cheese-filled ravioli, or lasagne. Although the sauce doesn't require much work, it does require some attention over the course of a morning or afternoon. Freeze extra in one-half pint or pint containers. Feel free to halve the amount of meat if you like. Even if you do, this is a meaty sauce, and it should be a meaty-tasting one.

2 tablespoons olive oil

1 small onion, minced

1 carrot, peeled and minced

1 celery stalk, minced

¼ cup minced bacon or pancetta

½ pound lean ground pork
(or use all beef)

½ pound lean ground beef

¾ cup dry white wine (or juice from
the tomatoes)

1 (28- or 35-ounce) can whole plum
tomatoes, drained (reserve juice,
if needed instead of wine)

1 cup Quickest Chicken Stock
(page 17) or store-bought beef
or chicken broth

Salt and freshly ground black pepper
to taste

1 cup cream, half-and-half, or milk

1 pound fresh or cut pasta,
like ziti or shells

Freshly grated Parmesan cheese (optional)

1 Put the olive oil in a large, deep skillet or saucepan. Turn the heat to medium-low and, 1 minute later, add the onion, carrot, celery, and bacon or pancetta. Cook, stirring occasionally, until the vegetables are tender, about 10 minutes.

2 Add the ground meat and cook, stirring and breaking up any clumps, until all traces of red are gone, about 5 minutes. Add the wine or tomato juice, raise the heat a bit, and cook, stirring occasionally, until most of the liquid is evaporated, about 5 minutes.

3 Crush the tomatoes with a fork or your hands and add them to the pot; stir, then add the stock. Turn the heat to low and cook at a slow simmer, stirring occasionally and breaking up the tomatoes and any clumps of meat that remain. After an hour or so, add salt and pepper. Cook for at least another hour, until much of the liquid has evaporated and the sauce is very thick. (This sauce may be covered and refrigerated for a day or two, or put in a closed container and frozen for several weeks. Reheat before completing.)

4 Add the cream, half-and-half, or milk and cook for another 15 to 30 minutes, stirring occasionally; taste and add more salt and/or pepper as needed. Meanwhile, bring a large pot of water to a boil and salt it. Cook pasta in lightly salted boiling water until tender but not mushy. Drain and top with warm sauce (reserve extra sauce for another use). Serve immediately, passing grated Parmesan, if you like, at the table.

Classic Lasagne, Bolognese-Style

Makes about 6 servings
Time: 45 minutes (with premade sauce)

This is the traditional Italian lasagne, made with a creamy white sauce, rather than ricotta and mozzarella cheese (see variation). Lasagne is not difficult to make; just plan ahead to have all the parts ready before assembling.

At least 5 quarts water

12 store-bought fresh lasagne or dried lasagne noodles

1 recipe béchamel sauce (page 31), about 1 cup

2 tablespoons softened butter (preferred) or extra-virgin olive oil

3 cups, more or less, meat sauce, from Pasta with Meat Sauce (page 29)

1½ cups freshly grated Parmesan cheese

Freshly ground black pepper to taste

Salt, if needed

1 Set at least 5 quarts of water in a large pot over high heat. When it comes to a boil, salt it.

2 Cook the noodles a few at a time; keep them underdone (if they are fresh, this means little more than 1 minute of cooking time). Drain carefully in a colander, then allow to rest on towels while you prepare the béchamel sauce. Preheat the oven to 400°F.

3 Smear the bottom of your baking pan with the butter or oil, then place a layer of noodles, touching but not overlapping. Trim any overhanging edges. Cover the noodles with about one-quarter each of the béchamel, meat sauce, and Parmesan, then with a light sprinkling of black pepper (between the meat sauce and the Parmesan, there should be enough salt, but if you feel it is under-seasoned, add a little salt to each layer also). Make four layers, ending with a sprinkling of Parmesan. (The dish can be prepared in advance up to this point, then well wrapped and refrigerated for a day or frozen for a month; defrost in the refrigerator for a day before cooking if possible.)

4 Bake for about 20 to 30 minutes, until the lasagne is bubbly. Remove from the oven and let rest for 5 minutes before cutting and serving. Or let cool completely, cover well, and refrigerate for up to 2 days, or freeze for up to a month.

Classic Lasagne, Italian-American-Style: Omit the béchamel. In Step 3, on each layer of the first three layers of noodles, spread about 1 cup of ricotta (thinned, if necessary, with some of the sauce). Top the ricotta with meat sauce, the meat sauce with about 1 cup of grated mozzarella, the mozzarella with a sprinkling of Parmesan. On the top layer, omit the ricotta.

Béchamel Sauce

Makes about 1 cup • **Time:** 10 to 20 minutes

Béchamel sauce is a basic French white sauce made with milk, butter, and flour. It can be served over simply cooked vegetables and is also used by cooks in Bologna for classic lasagne, where it's called *besciamella*.

1¹/₂ tablespoons butter

1¹/₂ tablespoons flour

1 to 1¹/₂ cups milk

Salt and freshly ground black pepper to taste

1 In a small saucepan, heat the butter over medium-low heat. When the foam begins to subside, stir in the flour. Turn the heat to low and cook, stirring with a wire whisk almost constantly, until the flour-butter mixture darkens, at least 3 minutes.

2 Stir in the milk, a little bit at a time, still whisking. When about 1 cup of the milk has been stirred in, the mixture will be fairly thick. Add more milk, a little at a time, until the consistency is just a little thinner than you like, then cook, still over low heat, until the mixture is the thickness you want.

3 Season to taste and serve immediately or keep warm over gently simmering water for up to an hour, stirring occasionally.

Preparation Tip: Lasagne is incomparably better with fresh noodles (these may be store-bought, of course) than dried. But no matter which noodles you choose, undercook them quite a bit. They will continue to cook in the oven.

Cooking Tip: Keep the sauce in the correct proportion to the noodles. The pasta to sauce (including solids) ratio should be, on average, 1 pound of raw pasta to about 1 quart of sauce. The noodles will absorb liquid, so you need enough sauce to keep the lasagne from being dry. But you also don't want so much sauce that the noodles are swimming in it when you remove the lasagne from the oven.

Stir-Fried Chinese Noodles with Vegetables

Makes about 4 servings • **Time:** 20 to 30 minutes

You can make Chinese-style stir-fried noodles with dried wheat or rice noodles, or with fresh egg noodles. And this recipe can be made with virtually any green vegetable. For example, I've used asparagus here; substitute at will, making sure the vegetable is cut into bite-sized pieces and cooked until tender before proceeding. If you'd like to use sautéed rather than parboiled vegetables, see the first variation (page 33). You can also combine these noodles with almost any stir-fried dish.

1 pound asparagus, more or less, no thicker than a pencil

1 pound Chinese wheat noodles, of spaghetti-like thickness

3 tablespoons peanut (preferred) or other oil

1 tablespoon minced garlic

1 tablespoon peeled and minced fresh ginger

$1/2$ cup Quickest Chicken Stock (page 17) or store-bought chicken or vegetable broth, or reserved cooking water

1 tablespoon soy sauce

$1/4$ cup minced scallion or chives

1 tablespoon dark sesame oil (optional)

1 Bring a large pot of water to a boil; salt it. Meanwhile, break the bottoms of the asparagus (they usually snap right at the point where the stalk is tender enough to eat); cut them into 1- to 2-inch lengths. When the pot of water is boiling, blanch the asparagus just until they begin to become tender, 1 to 3 minutes depending on their thickness. Remove them from the water with a slotted spoon and quickly plunge into ice water to stop the cooking.

2 Using the same water, cook the noodles, stirring occasionally and beginning to taste after 4 or 5 minutes (less time if you're using fresh noodles). When they are just tender, drain thoroughly, reserving $1/2$ cup cooking liquid if you do not have any stock. Toss with 1 tablespoon of the peanut or other oil (a little more if you are not proceeding with the recipe right away), and set aside.

3 Just before you are ready to eat, heat a large skillet or wok (preferably non-stick) over medium-high heat for 3 or 4 minutes. Add the remaining oil, then the garlic and ginger; let sizzle for about 15 seconds, then toss in the noodles. Raise the heat to high and let the noodles sit for about 1 minute, until they begin to brown on the bottom. Toss once or twice and allow to sit again. Add the stock or cooking water and stir, scraping to loosen any bits that may have stuck to the bottom. Add the (drained) asparagus and stir a few times; add the soy sauce and scallion or chives, and the sesame oil if you are using it. Stir and serve.

Shopping Tip: Generally, when calling for sesame oil, cookbooks (including this one) mean dark, roasted sesame oil, the rich, distinctive oil sold in Asian food stores and many supermarkets. Unroasted sesame oil is a light cooking oil, not unlike corn or sunflower, and is not a good substitute.

Stir-Fried Noodles with Stir-Fried Vegetables:
Omit asparagus. Use about 1 pound of tender vegetables, such as spring onions, leeks, broccoli raab, celery, bean sprouts, Napa cabbage, bok choy, snow peas, or a combination. Trim and chop into small pieces if necessary; cook them in a large non-stick skillet or wok over high heat with 2 or 3 tablespoons of peanut oil. Stir every 10 seconds or so until vegetables are brown and tender. Cook the noodles as in Step 2, then substitute this mixture for the asparagus in Step 3.

Stir-Fried Noodles with Meat or Shrimp: Omit asparagus. Mince 2 or 3 shiitake mushrooms (or substitute dried; soak them in hot water for 10 minutes, then drain and mince), 1 small onion, and 2 or 3 scallions. Cook this mixture, stirring, over medium-high heat in 1 tablespoon peanut oil until the onion is translucent; add $1/2$ pound ground, minced, diced, or sliced turkey, chicken, pork, or beef (leftovers are okay, too), or $1/2$ pound peeled shrimp, cut into pieces if they are large. Raise the heat to high and cook, stirring almost constantly, until browned. Add 2 tablespoons soy sauce and $1/2$ cup stock or water; taste and add salt as necessary. Cook the noodles and toss with the oil as in Step 2, then substitute this mixture for the asparagus in Step 3, and finish as directed.

The Basics of Asian Noodles

Noodles in China, Japan, and Southeast Asia are often made from ingredients other than wheat; rice noodles are especially common. These may be soaked rather than boiled before combining with other foods, but are best when soaked, then boiled for a minute or two. Most Asian noodles, though, are made from wheat, or wheat and eggs, and are not that much different from the European noodles to which most Americans are accustomed.

Like the Italians, the Chinese rely primarily on two kinds of noodles: white wheat noodles, made with flour and water, and yellow egg noodles. You can find both varieties fresh in supermarkets and, of course, Asian food stores.

Cold Noodles with Sesame or Peanut Sauce

Makes 4 to 6 servings • **Time:** About 30 minutes, plus chilling time, as needed

A wonderful starter or side dish; the noodles and sauce each can be made in advance and combined at the last minute. Add shredded cooked chicken and/or diced seeded cucumber to this to add substance and crunch. These are often served chilled, but can also be served freshly made.

12 ounces fresh egg noodles, or any dried noodles, such as spaghetti

2 tablespoons dark sesame oil

$1/2$ cup sesame paste (tahini) or natural peanut butter

1 tablespoon sugar

$1/4$ cup soy sauce

1 tablespoon rice or wine vinegar

Hot sesame oil, chile-garlic sauce, Tabasco, or other hot sauce to taste

Salt and freshly ground black pepper to taste

At least $1/2$ cup minced scallions for garnish

1 Cook the noodles in boiling salted water until tender but not mushy. Drain, then rinse in cold water for 1 or 2 minutes. Toss with half the sesame oil and refrigerate up to 2 hours, or proceed with the recipe.

2 Beat together the tahini or peanut butter, sugar, soy sauce, and vinegar. Add a little hot sauce and salt and pepper; taste and adjust seasoning as necessary. Thin the sauce with hot water, so that it is about the consistency of heavy cream.

3 Toss together the noodles and the sauce, and add more of any seasoning if necessary. Drizzle with the remaining sesame oil, garnish, and serve.

Cooking Tip: Unless you know you really love your food with a lot of heat, when adding hot sesame oil, chile-garlic sauce, Tabasco, or other hot sauces to dishes, start out by adding $1/4$ teaspoon at a time. In this sauce, if you find you've added too much, add a little more sesame paste or sugar to counter the heat.

3 | Fish

You may be a big fan of shrimp scampi or gravitate to grilled tuna in restaurants, but you may also be reluctant, even intimidated, by the thought of buying fish and cooking it at home. The truth is you can easily buy fish cleaned and ready-to-cook, so fish is simple and generally quite fast to prepare, and offers a host of health benefits. If you like fish, it's worth the effort to learn the basics.

Fish is different from other animals we eat for one main reason: sixty or more kinds, on a rotating basis, make common appearances in the supermarket. But because many fish are similar, they can also be readily substituted for one another; the differences are less significant than the similarities. And there's almost always some fish, in good shape, in any market, that will meet your current need. So, for example, if you're looking for fillet of sole and can't find it, there will be something else—flounder, sea bass, orange roughy, or other fillets—that will fit the bill.

Here's the quick, no-nonsense course in fish-shopping; there are more details in the discussions of individual fish:

- Avoid fish counters that smell or look dirty. I'd like to think that these days you won't encounter such a disgrace, but if you do, run, don't walk, in the other direction.

- Generally, steer clear of prewrapped fish. It might be good, and there's nothing intrinsically wrong with it, but it's difficult to evaluate. If you've had good experience with it in a given market, you're lucky; but I usually don't take a chance unless I'm sure.

- Trust your instincts. Good fish looks good, has firm, unmarred flesh, and smells like fresh seawater. If your supermarket fishmonger won't let you smell the fish, and it passes the appearance tests, try buying it, opening the package right on the spot, and, if the smell is at all off, handing it right back. If you're reluctant to do that, remember that if any fish doesn't meet your expectations when you cook it, bring it back to the supermarket for an exchange or a refund. Demand quality.

Broiled Flatfish or Other Thin White Fillets

Makes 4 servings • **Time:** 15 minutes

Simple, fast, delicious. What more can you ask for? All-important: The fish must smell of seawater, no more. There are many fish from which fillets are cut, so ask your fishmonger for suggestions if you want to try something other than the thin fillets listed here.

> About 1½ pounds fillets of flounder, sole, red snapper, or sea bass, cut about ¼ inch thick, scaled or skinned
>
> 1 tablespoon olive oil or melted butter, plus a little more for the pan
>
> Salt and freshly ground black pepper to taste
>
> Lemon quarters or a sprinkling of vinegar

1 Preheat the broiler. It should be very hot, and the rack should be as close to the heat source as you can get it—even 2 inches is not too close. (You can also bake the fish at 450°F; it will take 1 or 2 minutes longer.)

2 Lightly grease a baking sheet or broiling pan. Lay the fillets on it, then brush with the tablespoon of oil or butter. Sprinkle with salt and pepper.

3 Broil the fish for 2 to 4 minutes (without turning), depending on the heat of your oven and the distance from the heat source. (If the fish is thicker than ¼ inch, adjust cooking time accordingly, but few of these fillets will take more than 5 minutes in most ovens.) When the fish is done, it should be firm and barely cooked through; the edges will flake, but the center should still show a little resistance. If there is a little translucence in the very middle, it will disappear by the time you get the fish onto a plate.

4 Remove the fish with a spatula and serve immediately, squeezing lemon juice or drizzling vinegar over the fillets at the table. Serve immediately.

Shopping Tip: Some thin fillets are sturdier and firmer than others; generally, these will be easier to handle. The more delicate ones are more tender and quicker-cooking.

Sturdier are: Catfish; Red Snapper; Rockfish; Sea Bass;

More Delicate are: Flatfish of any type, such as Flounder, Fluke, Sole; Haddock; Large- or Small-Mouth Bass (freshwater).

Four Ideas for Broiled Fillets

1. Brush lightly, before and after cooking, with butter, oil, or vinaigrette.

2. Broil plain, as in the master recipe, and serve with any store-bought salsa.

3. Serve over a bed of lightly dressed greens.

4. Use cold or hot in sandwiches, with mayonnaise (see page 7 for homemade) or other dressing.

Broiled Flatfish or Other White Fillets with
Garlic-Parsley Sauce: Steps 1 and 2 remain
the same; use olive oil. Combine 1 teaspoon
minced garlic, $1/3$ cup extra-virgin olive oil,
$1/4$ cup freshly squeezed lemon juice, $1/2$ cup
minced fresh parsley leaves, and a little salt
and pepper. Spoon some of this mixture
over the fish. Proceed with Steps 3 and 4
as directed; pass the rest of the sauce at
the table.

The Basics of Thin White Fish Fillets

Thin white fish fillets are all stark-white, or
nearly so. They are usually under an inch
thick, ranging from flounder and other flatfish, which are often a $1/4$ inch thick or so, to
red snapper, whose fillets can reach an inch
in thickness. They are all tender, some more
than others. Sturdier ones can be substituted in the recipes that work for the more
tender ones. (The converse is not true; but
you can substitute one sturdy fish for
another.) All of these fish, regardless of their
texture, are mild-flavored.

These fish cook very quickly. A $1/4$-inch-
thick flounder fillet can cook through in
2 minutes. Even a relatively thick piece of
red snapper will be done in less than 10 minutes. How do you know when they're done?

By the time the outside of a thinner fillet
is opaque, the inside is very nearly done.

This is absolutely true if you turn the fish
over, as you do in a pan. But even in a
broiler or oven, external opacity is a sign of
internal doneness.

With thinner fillets, when the thinnest
part flakes, the thicker part is done. When
the thicker part flakes, it's overcooked.

With thicker fillets, you can roughly esti-
mate doneness by timing: about 8 minutes
is the longest you want to cook any fillet
less than 1 inch thick. In addition, take a
peek between the flakes of the fish; if most
of the translucence is gone, and the fish is
tender, it's done.

Remember, all food continues to cook
between stove or oven and table, so fish
fully cooked in the kitchen will likely be
slightly overcooked at the table.

Sautéed Flatfish or Other Thin White Fillets

Makes 2 servings • **Time:** 20 minutes

This classic preparation for fillets of flatfish ("sole meunière") works equally well for any thin fillets. Note that this is for two people. If there is a disadvantage to this recipe, it is that the thinness of the fillets makes pan-cooking difficult—they simply take up too much room. Cook in batches if you're going to double the recipe. And serve the fish hot, hot, hot.

About ¹/₂ to ³/₄ pound fillets of flounder, sole, red snapper, or sea bass, cut about ¹/₄ inch thick, scaled or skinned

Salt and freshly ground black pepper to taste

1 tablespoon extra-virgin olive oil

4 tablespoons (¹/₂ stick) butter

Flour for dredging

2 tablespoons freshly squeezed lemon juice

Minced fresh parsley leaves for garnish

Lemon wedges

1   Heat two dinner plates in a 200°F oven. Season the fillets with salt and pepper.

2   Heat a large skillet, preferably non-stick, over medium-high heat for 2 or 3 minutes. Add the oil and half the butter. When the butter foam subsides, dredge the fillets, one by one, in the flour, shaking off any excess, and add them to the pan. Raise the heat to high and cook the fillets until golden on each side, 4 to 5 minutes total. Remove to the warm serving plates.

3   Turn the heat to medium and add the remaining butter to the pan. Cook until the butter foams, 1 or 2 minutes. Add the lemon juice, and cook, stirring and scraping the bottom of the pan, for about 15 seconds. Pour the sauce over the fillets.

4   Garnish and serve immediately with the lemon wedges.

Shopping Tip: Most fillets and steaks are cut before they even reach a supermarket fish counter. If you don't like the way they look, move on, or ask if there are fresher specimens in the back (there almost always are).

Sautéed Flatfish or Other White Fillets with Soy Sauce: Steps 1 and 2 remain the same; use peanut or vegetable oil in place of the butter. In Step 3, add an additional tablespoon of oil to the pan and, over medium heat, add 1 teaspoon minced garlic, 1 tablespoon peeled and minced or grated fresh ginger, 2 minced scallions; cook, stirring, about 30 seconds. Add ¹/₂ cup any broth, white wine, or water, and let it bubble away for 30 seconds or so. Add 2 tablespoons soy sauce and the juice of 1 lime. Pour this sauce over the fish. Serve with lime wedges.

Red Snapper or Other Fillets in Packages

Makes 6 servings • **Time:** 1 hour

Cooking *en papillote* is fun and virtually foolproof. Since all of the fish's essences are locked within the package, moistness is guaranteed. But because you can't peek into all the packages to judge doneness, I wouldn't make this with very thin fillets, which are likely to overcook. It's a fine recipe for thicker fillets such as red snapper, or catfish or sea bass; simply increase the cooking time by 4 or 5 minutes per 1/2 inch of thickness.

About 1 pound waxy red or white potatoes, peeled and sliced as thinly as possible (you want 24 to 36 slices)

6 red snapper fillets or other sturdier thin white fillets, 4 to 6 ounces each, scaled or skinned

2 or 3 large tomatoes, cored and cut through the equator into 1/4-inch-thick slices (you want 12 slices)

Salt and freshly ground black pepper to taste

24 fresh basil leaves

About 2 tablespoons olive oil

1 Preheat the oven to 450°F. Cut six 18-inch-squares of aluminum foil or parchment paper; then fold each in half to make a double layer. On each piece, place a thin layer of 4 to 6 potato slices, roughly the same size as the fillet; top with a piece of fish, 2 slices of tomato, salt, pepper, 4 basil leaves, and a drizzle of oil. Fold over the foil and crimp the edges to seal into packages and place them in a single layer in a large baking dish.

2 Bake for about 20 minutes, turning the pan in the oven after 10 minutes to ensure even cooking. Check the fish in one package; the snapper will be white, opaque, and tender when done, the tomato will have liquefied, and the potato will be cooked. Serve the packages closed, allowing each diner to open his or her own at the table.

Red Snapper or Other Fillets in Packages with Carrots and Zucchini: In Step 1, replace the potatoes with a bed of about 1/2 cup mixed julienned carrots and zucchini, sprinkled with a few drops of balsamic vinegar; top with a drizzle of olive oil, chopped fresh tarragon, and a thin slice of lemon. Step 2 remains the same.

Broiled Cod or Other Thick White Fillets

Makes 4 servings
Time: 20 minutes, plus time to preheat the broiler

As long as your fish is good and fresh, you need do no more than this; it will be delicious. There are, however, an infinite number of variations. I give some of them here; for others, see Four Ideas for Broiled Fillets, page 36.

1 or 2 cod fillets, at least 1 inch thick, weighing about 1½ pounds total

1 tablespoon olive oil or butter, plus a little more for the pan

Salt and freshly ground black pepper to taste

1 lemon, quartered

1   Preheat the broiler. It should be very hot, with the rack about 4 inches from the heat source. (You can also bake the fish at 450°F; it will take 1 or 2 minutes longer.)

2   Lightly grease a baking sheet or broiling pan. Lay the fillets on it, then brush with the tablespoon of oil or butter. Sprinkle with salt and pepper.

3   Place the pan in the broiler. Change its position every 2 minutes or so in order to brown the fish evenly, and baste once or twice with the melted fat from the bottom of the pan.

4   Generally, when the top of the fish is nicely browned, the fish is cooked through, or nearly so; as a general rule, figure about 8 to 10 minutes per inch of thickness, measured at the thickest point. If the fish is browning too quickly, turn off the broiler and finish the cooking with the oven set at 500°F. Most fillets are done when they offer no resistance to a thin-bladed knife and are opaque, or nearly so, throughout; avoid overcooking. Serve with lemon quarters.

Shopping Tip: Firm thick fillets like Grouper, Monkfish, and Striped Bass require longer cooking to become tender, but are sturdy enough to grill; more delicate ones, such as Cod, Red Snapper, Turbot, and Orange Roughy, can be broiled or baked but are difficult to grill.

Broiled Cod or Other Thick White Fillets with Flavored Bread Crumbs: Steps 1, 2, and 3 remain the same. While the fish is cooking (or before), heat 2 to 4 tablespoons of butter or oil in a medium skillet over medium heat; when hot, toss in ½ to 1 cup plain bread crumbs, with or without 1 teaspoon of minced garlic and ¼ cup minced fresh parsley leaves. Spread the bread crumbs on top of the fish about 2 minutes before it finishes cooking in Step 4.

Broiled Cod or Other Thick White Fillets with White Wine and Herbs: A low-fat variation. Steps 1 and 2 remain the same; omit the butter or oil if you like. In Step 3, douse the fish with ¼ cup dry white wine and a sprinkling of minced fresh herbs—tarragon, rosemary, parsley, chives, basil, chervil, savory, etc.—about halfway through the cooking. A teaspoon or so of minced garlic may be added at the same time. Step 4 remains the same; serve with the liquid and good crusty bread.

The Basics of Thick White Fish Fillets

By definition, thick white fillets are all white, tender, and mild-flavored, and at least an inch thick (and often even up to 2 inches thick).

You must take care to cook thick fillets thoroughly. This has a couple of advantages: It means that in broiling, and even roasting, you're likely to use cooking times that are long enough to assure browning. With the firmest fillets, it also means that they'll have plenty of time to crisp up in a skillet, yet remain sturdy enough to turn without breaking.

These fish cook quickly, at a rate of 8 to 10 minutes per inch of thickness with most cooking methods. To check if they are done:

Begin checking the fish after about 7 minutes of cooking time per inch of thickness. First, insert a very thin-bladed knife or skewer into the thickest part. If it penetrates with little or no resistance, the fish is done, or nearly so.

Use the same blade to gently pry open the fish at its thickest part and peek in there (a flashlight can be helpful here if your kitchen light is not direct). Once it is opaque throughout, the fish is completely done. You can stop cooking just before this point—when a bit of translucence remains—and the fish will finish cooking on the way to the table.

Note that some of these fish—striped bass, for example, or grouper—are large enough so that you can ask for a "center cut" of the fillet. It will be of fairly even thickness throughout, minimizing the differences in doneness between portions of the fish. A portion of a cod fillet can also be cut to more or less uniform thickness.

Grilled Swordfish, Tuna, Salmon, or Other Steaks

Makes 4 servings
Time: 45 minutes, plus time to preheat the grill

Nothing simpler, few things better. The marinade just gives a bit of tang to the browning crust; you could eliminate it, and brush the grilling fish with a bit of olive oil or soy sauce if you prefer.

> 2 (1-inch-thick) swordfish, tuna, salmon, or other fish steaks, a total of 1½ to 2 pounds
>
> Juice of 1 lime
>
> 2 tablespoons soy sauce
>
> Lime or lemon wedges

1 Start a charcoal or wood fire or preheat a gas grill or broiler; the fire should be quite hot and the rack should be fairly close to the heat, 3 or 4 inches at most.

2 Soak the steak in a mixture of the lime juice and soy sauce for 15 to 30 minutes, if desired.

3 Grill the fish, brushing once or twice with the soy-lime mixture. After 4 minutes, the fish should be nicely browned; turn it. Three minutes later, check the fish for doneness by peeking between the layers of flesh with a thin-bladed knife—when the knife meets little resistance and just a touch of translucence remains, the swordfish is done. Serve immediately, with lime or lemon wedges.

Shopping Tip: Firm steaks are ideal for grilling, and include Swordfish, Tuna, Salmon, and Tilefish. More delicate steaks, like Bluefish (strong-flavored), Cod, and Halibut, can also be grilled, but handle them carefully.

Herb-Rubbed Grilled Swordfish, Tuna, or Other Steaks: Step 1 remains the same. In Step 2, omit the marinade and, before grilling, rub the fish with a mixture of 1 tablespoon grated or minced lemon peel, 1 teaspoon coarse salt, 1 large minced clove garlic, and 2 tablespoons minced mixed fresh herbs, such as parsley, chives, basil, sage, thyme, and/or rosemary. Grill as in Step 3 and serve with lemon wedges.

Three Ideas for Grilled or Broiled Fish Steaks

1. Serve hot on a lightly dressed bed of greens.
2. Chill and use in a sandwich.
3. Drizzle with soy sauce or dark sesame oil.

The Basics of Fish Steaks

All fish steaks can be grilled, although the more delicate fish such as halibut and cod need care, not only to prevent them from falling apart, but because they overcook and dry out easily. First-time fish grillers are better off with the sturdy, flavorful, nearly foolproof steaks of tuna and swordfish.

Steaks can also be cooked by any other method; broiling, roasting, and pan-cooking are the easiest and the best. Generally, they all take about the same length of time; when roasting, I usually add 2 or 3 minutes extra.

Because they are of uniform thickness, or nearly so, steaks cook evenly and at a fairly uniform rate. Some steaks—most notably swordfish and tuna—are better when they're cooked to a medium, and even a medium-rare stage, than when they are cooked to well done. Others, such as halibut and cod, become quite dry if they're overcooked.

To check doneness, begin checking the fish after about 7 minutes of cooking time per inch of thickness. Cod and halibut are done when a thin-bladed knife passes easily through the center. To confirm, take a very thin-bladed knife, and make a small cut near the center of a steak. Pry the flesh apart and peek in there to judge the level of doneness; all translucence should be gone.

Swordfish is at its most moist if you stop cooking when just a little translucence remains in the center; cook it to the well-done stage if you prefer, but get it off the heat quickly or it will be dry. Tuna is best when still red to pink in the center. Fully cooked tuna is inevitably dry.

Pan-Grilled Salmon Fillets

Makes 4 servings • **Time:** 20 minutes

This is an easy salmon recipe, which sacrifices the skin in order to leave the flesh moist. It will, however, create a fair amount of smoke, so turn on the exhaust fan if you have one.

1 to 1¼ pounds salmon fillet, preferably in two pieces of equal thickness, skin on (scaling is not necessary), pin bones removed

Salt and freshly ground black pepper to taste

Minced fresh parsley leaves for garnish

Lemon wedges

1 Preheat a large ovenproof skillet (cast iron is fine) for 3 or 4 minutes over medium-high heat. Preheat the broiler as well, positioning the rack about 4 inches beneath the heat source.

2 Place the salmon fillets in the skillet, skin side down. Leave the heat on medium-high. Sprinkle with salt and pepper and cook, undisturbed, for about 6 minutes, or until the salmon flesh turns opaque about halfway up the fish.

3 Move the fish to the broiler and leave it there for 2 or 3 minutes, just until the top browns. The fish should still be moist and slightly undercooked in the middle.

4 Remove the fish, garnish, and serve with lemon wedges.

Shopping Tip: In late spring through late summer, when wild salmon is in season, look for it; the best species are King (Chinook) and Sockeye (Red), but Coho (Silver) is also good, and Chum is acceptable. The rest of the year, rely on farm-raised salmon.

Pan-Grilled Salmon Fillets with Sesame Oil Drizzle: Steps 1, 2, and 3 remain the same; omit the salt, or at least go easy on it. While the fish is cooking, warm 2 teaspoons dark sesame oil and 1 teaspoon vegetable oil in a small saucepan over low heat. When they're hot, add 2 teaspoons soy sauce. When the fish is done, drizzle this sauce over it. Garnish with minced parsley, minced cilantro, or minced lemon zest; serve with wedges of lemon or lime.

REMOVING PIN BONES

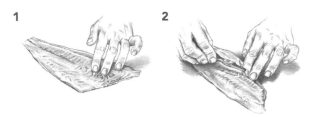

(Step 1) Fillets of many fish, no matter how skillfully handled, may contain long bones along their center, which must be removed by hand. Feel with your fingers to see if your fillet contains pin bones. **(Step 2)** remove them with needle-nose pliers or similar tool.

The Basics of Salmon

Salmon is distinctively rich, oily, and sometimes downright fatty, full of flavor but almost never "fishy."

It is most often sold as steaks and fillets (There are sometimes large "pin bones" that run down the center of imperfect fillets, but you can remove these in the kitchen. See illustration.) Salmon's ease of cooking and good flavor are largely thanks to its high fat content, which seems to be associated with combating rather than encouraging disease. It cooks easily, whether grilled, roasted, or poached.

Fish markets often scale fish before cutting it up but supermarkets usually don't. The easiest solution is to cook the fish with the scales on and discard the skin. This works well for salmon, because the scales give added protection against overcooking,

and the skin peels right off afterward, taking the scales with it. On the other hand, salmon skin is good to eat, so if you can get it scaled (or scale it yourself—all you do is run a spoon or other dull implement against the grain of the scales, and they'll come flying off) you'll have better eating.

The cooking time for salmon varies according to your taste. I prefer my salmon cooked to what might be called medium-rare to medium, with a well-cooked exterior and a fairly red center. Given that, I always look at the center of a piece of salmon to judge its doneness. Once again, remember that fish retains enough heat to continue cooking after it has been removed from the heat source, so stop cooking just before the salmon reaches the point you'd consider it done.

Shrimp Cocktail

Makes 4 servings
Time: 20 minutes, plus chilling time, as needed

Almost any shrimp recipe can be made into an appetizer, but this classic is never anything but.

1 pound large shrimp (about 20 per pound), preferably with their peels on

1/2 cup ketchup

1 teaspoon chile powder

3 tablespoons freshly squeezed lemon juice

Salt and freshly ground black pepper to taste

1 tablespoon Worcestershire sauce, or to taste

Several drops Tabasco or other hot sauce

1 tablespoon prepared horseradish, or to taste

1 tablespoon finely minced onion (optional)

Iceberg lettuce (optional)

1   Place the shrimp in a medium pot of salted water to cover and turn the heat to high; when it boils, reduce the heat to medium-low and cook just until the shrimp are pink all over, 3 to 5 minutes. Turn off the heat and rinse immediately in cold water. Peel and devein the shrimp (see "Preparing Shrimp").

2   In a medium bowl, combine all the other ingredients (except the lettuce); taste and adjust seasoning. If possible, chill both shrimp and sauce at least 2 hours.

3   Serve individual portions of shrimp, on a bed of lettuce if you like, with a small bowl of sauce.

Shopping Tip: Shrimp should have no black spots, or melanosis, on their shells, which indicate that a breakdown of the meat has begun. Be equally suspicious of shrimp with yellowing shells. And, like most seafood, shrimp should smell of salt water and little else.

PREPARING SHRIMP

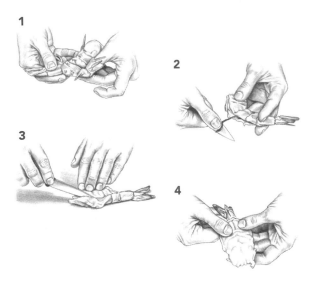

(Step 1) To peel shrimp, grasp the feelers on the underside and pull the peel away from the meat.
(Step 2) Should you choose to devein, make a shallow cut on the back side of each shrimp, and then remove the long, black, threadlike vein.
(Steps 3–4) To butterfly shrimp, cut most of the way through the back of the shrimp and open it up.

The Basics of Shrimp

Shrimp, the most popular non-canned seafood in America, can be domestic or imported, wild or farm-raised. Almost all shrimp is frozen before sale, and it makes some sense to buy frozen shrimp rather than those that have been thawed. Since the shelf life of previously frozen shrimp is not much more than a couple of days, buying thawed shrimp gives you neither the flavor of fresh nor the flexibility of frozen. Stored in the home freezer, shrimp retain their quality for a month or more.

Despite the popularity of shrimp, there are few rules governing its sale. Small, medium, large, extra-large, jumbo, and other size classifications are subjective.

Small shrimp of fifty to the pound are frequently labeled "medium," as are those twice that size, so learn to judge shrimp size by the number it takes to make a pound, as retailers do. Shrimp labeled "16/20," for example, require sixteen to twenty individual specimens to make a pound. Those labeled "U-20" require fewer (under twenty) to make a pound. Shrimp of about twenty to about thirty per pound usually give the best combination of flavor, ease (peeling tiny shrimp is a nuisance), and value.

The best way to defrost shrimp is in the refrigerator, which takes a while, or under cold running water, which is faster.

Shrimp, My Way

Makes 4 servings • **Time:** About 30 minutes

This pan-cooked and broiled shrimp recipe
is so good it makes people go nuts; if you
like scampi, try this (or the scampi variation).
It pays to look for good, fresh paprika for
this recipe.

> ½ cup extra-virgin olive oil
>
> 3 or 4 big cloves garlic, cut into slivers
>
> 1½ to 2 pounds shrimp, in the 20 to
> 30 per pound range, peeled, rinsed,
> and dried
>
> Salt and freshly ground black pepper
> to taste
>
> 1 teaspoon ground cumin
>
> 1½ teaspoons fresh spicy paprika
>
> Minced fresh parsley leaves for garnish

1 Preheat the broiler and adjust the rack so that
it is as close to the heat source as possible.

2 Very gently, in a large, broad ovenproof skillet
or baking pan, warm the olive oil over low heat.
There should be enough olive oil to cover the bottom of the pan; don't skimp. Put the garlic in the
oil and cook for a few minutes, still over low heat,
until it turns golden.

3 Raise the heat to medium-high and add the
shrimp, salt, pepper, cumin, and paprika. Stir to
blend and immediately place under the broiler.
Cook, shaking the pan once or twice and stirring if
necessary, but generally leaving the shrimp undisturbed, until they are pink all over and the mixture
is bubbly. This will take from 5 to 10 minutes,
depending on the heat of your broiler. Garnish and
serve immediately.

Preparation Tips: You should peel shrimp if they
will be cooked in a sauce that will make it difficult to peel them at the table. You might also peel
them if you're feeling generous or energetic; it
saves your guests the hassle. For simple grilling or
pan-cooking, however, it's arguable that shrimp
with their peels on lose less liquid and flavor.

Devein shrimp only if you choose to. Some people won't eat shrimp that isn't deveined. Others
believe that the "vein"—actually the animal's
intestinal tract—contributes to flavor. It's a matter of personal taste.

Shrimp "Scampi": Don't preheat the broiler; use
a large, deep skillet instead. Step 2 remains
the same. In Step 3, omit the cumin and
paprika. When the shrimp turns pink on one
side, turn it over and add ¼ cup minced
fresh parsley leaves. Raise the heat slightly
and cook until the shrimp are done, about
2 minutes more. Stir in 1 tablespoon freshly
squeezed lemon juice, dry sherry, vinegar,
or white wine if you like and cook another
30 seconds before garnishing with more
parsley and serving.

Spicy Grilled or Broiled Shrimp

Makes 4 servings

Time: 20 minutes, plus time to preheat the grill

Be forewarned: This is the kind of dish that makes people eat more than they should. Make extra; I always do.

1 large clove garlic

1 tablespoon coarse salt

$1/2$ teaspoon cayenne

1 teaspoon paprika

2 tablespoons olive oil

2 teaspoons freshly squeezed lemon juice

$1^1/2$ to 2 pounds shrimp, in the 20 to 30 per pound range, peeled, rinsed, and dried

Lemon wedges

1 Start a charcoal or gas grill or preheat the broiler; in any case, make the fire as hot as it will get and adjust the rack so that it is as close to the heat source as possible.

2 Mince the garlic with the salt, mix it with the cayenne and paprika, then make it into a paste with the olive oil and lemon juice. Smear the paste all over the shrimp. Grill or broil the shrimp, 2 to 3 minutes per side, turning once. Serve immediately or at room temperature, with lemon wedges.

Preparation Tip: You might want to skewer these (or other) shrimp before grilling, either for appearance or ease of handling. Metal skewers, which get quite hot, are reusable. Wooden skewers, which are a little easier to handle and can be discarded after use, should be soaked in water to cover for at least 15 minutes before using, to inhibit burning.

Steamed Clams

Makes 4 servings

Time: 15 minutes, longer if you have time

Sometimes, steamed clams—often called "steamers"—are so sweet you'll swear you never had better seafood. In my experience, the best come from the North—Maine, the Maritime Provinces of Canada, and the Pacific Northwest. For more elaborate recipes, see the variations under Steamed Mussels (page 52).

> 4 to 6 pounds soft-shell clams ("steamers")
>
> ½ onion or several cloves garlic, lightly smashed
>
> Several sprigs fresh parsley
>
> 1 cup white wine or water
>
> Melted butter

1 Rinse the clams in a few changes of water, getting rid of the coarsest dirt. Then, if you have time, soak them for a few hours in cold salted (or sea) water to which a couple of handfuls of cornmeal have been added. Then rinse them again. If you don't have time, proceed.

2 Place the onion, parsley, and wine in a large, deep pot that has a lid over medium-high heat, along with the clams. Cover and turn the heat to high. Steam the clams, shaking the pot often until they open, 5 to 10 minutes.

3 Remove the clams with a slotted spoon; place them in a bowl. Use a mesh strainer lined with a paper towel to strain the broth into another bowl. Serve immediately, with melted butter. Eat by removing each clam from its shell, then taking the black membrane off its "neck" or "foot," dipping it in the broth to clean it of any remaining sand, then into the butter.

SHUCKING CLAMS

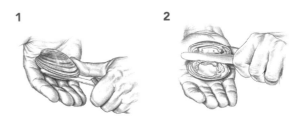

1   2

To open a clam, you must use a blunt, fairly thick knife; there is a knife made specifically for this purpose (called, not surprisingly, a "clam knife"), and it's worth having for this chore. **(Step 1)** Hold the clam in your cupped hand, and wedge the edge of the knife into the clam's shell opposite the hinge. Once you get it in there the clam will give up all resistance. **(Step 2)** Run the knife along the shell and open up the clam. Try to keep as much juice inside the shell as you can. Detach the meat from the shell and serve.

The Basics of Clams

Clams range from little ("littlenecks") to sea clams that weigh hundreds of pounds; they may be hard (littlenecks, cherrystones, or quahogs), or soft (steamers, razor clams, and other clams with fragile shells). The biggest and toughest are chopped into bits to be made into chowder. The choicest—essentially the smallest—are sold live, and are great raw, on the half-shell.

Buying clams is easy, since those in the shell must be alive. If hard-shells have died, the shells separate easily; otherwise, they're shut up pretty tight, and you cannot even slide their shells from side to side. Dead clams smell pretty bad, so it's unlikely you'll be fooled.

Never store clams in sealed plastic or under water; they'll die. Just keep them in a bowl in the refrigerator, where they will remain alive for several days.

Soft-shells usually contain large quantities of sand, and you must wash them well before cooking (soft-shells are never eaten raw). Hard-shells require little more than a cleaning of their shells. I use a stiff brush to scrub them under running water. To shuck them, see the illustrated steps. Serve with lemon if you like; sauces are superfluous. Small hard-shells—under 2 inches across—are also nice lightly steamed, like mussels.

Steamed Mussels

Makes 4 servings

Time: About 15 minutes, plus cleaning time

When mussels are good—fat and sweet—
one pound per person is just about right for
a main course. A little bit of saffron added to
the steaming liquid gives the broth a won-
drous flavor. Serve with crusty bread to soak
up the extra broth.

> 3 tablespoons extra-virgin olive oil
>
> 4 cloves garlic, smashed
>
> 1 medium onion, roughly sliced
>
> $1/2$ cup dry white wine
>
> $1/2$ cup roughly chopped fresh
> parsley leaves
>
> At least 4 pounds large mussels,
> well washed (see next page)

1 In a large pot over medium heat, heat the oil,
then add the garlic and onion and cook, stirring,
just until the onion softens.

2 Add the wine, parsley, and mussels, cover the
pot, and turn the heat to high. Steam, shaking the
pot frequently, until the mussels open, about 8 to
10 minutes. Use a slotted spoon to put the mussels
into a serving bowl; if you like, you can strain a
little of the liquid over them.

Mussels with Butter Sauce: Follow the basic
recipe and keep the mussels warm. Strain the
cooking liquid through a mesh strainer lined
with a paper towel into a medium saucepan
and bring it to a boil over medium-high heat.
Meanwhile, discard 1 shell of each mussel,
and arrange the remaining shells, with the
mussel meat, on a platter. Keep warm in a
low oven while the liquid reduces. When the
steaming liquid is reduced to about $1/4$ cup,
add 3 tablespoons butter, cut into bits, and
let it melt. Add 1 teaspoon minced garlic and
$1/4$ cup minced fresh parsley leaves. Cook
over medium heat for 1 or 2 minutes. Check
for salt, then drizzle the sauce over the
mussel meats and serve.

DEBEARDING MUSSELS

Most mussels have a "beard," a small amount of
vegetative growth extending from their flat side.
Pull or cut it off before cooking.

Mussels with Cream: Follow the recipe as directed and place the mussels in a warm, covered bowl. Strain the cooking liquid through a mesh strainer lined with a paper towel into a medium saucepan; bring it to a boil over medium-high heat. Add 1 teaspoon minced fresh tarragon leaves or ½ teaspoon dried tarragon. Reduce the liquid to about ½ cup, then turn the heat to low. Add 2 tablespoons butter, cut into bits. When it has melted, add 1 cup heavy cream or half-and-half. Heat but do not boil. Taste the sauce for seasoning (feel free to add a little more tarragon) and pour it over the mussels.

The Basics of Mussels

Mussels are usually much less expensive than clams, and can be as heavenly as a good lobster. They come from everywhere, from Maine to New Zealand. (In my opinion, they don't freeze well, but there are those who disagree.)

The biggest hassle about mussels is cleaning them. If possible, start with clean mussels (farmed mussels are almost always cleaner than wild mussels) instead of muddy ones. If you have the time, let them sit in a pot under slowly running cold water for 30 minutes or more. Then wash the mussels carefully, discarding any with broken shells, those whose shells remain open after tapping them lightly, or those which seem unusually heavy (chances are they're filled with mud). As you clean them, pull or scrape off the "beard"—the weedy growth attached to the bottom of shell—from each one. Rinse thoroughly.

Boiled or Steamed Lobster

Makes as many servings as desired
Time: 30 minutes or less

If you want to serve the lobster with drawn butter (lemon is just as good or better, in my opinion—lobster is plenty rich enough without butter), simply melt 2 tablespoons of butter per person over low heat and serve it in small bowls with the lobster.

For each person, choose a lobster that weighs 1½ pounds or more; a 3-pound lobster is enough for two people

Lemon wedges (optional)

1 In a large, covered pot (like one used for pasta), bring lots of water to a boil—or just 1 inch if you choose to steam—and add salt, a couple of handfuls or so (if you have access to clean seawater, that's a nice touch, as is steaming atop a pile of fresh seaweed).

2 Plunge the lobster(s) into the pot, cover, and cook about 8 minutes for its first pound—from the time the water returns to the boil—and then an additional 3 or 4 minutes per pound thereafter. Thus, a 3-pounder should boil for 15 to 20 minutes. Lobster is done when the meat becomes opaque and firm, and the coral—which you only find in females—turns, well, coral-colored (it stays dark red until it is cooked). None of this does you any good if the lobster is whole, since you can't see or feel the meat or the coral. One assurance: It's difficult to undercook a small lobster, if you use the timing guidelines above. If you're boiling a larger one, insert an instant-read thermometer into the tail meat by sliding it in between the underside of the body and the tail joint; lobster is done at 140°F.

3 Remove the lobsters, which will be bright red, and let them sit for 5 minutes or so before serving. If lobsters have been boiled, poke a hole in the cross-hatch right behind the eyes, and drain out the water. Eat.

EATING LOBSTER

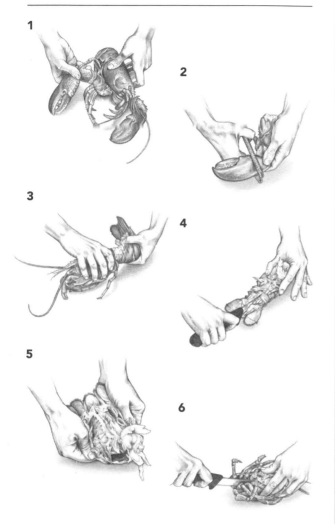

1

2

3

4

5

6

(Step 1) Twist the claws to remove them; they will come off easily. (Step 2) Use a nutcracker to split their shells and a pick to pull out the meat. (Step 3) Twist the lobster in half to separate the tail from the body. (Steps 4–5) Cut through the soft side of the tail and crack it open like a shrimp to remove the tail meat. (Step 6) Cut through the underside of the front part of the body; pick out the small bits of meat in there.

The Basics of Lobsters

When buying lobster, lift each one (make sure its claws are pegged or banded); if it doesn't flip its tail and kick its legs, look for another. I look for hard-shell lobsters; you can tell the difference with a little squeeze—soft shells will yield to pressure.

Two people sharing a three-pound lobster will get more meat of equally high quality than if each has his own pound-and-a-half lobster. There's less work, less waste, and more meat.

There are very few parts of a lobster that you cannot eat. You can even remove the tomalley (the green, liverlike organ) and the coral (the very dark red eggs, which turn bright red after cooking; found in females only) to use in sauces.

Should you boil or steam? If you're cooking one batch of lobsters—whatever fits in your pot—steam them; it's much easier, and, because the lobster absorbs less water, far less messy. But lobsters flavor the cooking water (you should consider saving it as broth), which in turn flavors the lobsters. So if you're cooking a bunch, boil them. And eat the last of the batch yourself.

Crab Cakes

Makes 4 servings
Time: 15 minutes, plus refrigeration time

If you ever make anything with crab, make crab cakes. They're simple to make and people love them. I like crab cakes that are mostly crab and seasonings, with a minimum of bread crumbs.

1 pound fresh lump crabmeat, picked over for cartilage

1 egg

$1/4$ cup minced red bell pepper

$1/2$ cup minced scallion

$1/4$ cup Mayonnaise (page 7), or prepared mayonnaise

1 tablespoon Dijon mustard

Salt and freshly ground black pepper to taste

2 tablespoons plain bread crumbs, or as needed

About 1 cup flour for dredging

1 teaspoon curry powder (optional)

2 tablespoons peanut, olive, or vegetable oil

2 tablespoons butter (or use all oil)

Lemon wedges and/or Real Tartar Sauce (page 7)

1   Mix together the crabmeat, egg, bell pepper, scallion, mayonnaise, mustard, salt, and pepper. Add sufficient bread crumbs to bind the mixture just enough to form into cakes; start with 2 tablespoons and use more if you need it.

2   Refrigerate the mixture until you're ready to cook (it will be easier to shape if you refrigerate it for 30 minutes or more, but it is ready to go when you finish mixing).

3   Season the flour with salt, pepper, and curry if you like. Preheat a large skillet, preferably non-stick, over medium-high heat for 2 or 3 minutes. Add the oil and butter and heat until the butter foam subsides. Shape the crabmeat mixture into four cakes, dredge each in the flour, and cook; if the crabcakes threaten to burn, lower the heat a bit. Turn once (very gently), until golden brown on both sides. Total cooking time will be about 10 minutes. Serve with lemon wedges.

Shopping Tips: You can buy fresh-picked crabmeat, refrigerated, in any good fish market and in many supermarkets. It keeps well for a few days, or may be frozen. Look for "lump" crabmeat, as opposed to "flake" crabmeat, which is essentially shredded. (If you can find "claw" crabmeat, even better, but it's unlikely, and it will cost a fortune.)

Canned crabmeat is not nearly as good, but you can make a halfway decent crabcake with it. Do not buy surimi, which is imitation crabmeat.

---

4 | Poultry

Chicken has become the preferred meat of many Americans. Not surprising, since it (and other birds, like turkey) is low in fat, cooks quickly, and has mild flavor and tender texture.

Most supermarket chicken is more than mild—it's downright bland. You must add flavor with herbs, spices, aromatic vegetables, small amounts of other meats, or through a flavor-enhancing cooking method, such as grilling. Fortunately, basic seasonings do wonderful things for chicken. Recipes can remain uncomplicated and still be quite delicious. Because chicken is essentially a blank slate, you have unlimited flavor options; and, as long as they're sensibly combined, the results will be just fine.

The results will be even better if you're able to start with a high-quality chicken. And chicken has become so popular that many supermarkets now offer some choices: two budget chickens (a store brand and a commercial brand); one kosher chicken; and one premium, "natural," or free-range chicken. Certainly from a flavor perspective, and quite possibly from those of environment and health, the alternatives are almost always better than mass-produced chickens.

It's worth noting that much of the chicken that is sold as "fresh" has actually been shipped at least partly frozen, which demonstrates that chicken freezes brilliantly. You can usually buy frozen birds (that's often the only way organic or kosher chickens are sold) with confidence, but, more important, this means that you can buy as much chicken as you can store when it's on sale and freeze it yourself. Just remove it from the package, then wrap it tightly in two layers of plastic, and place in the freezer, which should be as cold as you can make it.

Turkey may forever signify Thanksgiving, so you should know how to get a basic feast on the table, and roasted duck is such a luxuriously flavorful bird when roasted, it's worth trying, even if only for special occasions.

Grilled or Broiled Chicken Cutlets

Makes 4 servings
Time: 20 minutes, plus time for marinating, as needed, and to preheat the grill

Soy sauce makes a great non-fat basting liquid. If you prefer olive oil—which keeps the meat moister—use it in place of soy and finish the chicken with lemon juice. In all but the hottest weather, broiling is far easier than grilling.

4 boneless, skinless chicken cutlets
(2 breasts, halved), 1 to 1¹/₂ pounds,
rinsed and patted dry with paper towels

2 tablespoons soy sauce

Freshly ground black pepper to taste

1 tablespoon freshly squeezed
lime juice

1 teaspoon dark sesame oil (optional)

1 Start a charcoal or wood fire or preheat a gas grill or broiler. The fire should not be too hot, but the rack should be fairly close to the heat source, 4 inches or less. If necessary, you can pound the chicken slices lightly between two pieces of waxed paper so that they are of uniform thickness.

2 Brush the chicken pieces with the soy sauce and sprinkle it with pepper. If you have time, let the chicken marinate in the refrigerator for 1 hour or more.

3 Grill or broil the chicken very quickly; it should take no more than 3 or 4 minutes per side. Sprinkle with lime juice and sesame oil; serve hot or at room temperature.

Grilled or Broiled Chicken Cutlets in Sweet Soy Marinade ("Chicken Teriyaki"): In Step 2, immerse the chicken in a combination of 1 teaspoon dark sesame oil, ¹/₄ cup soy sauce, 1 tablespoon peeled and finely minced or grated fresh ginger, ¹/₄ cup minced scallion, both green and white parts, 1 teaspoon minced garlic, 1 tablespoon dry sherry, white wine, or water, and 1 tablespoon honey or sugar. (Marinate in refrigerator for 1 hour, if possible.) Remove the chicken from the marinade and boil the marinade for 1 minute. Grill or broil the chicken as in Step 3, brushing frequently with the marinade (omit the lime juice). Garnish with more minced scallion and serve.

Grilled or Broiled Chicken Cutlets with Basil and Tomato: In Step 2, immerse the chicken breasts in a combination of 1 tablespoon olive oil, ¹/₂ cup chopped fresh basil leaves, 2 tablespoons freshly squeezed lemon juice, and salt and pepper to taste. While the grill is preheating, cut a ripe medium tomato (peeled and seeded if you like, page 26) into little cubes, about ¹/₄ inch on each side. Remove the chicken from the marinade and boil the marinade for 1 minute. Grill or broil the chicken as in Step 3, brushing frequently with the marinade. Serve, garnished with the tomato cubes, some minced basil, and a drizzle of olive oil.

The Basics of Boneless Chicken Breasts

Boneless chicken breasts have become standard weeknight fare for many Americans, because they can be cooked in minutes using any of a number of techniques: on top of the stove in a skillet or wok (they're ideal for stir-fries), on a grill, under a broiler, or in the oven. They need little or no added fat. And they can take almost any seasoning. If there is a problem with them, it is that care must be taken not to overcook them or they will become tough and dry as jerky.

So use bold flavorings and keep the cooking time short, as little as 6 minutes for $1/2$-inch-thick boneless breasts. Generally, it's best to remove them from the heat when the inside is still a little pearly, rather than chalky-white. (It's not easy to use an instant-read thermometer on thin boneless breasts, but you can get an accurate reading by sliding the probe in from the end, rather than the top, and inserting it into the middle; breasts are done at 160°F.)

Any chicken cutlet recipe can also be used for turkey cutlets—or, for that matter, veal cutlets or thin-sliced pork. Most of them (especially those that add strong flavors) are also great with boneless thighs. You'll have to increase the cooking time somewhat, to around 6 to 8 minutes per side.

Sautéed Chicken Cutlets

Makes about 4 servings • **Time:** 20 minutes

This is among the simplest of recipes: It has no sauce and virtually no seasonings. But, given good chicken and care not to overcook, it is delicious.

4 boneless, skinless chicken cutlets (2 breasts), 1 to 1½ pounds, rinsed and patted dry with paper towels

Salt and freshly ground black pepper to taste

1 cup all-purpose flour, plain bread crumbs, seasoned bread crumbs, or cornmeal

2 tablespoons olive oil

1 tablespoon butter (or use all olive oil)

Lemon wedges

Minced fresh parsley leaves for garnish (optional)

1 Heat a large skillet, preferably non-stick, over medium-high heat for 2 or 3 minutes. While the skillet is heating, sprinkle the chicken breasts with salt and pepper and place the flour, bread crumbs, or cornmeal on a plate or in a shallow bowl.

2 Add the oil and butter, if any, to the skillet and swirl it around. When it is hot—a pinch of flour will sizzle—dredge a piece of the chicken in the coating, pressing it down a bit to coat evenly. Shake it a little so that excess coating falls off. Add the chicken piece to the pan, then move on to the next one. (Don't be tempted to dredge in advance and add all the pieces at once; the coating will become soggy, and the heat in the pan will drop too quickly.)

3 Cook the chicken, regulating the heat if necessary so that there is a good constant sizzle but no burning. After 2 minutes, rotate the chicken (do not flip) so that the outside edges are moved toward the center and vice versa. After 3 to 4 minutes, when the pieces are brown, turn them over.

4 Cook on the second side 3 to 4 minutes, until the chicken breasts are firm to the touch. If you are unsure whether they're done, cut into one with a thin-bladed knife; the center should be white (the barest trace of pink is okay, too—they will finish cooking on the way to the table). Serve with lemon wedges; garnish with parsley if you like.

Preparation Tip: To make your own seasoned bread crumbs, start with 3 or 4 slices of not-too-fresh bread. Whir them in a food processor with 1 clove of garlic and ½ cup fresh parsley leaves until fairly fine.

Extra-Crisp Chicken Cutlets: Use seasoned bread crumbs (see Preparation Tip) if possible. In Step 1, set up three bowls: one with all-purpose flour, one with a beaten egg, and one with the bread crumbs. In Step 2, when the fat is hot, dredge each piece of chicken first in the flour, as above, then in the egg, and finally in the bread crumbs, pressing to help them adhere. Proceed as above, lowering the heat a bit after the first minute or two in order to avoid burning the bread crumbs.

Chicken Parmigiana: Make Extra-Crisp Chicken Cutlets (page 60), cooking chicken just enough to brown it (don't worry about cooking it fully). Preheat the oven to 400°F. Spread about ¹/₂ cup of Easy Tomato Sauce (page 27) on the bottom of a 9-inch square baking dish. Place the cutlets on top of the sauce, and top with another cup of sauce. Sprinkle 1¹/₂ cups coarsely grated mozzarella over the sauce. Bake until the cheese melts and the sauce is hot, 10 to 15 minutes. Top with 1 or 2 tablespoons of minced parsley or oregano leaves and serve.

The Basics of Sautéed Chicken Cutlets

There are some things to bear in mind before you sauté chicken cutlets. (For general information about sautéing, see The Basics of Sautéing, page xii).

You must use a large enough skillet. It must be hot before you add the fat, and the fat must be hot before you add the meat (oil will shimmer and sizzle when you add a pinch of flour; the foam of butter will subside and it will begin to turn brown). This is not just to prevent sticking—a non-stick skillet will achieve that automatically—but to properly brown the meat. Too-cool temperatures, which can also result from adding too much meat to the pan too quickly, or from overcrowding, result in a soggy coating.

The process is fast: Thin slices will cook in 6 minutes, thicker ones in 10, and most in about 8. When they're firm, or an instant-read thermometer reads 160°F they're done.

I set the oven at about 200°F as I begin this cooking process. If you choose to make a sauce, a warm oven will hold the chicken perfectly as you do so. But even if you do not, it gives you the option of moving those pieces that finish cooking a little more quickly than others, whether because they are thinner or closer to the center of the pan, to a place where they will stay hot and crisp until you need them.

You can substitute turkey, pork, or veal cutlets in the recipe or variations.

Reduction Sauce or Pan Gravy

Makes ¹/₂ cup • **Time:** 10 minutes

A reduction or pan gravy is made after cooking, in the same skillet or roasting pan in which you cooked whatever it is you're dressing. You could do without sauce or use bottled, but this is an easy method for any pan-cooked food—poultry, fish, meats, and vegetables. Here we're using the reduction for sautéed chicken. Keep your food warm in a low oven if necessary while you prepare the sauce. Or just add the food back to the pan with the finished sauce and heat through for a minute or so.

Try making a reduction sauce with Sautéed Flatfish or Other Thin White Fillets (page 38); Sautéed Pork Chops (page 90); Lamb Shanks with White Beans (page 97); or Sautéed Summer Squash or Zucchini (page 136).

> 1 tablespoon minced shallot or onion
>
> ¹/₂ cup dry white (for fish, poultry, or vegetables) or red (for red meats) wine
>
> ¹/₂ cup Quickest Chicken Stock (page 17) or store-bought chicken, beef, or vegetable broth, or water, warmed
>
> 2 tablespoons softened butter (optional)
>
> Salt and freshly ground black pepper to taste
>
> A few drops of freshly squeezed lemon juice or vinegar (optional)
>
> Minced fresh parsley leaves for garnish

1 Pour off all but 1 or 2 tablespoons of the cooking fat (if there are dark, non-fatty juices in the skillet or roasting pan leave them in there). Turn the heat under the skillet or pan to medium-high and add the shallot and the wine. Cook, stirring and scraping, until most of the wine has evaporated, the shallot is soft, and the bottom of the pan is clean.

2 Add the stock and repeat; when there is just under ¹/₂ cup of liquid, turn off the heat. Add the butter, a little at a time, stirring well after each addition to incorporate it. Taste and season if necessary with salt, pepper, and/or lemon juice or vinegar.

3 Spoon this sauce over the meat, garnish, and serve.

Asian Sauce: Cook 1 tablespoon each minced garlic, ginger, and scallions (in place of shallot) until soft before adding the wine. Proceed as above, omitting butter. Once the heat is off, stir in 1 tablespoon soy or fish sauce (or Worcestershire sauce), and finish with a few drops of freshly squeezed lime juice. Garnish with minced cilantro leaves.

Mushroom Sauce: Before adding the wine, cook ¹/₂ cup chopped wild or domestic mushrooms along with 2 tablespoons shallots, until soft. Proceed as above. Best with ¹/₄ cup or more of heavy cream added at the last minute.

The Basics of Reduction Sauces

The drill for reduction sauces is straight-forward.

1. Remove the chicken, meat, fish, or vegetables from your roasting or sauté pan.
2. Add twice as much water or other liquid—such as wine or vermouth, milk or cream, or stock—as you would like sauce.
3. Turn the heat to high (if you're working with a large roasting pan, set it over two burners).
4. Stir, scraping the bottom of the pan to release any solids left from cooking, until the liquid is reduced in quantity by about half.
5. Stir in some softened butter, olive oil (preferably extra-virgin), or cream if you like.
6. Serve.

Every reduction sauce is a variation on these simple steps. Some are thickened by adding flour before the liquid, or a cornstarch mixture after the reduction; most are more heavily seasoned. But basically, that's about it.

Five Other Ideas for Reduction Sauces

1. Add ½ cup or more of minced aromatic vegetables—onion, shallots, mushrooms, celery, carrot, or a combination—to the fat remaining in the pan before adding the wine. Cook, stirring, until soft, then add liquid.
2. Substitute heavy cream for half or all of the stock.
3. Add minced herbs or ground spices at the beginning or the end of the sauce-making process. Those added at the beginning will become better incorporated, those at the end will retain more of their flavor. Add them twice if you like.
4. Add chopped or crushed tomatoes or tomato sauce in place of or in addition to some of the stock.
5. Add prepared Dijon or grainy mustard, along with some cream if you like, in place of or in addition to the optional butter.

Fried Chicken

Makes 4 to 6 servings • Time: About 30 minutes

Fried chicken isn't difficult, but it can be messy. I make two adjustments to make it a little less so: One, I use a minimum of oil (which still seems like a lot by today's standards). And two, I cover the skillet for the first few minutes, which reduces spattering substantially. Then I uncover the chicken to make sure it doesn't steam in its own juices, which would defeat the point of frying—namely, a super-crisp skin and moist interior. Like all good fried chicken dishes, this one is fine at room temperature.

Olive oil, peanut oil, lard, vegetable oil, or a combination for frying

2 cups all-purpose flour

1 tablespoon coarse salt

1 teaspoon freshly ground black pepper

2 tablespoons ground cinnamon

1 whole (3- to 4-pound) chicken, cut up, trimmed of excess fat, then rinsed and patted dry with paper towels

Lemon wedges (optional)

1 Heat about $\frac{1}{2}$ inch of the fat over medium-high heat in a deep-fryer, large, deep skillet, or broad saucepan that can later be covered. While it is heating, mix together the flour and seasonings in a plastic bag. Toss the chicken in the bag, two or three pieces at a time, until they are well coated with flour. Put them on a rack as you finish.

2 When the fat reaches 350°F, raise the heat to high and begin to slowly but steadily add the chicken pieces, skin side down, to the skillet (if you add them all at once, the temperature will plummet). When they have all been added, cover the skillet, reduce the heat to medium-high, and set a timer for 7 minutes. After 7 minutes, uncover the skillet, turn the chicken, and continue to cook, uncovered, for another 7 minutes.

3 Turn the chicken skin side down again and cook for about 5 minutes more, turning as necessary to ensure that both sides are golden brown.

4 As the chicken pieces finish cooking (the juices near the bone will run clear), remove them from the skillet and drain them on paper towels. Serve hot, warm, or at room temperature with lemon wedges, if desired.

Shopping Tip: Lard is an old-fashioned fat, but recent research indicates it's less harmful to your health than the frying and cooking fats that were developed to replace it, like margarine and vegetable shortening. It browns food beautifully and, used sparingly, is delicious. Look for it at the supermarket near the bacon.

Cooking Tips: Chicken should be fried at about 350°F, but slightly higher temperatures, up to 375°F, are okay. Use a frying thermometer for accuracy; too-low temperatures will result in soggy chicken. The temperature will plunge as soon as you begin to add the chicken, so keep the heat as high as possible at first to enable the temperature to recover as quickly as possible.

Don't crowd the chicken in the pan; if the chicken pieces touch each other, they won't brown.

Chile-Spiced Fried Chicken: Use peanut or vegetable oil. Season the flour with 2 tablespoons each chili powder and ground cumin, 2 teaspoons ground turmeric, $1/2$ teaspoon cayenne (optional), and salt and pepper; omit cinnamon. Proceed as above. Serve with lime wedges.

Roast Chicken Parts with Herbs and Olive Oil

Makes 4 to 6 servings • **Time:** 40 minutes

Roast chicken parts cook considerably faster than a whole roast chicken and also have more direct contact with the seasonings—for more flavor impact. You can use almost any mild green herb here, from parsley, basil, dill, or mint to more obscure herbs such as summer savory.

> ¼ cup extra-virgin olive oil or butter
>
> 1 whole (3- to 4-pound) chicken, cut up (legs cut in two) trimmed of excess fat, then rinsed and patted dry with paper towels
>
> Salt and freshly ground black pepper to taste
>
> ½ cup any mild fresh green herb or a combination of fresh herbs

1 Preheat the oven to 450°F. When it is hot, put 1 tablespoon of the oil or butter in a roasting pan and place it in the oven—leave it there for about 1 minute, or until the oil is hot or the butter melts.

2 Add the chicken, skin side up, season with salt and pepper, and return the pan to the oven. Combine the herb and the remaining oil or butter in the container of a small food processor and blend, or mince the herb and mix it with the oil or butter in a bowl.

3 After the chicken has cooked 15 minutes, spread about one quarter of the herb mixture over it, turn, add another quarter of the mixture, and roast another 10 minutes. Turn the chicken over again (now skin side up) and add another quarter of the herb mixture.

4 Cook until the chicken is done (you'll see clear juices if you make a small cut in the meat near the bone), a total of 30 to 40 minutes. Drizzle or spread with the remaining herb mixture and serve.

Shopping Tip: If you prefer just the breasts or the thighs, buy those at the supermarket. Just adjust the temperature—less time for all white meat; more for all dark meat.

Preparation Tip: Chicken thighs, and even breasts, occasionally have large pieces of fat attached to them; simply trim them off with a paring knife.

The Basics of Chicken Parts

Almost everyone buys bone-in chicken these days already: cut into eight pieces—two legs, two thighs, two breast halves, two wings, with the back usually discarded or saved for stock—it's incredibly convenient.

Because breasts and legs cook at different rates it sometimes makes sense to cook them separately, serving the breasts at one meal and the legs at another. Though it's also nice to give people a choice, there are times dark meat is preferable to breasts and vice versa.

In any chicken recipe, take care when cooking white and dark meat together, since white meat cooks so much faster.

Sometimes, the thickness of a bone-in breast compensates for the difference, and everything finishes at about the same time. You can also increase the likelihood of this by starting the legs a little before the breasts, and by keeping them in the hottest part of the pan (usually the center, if you're cooking on top of the stove).

Keep an eye on things and remove the breasts as soon as they're done, even if the legs have a few minutes more to go. When measured with an instant-read thermometer, breasts are done at 160°F, thighs closer to 165°F.

Stir-Fried Chicken with Broccoli or Cauliflower

Makes 4 servings, with rice
Time: 20 to 30 minutes

Here is a model recipe for making stir-fry with "hard" vegetables, those that must be parboiled before stir-frying. The extra step actually saves time—it's much faster to soften broccoli and like vegetables with a quick poaching than by stir-frying.

2 cups broccoli or cauliflower florets and stems, cut into bite-sized pieces

2 tablespoons peanut or other oil

2 tablespoons minced garlic

1 tablespoon peeled and grated fresh ginger

1 cup sliced onion

1/2 cup trimmed and chopped scallions, plus minced scallion greens for garnish

12 ounces boneless, skinless chicken breast, rinsed and patted dry with paper towels, and cut into 1/2- to 3/4-inch chunks

1 teaspoon sugar (optional)

2 tablespoons soy sauce

Salt and freshly ground black pepper to taste

1 tablespoon hoisin sauce (optional; available at Asian markets)

1/2 cup toasted cashews (optional)

1 tablespoon cornstarch (optional)

1/4 cup Quickest Chicken Stock (page 17) or store-bought chicken or vegetable broth, or water

1 Bring a medium pot of salted water to a boil; add the broccoli or cauliflower and cook for about 2 minutes, just long enough to remove the hardest crunch. Drain and plunge into cold water to stop the cooking; drain again.

2 Place a wok or large, deep skillet over high heat. Add half the oil, swirl it around, and immediately add half the garlic and ginger. Cook for 15 seconds, stirring, then add the onion and cook, stirring, for 2 minutes. Add the broccoli or cauliflower and 1/2 cup chopped scallions and cook over high heat until the broccoli or cauliflower browns and becomes tender but not at all mushy, about 5 minutes.

3 Turn the heat to medium and remove the vegetables. Add the remaining oil to the pan, then the remaining garlic and ginger. Stir, then add the chicken. Raise the heat to high, stir the chicken once, then let it sit for 1 minute before stirring again. Cook, stirring occasionally, until the chicken has lost its pinkness, 3 to 5 minutes.

4 Return the vegetables to the pan and toss once or twice. Add the sugar, if desired, and the soy sauce, and toss again. Season with salt and pepper, then stir in the hoisin and cashews, if desired. If using, combine the cornstarch with the stock or water and add to the pan. Otherwise, just add the liquid. Raise the heat to high and cook, stirring and scraping the bottom of the pan, until the liquid is reduced slightly and you've scraped up all the bits of chicken. If you've used cornstarch, the sauce will have thickened.

5 Garnish and serve immediately, scooping out some of the sauce with each portion of meat and chicken.

Shopping Tip: Hoisin is a blend of soy sauce, sugar, chiles, garlic, and other spices—the Chinese equivalent of ketchup. Try to find brands where soy is the first ingredient, and without artificial ingredients.

Preparation Tip: Ginger can be peeled with a vegetable peeler, a paring knife, or even a spoon (try it; it works well). Once peeled, it can be grated or minced.

Five Additions to Stir-Fried Chicken

1. Add 1 teaspoon dark sesame oil with the soy sauce.

2. Toss in $1/2$ to 1 cup raw or roasted peanuts when you return the vegetables to the pan.

3. Add $1/2$ to 1 cup canned coconut milk along with the soy sauce. (Omit stock or water.)

4. Add 1 cup cored and chopped fresh tomatoes when you return the vegetables to the pan.

5. Use snow peas, mushrooms, or other quick-cooking vegetables, alone or in combination, in addition to or in place of the broccoli or cauliflower.

Simple Roast Chicken

Makes 4 servings • **Time:** About 1 hour

We associate roast chicken with elegance, but it's also great weeknight food, since it takes just about 1 hour from start to finish. This method gives you a nicely browned exterior without drying out the breast meat, and it's easily varied (the variations I offer are a fraction of the possibilities). Use kosher or free-range chicken if at all possible.

1 whole (3- to 4-pound) chicken, trimmed of excess fat, then rinsed and patted dry with paper towels

3 tablespoons olive oil

2 teaspoons chopped fresh thyme, rosemary, marjoram, oregano, or sage leaves, or 1 teaspoon dried

Salt and freshly ground black pepper to taste

Chopped fresh herbs for garnish

1 Preheat the oven to 500°F.

2 Place the chicken, breast side up, on a rack in a roasting pan. Begin roasting. Mix together the olive oil, herb, salt, and pepper.

3 After the chicken has roasted for about 20 minutes, spoon some of the olive oil mixture over it; baste every few minutes. When the bird begins to brown, turn the heat down to 325°F, baste again, and roast until an instant-read thermometer inserted into the thickest part of the thigh reads 160° to 165°F. Total roasting time will be under an hour.

4 Before removing the chicken from the pan, tip the pan to let the juices from the bird's cavity flow into the pan (if they are red, cook another 5 minutes). Remove the bird to a platter and let it rest for about 5 minutes. While it is resting, pour the pan juices into a clear measuring cup, and pour or spoon off as much of the fat as you can. Reheat the juice, carve the bird (see illustrations on next page), garnish, and serve with the pan juices.

Shopping Tip: Kosher chicken, though variable in quality, usually comes from better breeds and is handled better through the slaughtering process. Free-range chicken, at least theoretically, comes from better breeds, is given better feed, and is handled well. None of this is guaranteed, but most experienced cooks agree that the least expensive chicken is also the least tasty and has the mushiest texture.

Three Ways to Flavor Roast Chicken

1. Use 3 tablespoons freshly squeezed lemon juice in addition to or in place of olive oil.

2. Combine 2 tablespoons to 1/3 cup any mustard with 2 tablespoons honey and baste the chicken with this mixture during the final stages of roasting.

3. Place 1/2 cup white wine and two cloves crushed garlic in the bottom of the roasting pan; baste with this in addition to or in place of the olive oil mixture above.

The Basics of Roast Chicken

The "secrets" of roast chicken are simple: Start with a good bird, time the cooking properly, and serve it promptly. The crisp skin and moist interior for which roast chicken is justly renown are fleeting qualities.

You don't need a rack to roast chicken, but elevating the bird above the floor of the roasting pan helps to keep its skin crisp and prevents it from sticking. I favor heavy, V-shaped racks because they make it a little easier to turn the bird. Vertical roasters and other gimmicky racks do not produce miracles.

An ordinary 9 × 13-inch roasting pan is fine for most chickens; in fact, you want to use the smallest roasting pan that will comfortably hold your bird, so you can concentrate the juices and keep them from burning. But you'll need a larger pan if you want to add roast vegetables to the mix.

If you use high heat for the roasting—and you should—the pan juices may begin to produce some smoke; to reduce this, just add a little water or wine (white or red, your choice) to the pan.

CARVING ROAST CHICKEN

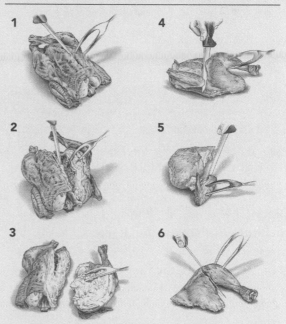

(**Step 1**) Cut straight down on either side of the breastbone, following the shape of the carcass. (**Step 2**) Continue to cut down toward the back until you reach the joints holding the thigh and wing to the carcass. (**Step 3**) Cut through those joints to free the entire half of the bird. (**Step 4**) Separate leg and breast sections by cutting through the skin that holds them together; hold the knife almost parallel to the cutting board, cut from the breast toward the leg, and you will easily find the right spot. (**Step 5**) Separate the wing from the breast if you like. (**Step 6**) Separate leg and thigh; the joint will offer little resistance once you find it.

Roast Turkey and Gravy, without Stuffing

Makes 4 servings
Time: 2¹/₂ to 5 hours, depending on size of the bird

Turkey—at least the whole bird—is rarely prepared except for feasts, so the next few pages offer typical Thanksgiving recipes including: gravy, stuffing, and cranberry sauce. (Look for vegetable side dishes in the Vegetables chapter.)

Basting helps improve the color and especially the flavor of the skin, and it also adds a little moisture. If the bird is under 10 pounds, roast it on its breast for the first hour, then flip it over for the second. If it's bigger than that, shield the breast with aluminum foil for the first couple of hours, then let it brown.

> 1 (8- to 20-pound) turkey, with giblets
>
> 1 whole onion, plus 1 to 2 cups chopped onions
>
> 1 whole carrot, unpeeled, halved if large, plus 1 to 2 cups peeled and chopped carrots
>
> Stems from 1 bunch parsley
>
> ¹/₂ teaspoon salt
>
> Freshly ground black pepper to taste
>
> 8 tablespoons (1 stick) butter, melted, or extra-virgin olive oil, approximately
>
> ¹/₂ to 1 cup chopped celery
>
> About 1 cup Quickest Chicken Stock (page 17) or store-bought chicken broth, or water, plus more as needed
>
> ¹/₄ cup cornstarch mixed with ¹/₂ cup cold water (per 3 cups gravy) (optional)

1 Make sure the turkey is thoroughly defrosted before starting. Preheat the oven to 350°F. Combine the turkey neck, wing tips, and gizzard (not the liver) in a medium saucepan. Add the whole onion, whole carrot, and parsley stems. Add water to cover, ¹/₂ teaspoon salt, and a few grindings of pepper. Bring to a boil, turn the heat to low, and simmer, adding water as necessary to keep the meat and vegetables covered. Skim any foam that arises to the top of the pot; after 1 hour of simmering, turn off the heat, cover, and refrigerate if the turkey will cook for a great deal longer. Reheat when you get to Step 5.

2 Fit a large roasting pan with a V-shaped rack if you have one; otherwise use a flat rack that rests a bit above the pan bottom. Brush the turkey with 1 tablespoon of the butter or oil and sprinkle it with salt and pepper. If you can handle the turkey easily, place it breast side down; if not, place it breast side up and cover it loosely with aluminum foil (remove the foil when about 1 hour of roasting time remains). Scatter the chopped onions, carrots, and celery around the turkey. Drizzle with 1 tablespoon of the butter or oil. Pour in about 1 cup of stock or water.

3 Roast, basting with a little additional butter or oil every 30 minutes and adding stock or water to the vegetables to keep them moist (better too wet than too dry in this case; you won't be eating them anyway). If you started the turkey with the breast down, flip it after an hour or so.

4 When the bird has about 1 hour of cooking to go (the internal temperature will be about 125°F), if the breast is not sufficiently browned (and it certainly won't be if you tented it with foil), turn the oven heat up to 400°F for the remaining cooking time. If at any time the bird appears to be browning too quickly, turn the heat back down (you can prop open the oven door for a couple of minutes to hasten the oven's cooling).

5 When the bird is done—an instant-read thermometer should read at least 165°F when inserted in mid-thigh—remove the bird to a platter but don't carve it until it has rested for at least 15 minutes. Reheat the giblet stock if necessary, then strain it into a bowl; then strain the vegetables that cooked with the bird into a larger bowl, pushing on them to extract as much liquid as possible. Combine these liquids. Mince the reserved liver.

6 Place the roasting pan over two burners on your stove, turn the heat to medium-high, and add 2 cups of the combined liquid and the reserved liver. Cook, stirring and scraping the bottom of the pan, until the liquid is reduced slightly. If your bird is small, season the gravy to taste and serve. If it is large, add as much more stock (using hot water to stretch it if necessary) as you like. If you want thicker gravy, combine $1/4$ cup cornstarch with $1/2$ cup cold water (per 3 cups of gravy) and stir it into the gravy until thickened.

7 Carve the turkey (page 74) and serve with the gravy.

Cooking Tip: Use the chart (below) to calculate roasting time, or figure 15 minutes per pound. For example, an 8-pound bird will take about $2^1/_2$ hours; a 16-pound bird should take just about 4 hours. Timing varies based on the frequency of basting and how much heat your oven loses, the original temperature of the turkey, and other factors. To be sure, use an instant-read thermometer, which should read 165° to 170°F in the thickest part of the thigh before you remove the bird from the oven.

Roast Turkey with Stuffing: Plan to use about 3 to 4 cups for a small bird, 6 to 8 cups for a larger one. Just before roasting, stuff the bird (or consider cooking the stuffing in a separate roasting pan, using some of the giblet stock to moisten it) and truss it if you like, or simply close the rear vent with metal skewers to keep the stuffing from falling out. Increase roasting time by about 5 minutes per pound, still relying primarily on the thermometer. In the interests of simplicity, I roast stuffed birds breast side up the entire time, shielding the breast with aluminum foil until the bird is almost cooked.

Timing Chart for Roasting Turkey and Other Large Birds

Weight	Roasting Time (Unstuffed)	Roasting Time (Stuffed)
6–8 pounds	2–$2^1/_2$ hours	$2^1/_2$–3 hours
10–12 pounds	3–$3^1/_2$ hours	4 hours+
14–18 pounds	$3^1/_2$–4 hours	5–6 hours
18 pounds+	4 hours+	6 hours+

CARVING TURKEY

1

First, remove the leg-thigh section by cutting straight down between the leg and carcass, and through the joint holding the thigh to the carcass. Set aside for the moment.

2

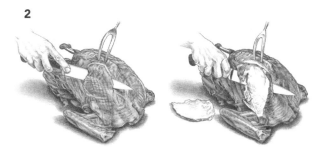

At this point you have two options: Either cut thick slices of white meat from the breast, or remove the breast entirely from the carcass and slice it as you would a boneless roast.

3

Cut the wing from the carcass.

4

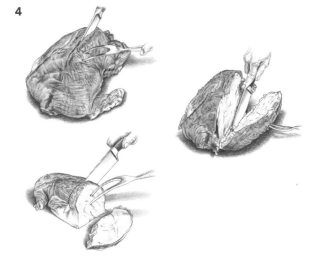

Carve the leg-thigh sections, repeat on the other side of the bird, and serve.

My Favorite Bread Stuffing

Makes about 6 cups, enough for a 12-pound bird
Time: 20 minutes, plus baking time

This wonderful recipe, based on a James Beard classic, is so great that I refuse to compromise when I make it (despite all the butter). I'd rather skip dessert than miss out on this yearly treat.

> ¹/₂ pound (2 sticks) butter
>
> 1 cup minced onion
>
> ¹/₂ cup pine nuts or chopped walnuts
>
> 6 to 8 cups fresh bread crumbs (page 100)
>
> 1 tablespoon minced fresh tarragon or sage leaves or 1 teaspoon dried crumbled tarragon or sage
>
> Salt and freshly ground black pepper to taste
>
> ¹/₂ cup minced scallions
>
> ¹/₂ cup minced fresh parsley leaves

1 Melt the butter over medium heat in a large, deep skillet, Dutch oven, or casserole. Add the onion and cook, stirring, until it softens, about 5 minutes. Add the nuts and cook, stirring almost constantly, until they begin to brown, about 3 minutes.

2 Add the bread crumbs and the tarragon or sage and toss to mix. Turn the heat to low. Add the salt, pepper, and scallions. Toss again; taste and adjust seasoning if necessary. Add the parsley and stir. Turn off the heat. (You may prepare the recipe in advance up to this point; refrigerate, well wrapped or in a covered container, for up to a day before proceeding.)

3 Pack this into the turkey if you like, or simply put it in an ovenproof glass or enameled casserole and bake it with the turkey during the last 45 minutes of cooking.

Traditional Cranberry Sauce

Makes about 1 quart
Time: 20 minutes, plus time to chill

This traditional cranberry sauce will gel upon cooling. If you want a less-sweet sauce, reduce the sugar. (It will be runnier.) If you want a very firm sauce, make the variation.

> 4 cups (about 1 pound) fresh cranberries, picked over and washed, or frozen cranberries
>
> 1¹/₂ cups sugar
>
> 2 cups water

1 Combine all ingredients in a medium saucepan and turn the heat to medium-low. Cover and cook, stirring occasionally, until the berries are broken, 10 to 15 minutes.

2 Transfer to a bowl; cool, then chill (in the refrigerator up to a week) until ready to serve.

Very Firm Cranberry Sauce or Cranberry Jelly:
Increase sugar to 2 cups. For sauce, proceed as above. For jelly, cook 5 minutes longer, stirring frequently. Pass through a sieve into a mold, bowl, or jelly jars and cool, then chill until firm. Slice to serve.

Basic Roast Turkey Breast, on the Bone

Makes 8 or more servings • **Time:** About 1 hour

At 3 to 6 pounds, a turkey breast can feed a small party and requires less effort for holiday meals, if you're not feeding a big crowd. It can also give plenty of leftovers for turkey sandwiches made with real turkey. And the roasting is a breeze. You can also use any of the variations for whole roast chicken on page 70, adjusting cooking time accordingly.

> 1 (3- to 6-pound) turkey breast
>
> About 3 tablespoons olive oil or melted butter for basting
>
> Salt and freshly ground black pepper to taste

1 Preheat the oven to 450°F. Place the turkey on a rack in a roasting pan.

2 Brush the turkey with oil or butter and season it with salt and pepper. Place it in the oven. Roast for about 45 minutes, basting every 15 minutes or so, then begin checking every few minutes with an instant-read thermometer. The turkey is ready when the thermometer reads 160°F. Let the turkey rest for 5 to 10 minutes before carving and serving.

Herb-Roasted Boneless Turkey Breast

Makes 8 or more servings · Time. About 1 hour

Among the many turkey parts now being sold are boneless breasts. They're better for roasting than boneless chicken breasts, because they don't dry out nearly as fast.

3 tablespoons minced fresh herbs: tarragon, summer savory, dill, chervil, basil, fennel leaves, or a combination

$1/2$ cup minced fresh parsley leaves, plus a little more for garnish

Salt and freshly ground black pepper to taste

2 filleted turkey breast halves, about 3 pounds total

1 tablespoon softened butter or extra-virgin olive oil

1 cup Quickest Chicken Stock (page 17) or store-bought chicken or vegetable broth, or water, plus a little more if needed

1   Preheat the oven to 450°F. Mix together the herbs (except the parsley for the garnish), salt, and pepper. Rub the turkey breasts all over with the fat, then with the herb mixture.

2   Place the turkey in a baking dish, and put the baking dish in the oven. Add about $1/3$ cup of stock or water to the bottom of the pan. Roast the turkey, basting every 10 minutes or so and adding more stock or water if necessary, until it is cooked through, about 30 minutes. (If you are unsure whether it's done, cut into it; the center should be white. An instant-read thermometer will show 160°F.)

3   Remove the turkey to a plate. Add the remaining liquid to the dish (or add an additional $1/2$ cup if you've already used up all the liquid) and cook, stirring and scraping the bottom of the pan, until the liquid is reduced slightly. Slice the turkey and spoon the sauce over it. (There will just be enough to give it a nice glaze.) Garnish with parsley and serve.

Basic Roast Duck

Makes 2 to 4 servings • **Time:** About 1¼ hours

If you're feeling adventurous or just love the taste of duck, here's the simple way to make it.

Duck is fatty—amazingly so, if you're used to chicken—which means it must be treated differently from other birds. It also means it develops a beautifully crisp, dark skin.

Note that a duck doesn't easily serve four, but it can be done if your co-eaters are not big on meat and you make a point of providing plenty of side dishes.

> 1 (4- to 5-pound) duck, excess fat removed, rinsed and patted dry with paper towels
>
> Salt and freshly ground black pepper to taste
>
> 1 tablespoon soy sauce (optional)

1 Preheat the oven to 350°F. Prick the duck skin all over with a sharp fork, skewer, or thin-bladed knife; try not to hit the meat (the fat layer is usually about ¼ inch thick). Season the duck with salt and pepper and place it, breast side down, on a rack in a roasting pan.

2 Roast the duck for 15 minutes, prick the exposed skin again, then roast another 15 minutes. Brush with a little soy sauce, if desired, and then turn it breast side up. Prick again, brush with a little more soy sauce, then roast until the meat is done, about another 45 minutes; all juices, including those from the center vent, should run clear, and the leg bone should wiggle a little in its socket. When the bird is done, an instant-read thermometer inserted into the thigh will measure about 180°F. Raise the heat to 400°F for the last 10 minutes of cooking if the duck is not as brown as you'd like.

3 Carve the duck the same way you would a chicken (page 71) and serve.

Cooking Tip: Pricking the skin is the fastest, easiest way to rid duck of its excess subcutaneous fat.

5 | Meat

Americans are eating less meat than we did 20 years ago, but it remains the centerpiece of many dinners, whether celebratory or quick—with beef, pork, and lamb still popular favorites. Although some people have philosophical problems with it, it's inarguable that meat is filling, usually requires little work, and is an excellent source of protein.

Most meat tastes best when it's browned, because the process of browning creates literally hundreds of flavor compounds. You can brown by grilling, broiling, pan-grilling, roasting, or sautéing, usually with added fat. The first four of these techniques are not merely the initial process of a given recipe but the entire technique; that is, when you brown meat by grilling, broiling, pan-grilling, or roasting, you usually finish cooking it that way also.

That is sometimes the case with sautéing too. But when you're braising or stewing (cooking in liquid) meat (or poultry, for that matter), you frequently want to give it an initial browning to heighten flavors. Two notes about this: First, this step can be skipped. The initial browning is more noticeable in some final dishes than in others but, given that most braised recipes have several added flavors, it isn't always essential. So if you're pressed for time, skip the browning step; it's unlikely that you'll be disappointed by the results. If you do choose to brown meat before proceeding with cooking, you should try it with the oven. It's easier to brown a large quantity of meat at high heat (450° to 500°F) in the oven than on top of the stove, and it is also far less messy. In addition, you can usually use less fat in the process. Once you try it, you'll probably become a convert.

A note about portion size: One way Americans have addressed health issues related to the fat content of meat, is by reducing portion size. To that end, I assume in my recipes that a pound of meat serves three to four people rather than the two or three it did not long ago. You can, of course, change proportions to reflect your personal style.

Grilled Steak, American-Style

Makes 2 to 4 servings

Time: About 10 minutes, plus time to build the fire

Straightforward and simple. Start with the right steak (one labeled "prime," if you can find it, is worth it in this instance) and don't overcook. In this single case, pan-grilling is closer to grilling than broiling, since most home broilers just don't get hot enough.

> 2 strip, rib-eye, or other steaks,
> 8 ounces each and about 1 inch thick
>
> Salt and freshly ground black pepper
> to taste

1 Remove the steaks from the refrigerator and their packaging if you have not already done so. Build a medium-hot charcoal fire or crank a gas grill as high as it will go; you should not be able to hold your hand 3 inches above it for more than 2 or 3 seconds (see The Basics of Grilling and Broiling, page xi). The rack should be 3 or 4 inches from the top of the coals.

2 Dry the steaks with paper towels. Grill them without turning for 3 minutes (a little more if they're over an inch thick, a little less if they're thinner or you like steaks extremely rare). Turn, then grill for 3 minutes on the other side. Steaks will be rare to medium-rare.

3 Check for doneness. If you would like the steaks better done, move them away from the most intense heat and grill another minute or two longer per side; check again. When done, sprinkle with salt and pepper and serve.

Grilled Porterhouse (T-bone) Steak: These are best when very thick, 1 1/2 inches or more, and weigh about 2 pounds, in which case they will easily serve 4 to 6 people. In Step 2, grill for 4 to 5 minutes per side, taking care not to burn the meat; the leaner tenderloin (the smaller of the two pieces on either side of the bone) is best very rare, so keep it toward the coolest part of the fire. Check for doneness, preferably with an instant-read thermometer and in both the sirloin and the tenderloin sections. If not done to your liking, move the steak to a cooler part of the grill and cook for another 2 to 3 minutes per side before checking again.

Broiled Steak: See The Basics of Grilling and Broiling, page xi, and remember that a broiler is little more than an upside-down grill. The major difference is that melting fat can build up in your broiling pan and catch fire, so it's best to broil on a rack. Turn the broiler to maximum, preheat it, and broil 3 to 4 inches from the heat source (any more, and you won't brown the steak; any less, and you'll burn it). Proceed as for grilling, with this exception: If your broiler heat is not intense enough to brown the steak well, don't turn it, but cook it the entire time on one side only. It will cook reasonably evenly, and should develop a nice crust on the top.

Pan-Grilled Steak: See Pan-grilling, page xii. A terrific option for 1-inch-thick steaks (not much thicker, though), as long as you have a decent exhaust fan. Preheat a cast-iron or other sturdy skillet just large enough to hold the steaks over medium-high heat for 4 to 5 minutes; the pan should be really hot—in fact, it should be smoking. Sprinkle its surface with coarse salt and put in the steaks. Clouds of smoke will instantly appear; do not turn down the heat. The timing remains the same as for grilled steaks.

The Basics of Steaks

A "good" steak means the right cut, which you can ruin only by cooking it to a point of doneness that doesn't please you. If you're unsure of your timing, aim to undercook by a wide margin, then use a thin-bladed knife to peek inside the meat and check for doneness; you can always throw the steak back on for a couple of minutes. Some beef cuts that are both tender and tasty:

Strip steaks (also called shell, club, New York, or top loin), which are usually sold boneless and make the ideal individual steak; *porterhouse* (*T-bone*), a bone-in steak that contains mostly sirloin but also a bit of the tender but less flavorful tenderloin; *rib-eye*, the boneless center of the rib, are also very tender and very flavorful, and make good individual steaks. *Skirt steak*, if you can find it (it's the steer's diaphragm, so only one per animal), is less tender, but delicious; do not overcook it.

Steaks simply labeled "sirloin" and sold bone-in or bone-out, are riskier; some are better than others and generalizations are difficult. But they're usually decent, and the worst that can happen is that they are on the chewy side. This is also the case with flank steak, which is guaranteed to be chewy but flavorful.

Chuck is a great meat for grinding or cooking with liquid. Don't grill it.

Classic Beef Stew

Makes 4 to 6 servings
Time: $1^1/_2$ to 2 hours, largely unattended

**Browning the beef before braising adds
another dimension of flavor, but isn't
absolutely necessary. Skipping browning,
while not strictly by the book, saves both
time and mess.**

2 tablespoons canola or other neutral
oil, or olive oil

1 clove garlic, lightly crushed,
plus 1 tablespoon minced garlic

2 to $2^1/_2$ pounds beef chuck or round,
trimmed of surface fat and cut into
1- to $1^1/_2$-inch cubes

Salt and freshly ground black pepper
to taste

2 large or 3 medium onions,
cut into eighths

3 tablespoons flour

3 cups Quickest Chicken Stock
(page 17) or store-bought chicken,
beef, or vegetable broth, or water,
or wine, or a combination

1 bay leaf

1 teaspoon fresh thyme leaves
or $1/_2$ teaspoon dried thyme

4 medium-to-large potatoes,
peeled and cut into 1-inch chunks

4 large carrots, peeled and cut into
1-inch chunks

1 cup fresh or frozen (thawed) peas

Minced fresh parsley leaves for garnish

1 Heat a large casserole or deep skillet that
can later be covered over medium-high heat for
2 or 3 minutes; add the oil and the crushed garlic
clove; cook, stirring, for 1 minute, then remove
and discard the garlic. Add the meat chunks to the
skillet a few at a time, turning to brown well on all
sides. Do not crowd or they will not brown properly; cook them in batches if necessary. Season the
meat with salt and pepper as it cooks.

2 When the meat is brown, remove it with a slotted spoon. Pour or spoon off most of the fat and
turn the heat to medium. Add the onions. Cook,
stirring, until they soften, about 10 minutes. Add
the flour and cook, stirring, for about 2 minutes.
Add the stock or water or wine, bay leaf, thyme, and
meat, and bring to a boil. Turn the heat to low and
cover. Cook, undisturbed, for 30 minutes.

3 Uncover the pan; the mixture should be quite
soupy (if it is not, add a little more liquid). Add the
potatoes and carrots, turn the heat up for a minute
or so to resume boiling, then lower the heat and
cover again. Cook 30 to 60 minutes until the meat
and vegetables are tender. Taste for seasoning and
add more salt, pepper, and/or thyme if necessary.
(If you are not planning to serve the stew immediately, remove the meat and vegetables with a slotted
spoon and refrigerate them and the stock separately. Skim the fat from the stock before combining it with the meat and vegetables, reheat, and
proceed with the recipe from this point.)

4 Add the minced garlic and the peas; if you are
pleased with the stew's consistency, continue to
cook, covered, over low heat. If it is soupy, remove
the cover and raise the heat to high. In either case,
cook about 5 minutes more, until the peas have
heated through and the garlic flavors the stew.
Remove the bay leaf, garnish, and serve.

The Basics of Beef Cuts

The more tender beef cuts—such as sirloin, tenderloin, and rib eye—are best grilled or roasted, and cooked rare. The tougher cuts—like chuck and brisket—need to be broken down with long cooking and moist heat.

If a piece of beef is cut thinly, it can be called a steak; a thick piece can be called a roast or a pot roast. Here's information about the most basic cuts, the best preparations, and what to ask for or look for on the label.

Chuck The neck/shoulder area. *Best cooking options:* roasts (shoulder roast, arm roast, blade roast); stir-fries and stews (boneless chuck). Except in stir-fries, almost always best when cooked slowly and thoroughly.

Rib Ribs number 6 through 12 comprise one of the most valuable parts of the steer. *Best cooking options:* steaks (rib or rib-eye steaks); roasts (rib roast). Best rare to medium-rare, about 125°F.

Loin, or Short Loin Directly behind the rib, in two sections: top (shell) and bottom (tenderloin). *Best tenderloin cooking options:* steaks (filet mignon); roasts (whole tenderloin). *Best shell cooking options:* steaks (New York strip or shell steaks, club steaks, or strip loin steaks); porterhouse (T-bone) steaks are part tenderloin, part shell. Best cooked rare to medium rare.

Flank Under the loin. *Best cooking options:* steaks, stir-fries (flank steak, skirt steak). Needs a tiny bit more cooking than loin cuts; best medium rare.

Sirloin Behind the loin and the flank. *Best cooking options:* steaks (may be labeled "sirloin"; look for pin-bone, flat-bone, then round-bone); roasts (top and bottom butt roast, or rump roast). Best rare to medium rare.

Round Rear end of the cow. *Best cooking options:* burgers, stuffings (ground meat); stir-fries (stir-fry meat). In burgers, best cooked rare; in stir-fries, medium to well done.

BEEF CUTS

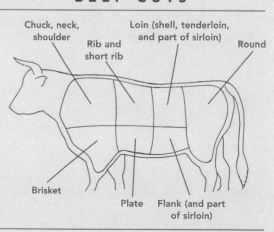

Chuck, neck, shoulder

Loin (shell, tenderloin, and part of sirloin)

Rib and short rib

Round

Brisket

Plate

Flank (and part of sirloin)

Classic Burger

Makes 4 servings
Time: 20 minutes, plus time to preheat the grill

Like steak, burgers need not be grilled; they're terrific made in a heavy skillet sprinkled with salt (see Step 1). If you like cheeseburgers, add cheese as soon as you turn the meat.

1¼ to 1½ pounds ground chuck or sirloin, not too lean

1 teaspoon salt, plus more if you're pan-grilling

1 Handle the meat as little as possible to avoid compressing it; shape it lightly into 4 burgers, about 4 to 5 inches across, sprinkling with salt as you do so. Start a charcoal or wood fire or preheat a gas grill; if you're cooking on a stove top, preheat a large, heavy skillet (cast iron is best) over medium-high heat for 3 or 4 minutes; sprinkle its surface with coarse salt.

2 The fire should be quite hot; you should barely be able to hold your hand 3 or 4 inches over the rack. Put the burgers on the rack and grill about 3 minutes per side for very rare, and another minute per side for each increasing stage of doneness, but no more than 10 minutes total unless you like hockey pucks. Timing on the stove top is exactly the same.

3 Serve on buns, toast, or hard rolls, garnished as you like.

Four Ideas for Flavoring Burgers

Gently mix any of these into ground meat before cooking it:

1. 2 tablespoons minced fresh parsley, basil, chervil, or other herbs, along with ¼ teaspoon or more minced garlic.

2. ¼ cup minced onion, shallot, or scallion or one teaspoon peeled and minced or grated fresh ginger, or ground ginger.

3. 1 tablespoon soy, Worcestershire, steak, or other flavored sauce, or Tabasco or other hot sauce to taste.

4. 1 teaspoon curry powder, chile powder, or other spice mixtures to taste.

The Basics of Burgers

Ground chuck—which generally corresponds to the "80 percent lean" ground meat sold in supermarkets—makes very good burgers; the fat acts to keep it moist. Of course you can use more expensive round or sirloin as well, but beware that the leaner the burger the more important it is to serve it rare, because fat keeps overcooked burgers somewhat juicy, while lean simply dries out.

Given concerns about the safety of store-ground meat—pre-ground meat has been linked to contamination by the salmonella and E. coli bacteria—you might want to try grinding your own meat for burgers. It's easy: Buy a chuck roast, cut it into 1- to 2-inch cubes, and pulse a small batch—about $1/2$ pound—at a time in the food processor. Don't pulverize the meat and it'll be wonderful. Freeze what you don't use immediately.

If you do buy pre-ground meat, most authorities recommend that you cook it to well done—160°F—to kill the harmful bacteria. Do this once and you're likely to begin grinding your own meat, since well-done hamburgers are often too dry to eat.

Prime Rib Roast

Makes about 6 servings
Time: About 1¹/₂ hours, largely unattended

This is a recipe for feeding a small crowd. It features a simple roasting technique: high heat to sear the meat, lower heat to cook it through. If you want a really crisp exterior, turn the heat back to 450°F for a few minutes right at the end of cooking; this won't affect the internal temperature too much.

1 (3-rib) roast, about 5 pounds,
trimmed of excess but not all fat

Salt and freshly ground black pepper
to taste

1 or 2 cloves garlic (optional)

1 cup red wine, Quickest Chicken Stock
(page 17) or store-bought broth,
or water

1   Bring the meat to room temperature by removing it from the refrigerator at least an hour before cooking, preferably two. Preheat the oven to 450°F.

2   Place the meat, bone side down, in a large roasting pan. Season it with salt and pepper. If you like garlic, peel the cloves and cut them into tiny slivers; use a boning or paring knife to poke small holes in the meat and insert the garlic into them.

3   Place the roast in the oven and cook for 15 minutes, undisturbed. Turn the heat down to 350°F and continue to roast for about 1 hour; check in several places with a meat thermometer. When no spot checks in at under 125°F, the meat is rare (120°F if you like your meat really rare and your guests are of the same mentality); cook another 5 or

10 minutes if you like it better done, then check again, but in no case let the temperature of the meat go above 155°F.

4   Remove the meat from the oven. Pour off all but a few tablespoons of the fat and place the roasting pan over a burner set to high. Add the liquid and cook, stirring and scraping up any brown bits, until it is reduced by half. Slice the roast and serve, splashing a little of the sauce on the meat platter and passing the rest at the table.

Prime Rib for a Big Crowd: With bigger roasts, 5 ribs or more, make sure to allow plenty of time to let the meat reach room temperature. In Step 2, use more garlic if you like. In Step 3, increase initial browning time to 20 minutes. After that, cooking instructions remain the same, and cooking time will be only marginally longer, but be sure to use an instant-read thermometer in several different places to check the meat. Increase the liquid in Step 4 to at least 2 cups.

Boneless Prime Rib: Have the butcher tie it so that it is of roughly uniform thickness. Cook as above, using a meat thermometer to gauge doneness; total weight won't matter much since there is no bone and the roast is relatively thin. A 3-pound boneless roast is almost certain to be done in less than an hour, so plan accordingly and watch it carefully; a 5- or 6-pound roast won't take a whole lot longer.

The Basics of Roast Beef

Roasting must start with tender meat, because dry cooking does little to tenderize it. You have four good choices:

Prime rib   Usually so big that if you cook the deepest center to rare, you will still have some medium well done areas, pleasing everyone. And so juicy that even well done (not overcooked) meat is tender and moist. For the best roast, request the small end (the twelfth through the seventh ribs) and ask the butcher—even at the supermarket—to cut a "short roast" for you, removing the short ribs. For rare meat, figure about 15 to 20 minutes per pound roasting, but see the recipe for details. The rarest part should be no less than 120°F when done.

Boneless prime rib   Neither as flavorful as prime rib with the bone, nor as much fun, but a lot easier to carve and faster to cook.

Fillet of beef   This is the whole tenderloin; it's wonderfully tender, but does not have a lot of intrinsic flavor. Unlike prime rib, which requires no saucing whatsoever, you should make a sauce if you want a roast fillet. (See Reduction Sauce or Pan Gravy, page 62.) Cooks quickly and easily, and best served very rare, no more than 125°F.

Whole strip   This is usually reserved for steaks, but it can also be left whole. For roasts, it is boned (and called a "shell" as often as it is a "strip"). Delicious but expensive. Best rare to medium-rare, about 125°F.

All beef is rare at 125°F (120°F for really rare); there are noticeable differences in meat color for each 5 degrees difference in temperature. I'd never cook anything beyond 155°F, although some cooks suggest cooking roast beef to 170°F for well done. Large roasts will rise at least 5 degrees in temperature between the time you remove them from the oven and the time you carve them.

CARVING A RIB ROAST

For a bone-in prime rib, cut close to the bone, between the ribs, for the first slice.

Unless you want huge portions, the second slice is boneless.

Pot Roast

Makes 6 to 8 servings
Time: 2$\frac{1}{2}$ to 4 hours, largely unattended

Use low heat when simmering this meat, and don't cook it forever; pot roast need not be overcooked to be tender and delicious. If you have time—a day or more—try the Vinegar-Marinated Pot Roast variation (page 89); its flavor is quite special. If you don't have extra time but want a different type of roast, rub the meat with one tablespoon of mild chile powder (add some cayenne if you like hot food) along with the bay leaf.

> 1 clove garlic
>
> 1 (3- to 4-pound) piece chuck or rump roast, tied if necessary
>
> 1 bay leaf
>
> Salt and freshly ground black pepper to taste
>
> 2 tablespoons olive or peanut oil
>
> 2 cups chopped onions
>
> 1 cup peeled and chopped carrot
>
> 1 celery stalk, chopped
>
> $\frac{1}{2}$ cup red wine or water
>
> 1 cup Quickest Chicken Stock (page 17) or store-bought chicken, beef, or vegetable broth, or water

1 Peel the garlic clove and cut it into tiny slivers; insert the slivers into several spots around the roast, poking holes with a thin-bladed knife. Crumble the bay leaf as finely as you can and mix it with the salt and pepper. Rub the meat all over with this mixture.

2 Heat the oil over medium-high heat in a Dutch oven or other heavy pot that can later be covered; brown the roast on all sides, taking your time. Adjust the heat so the meat browns but the fat does not burn. Remove the meat to a platter and add the vegetables to the Dutch oven. Cook them over medium-high heat, stirring frequently, until softened and somewhat browned, about 10 minutes.

3 Add the red wine, and cook, scraping the bottom of the pot with a wooden spoon, until the wine has just about evaporated. Add about half the stock or water, return the roast to the pot, and turn the heat down to very low.

4 Turn the meat every 15 minutes and cook until it is tender—a fork will pierce the meat without pushing too hard and the juices will run clear—about 1$\frac{1}{2}$ to 2$\frac{1}{2}$ hours, but possibly longer if your roast is higher than it is long (very thick roasts may require as long as 4 hours if you keep the heat extremely low). Add a little more stock if the roast appears to be drying out, an unlikely possibility (and a sign that your heat is too high). Do not overcook; when the meat is tender, it is done.

5 Remove the meat from the pot and keep it warm. Skim the fat from the surface of the remaining juice. Turn the heat to high and cook, stirring and scraping the bottom of the pan, until the liquid is thick and almost evaporated. Check for seasoning. Slice the meat and serve it with the pan juices.

Shopping Tips: If a boneless roast is produced from a cut that originally had a bone, it's usually tied in order to have a uniform shape. A butcher will do this for you.

Whenever you're cooking with red wine, avoid the "cooking wine" sold in the vinegar section of supermarkets. Use something decent, not necessarily the wine you're drinking, but a wine you're willing to drink.

Vinegar-Marinated Pot Roast (Sauerbraten): In a covered pot or other container (or a heavy plastic bag), marinate the meat in a mixture of 2 cups red wine (or water); 1/2 cup red wine vinegar; 3 cloves (or a pinch of ground cloves); 5 juniper berries; 5 peppercorns; and half the onions, carrot, and celery. Refrigerate, turning occasionally, for 1 to 3 days. Remove from the marinade and strain out the vegetables, reserving the liquid and discarding the vegetables. Dry the meat well and proceed as in Step 1 (page 88). In Step 2, use the remaining fresh vegetables, adding more if you like. Use the reserved marinade in Step 3 in place of the red wine and stock, and proceed as directed.

The Basics of Pot Roasts

Here, chuck, rump, or brisket are best, although cuts of shank, or shin, or oxtails can also be used in any of these recipes. As with stews, cooking time will vary from one cut to another. Keep the heat very low and allow plenty of time, testing for doneness every 15 minutes or so after the first hour.

Although some people believe it's impossible to overcook pot roasts, I'm not one of them; when the meat is tender, it is done. Hold it in the warm liquid for a while if you like (you can even slice it and let the slices rest in the gravy), but don't plan to hold it for too long. This is especially true for chuck and rump; brisket, which is laced throughout with fat, is the most forgiving of the cuts and can stand a little overcooking.

Sautéed Pork Chops

Makes 4 servings • **Time:** 30 minutes

A simple method that always gives good results, no matter what seasonings you add. Use center-cut loin chops, whenever possible.

4 center-cut loin pork chops, about 1 inch thick, trimmed of excess fat

Salt and freshly ground black pepper to taste

2 tablespoons olive oil, plus more if not using butter

$1/2$ cup dry white wine

1 teaspoon minced garlic or 2 tablespoons minced shallot, onion, or scallion

$1/2$ cup Quickest Chicken Stock (page 17) or store-bought chicken, beef, or vegetable broth, or water, plus more if needed

1 tablespoon butter (you can use more olive oil instead, especially if it's flavorful)

1 tablespoon freshly squeezed lemon juice or wine vinegar

Minced fresh parsley leaves for garnish

1 Sprinkle the chops with salt and pepper. Place a large skillet over medium-high heat for 2 or 3 minutes. Add the 2 tablespoons olive oil; as soon as the first wisps of smoke rise from the oil, add the chops and turn the heat to high. Brown the chops on both sides, moving them around so they develop good color all over. The entire browning process should take no longer than 4 minutes, and preferably less.

2 Reduce the heat to medium. Add the wine and the garlic and cook, turning the chops once or twice, until the wine is all but evaporated, about 3 minutes. Add $1/2$ cup of stock or water, turn the heat to low, and cover. Cook for 10 to 15 minutes, turning the chops once or twice, until the chops are tender but not dry. When done, they will be firm to the touch, their juices will run just slightly pink and, when you cut into them (which you should do if you're at all unsure of their doneness), the color will be rosy at first glance but quickly turn pale.

3 Remove the chops to a platter. If the pan juices are very thin, cook, stirring and scraping the bottom of the pan, until the liquid is reduced slightly. If they are scarce (unlikely), add another $1/2$ cup of stock or water; cook, stirring and scraping the bottom of the pan, until the liquid is reduced slightly. Then stir in the butter or oil over medium heat; add the lemon juice, pour over the chops, garnish, and serve.

Pork Chops with Apples: Steps 1 and 2 remain the same. In Step 3, after removing the chops, cook 2 cups peeled, cored, and sliced apples (or 1 cup dried fruit, soaked in water to cover for about 15 minutes) in the remaining liquid, stirring and scraping the bottom of the pan as the apples cook and adding about $1/2$ cup more liquid (white wine or stock) if necessary. When the apple slices are soft, about 5 minutes, stir in 1 tablespoon lemon juice (omit butter), pour over the chops, garnish, and serve.

Pork Chops with Mustard: Steps 1 and 2 remain the same. In Step 3, stir in 1 tablespoon or more of Dijon mustard with the lemon juice (some capers are good here, too, as is a dash or two of Worcestershire sauce). Finish as above.

The Basics of Pork

When fat was declared "bad," pork breeders created "the other white meat." As a consequence, pork has been made so lean that it must be cooked quickly to keep it from drying out.

You might wonder how you can cook pork quickly if it must be cooked well done, but in reality many pork cuts taste best when still on the pink side, at around 150°F. Since trichinae—which causes the dread trichinosis—is killed at 137°F, eating medium pork is widely considered safe. (Other bacteria, including salmonella, may not be killed at this temperature; if this concerns you, cook pork to 160°F—well done—but note that you should be doing the same for beef.)

It's not as difficult to buy the right cut of pork as it is of beef, but here are the most basic cuts, simplest preparations (and what to ask for or look for on a label).

Shoulder   Also called butt, this is fatty and delicious. *Best cooking options:* roasts, braises, stir-fries. Best well-done, about 150°F.

Loin   Behind the shoulder. *Best cooking options:* roasts, chops (rib-end—from the shoulder end, loin- or rump-end—from the rear end, and center loin or center-cut loin or center-cut rib); sautéing (pork tenderloin; pork medallions). Stop the cooking at about 135 to 140°F; if you let it rest, the temperature will rise about 10 degrees, just short of well done.

Belly   The cut that contains spareribs and bacon. (For cooking bacon, see The Basics of Bacon, page 183.) *Best cooking options:* ribs, parboiled or grilled; bacon, fried. Best well-done.

Ham   The rear legs; almost always cured, though fresh ham is similar to pork shoulder, if a bit leaner. Cook fresh ham in the same way as shoulder; cured ham should just be heated through.

PORK CUTS

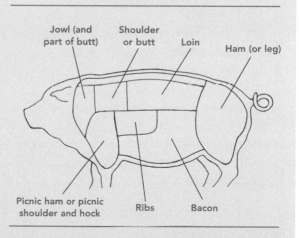

Jowl (and part of butt)

Shoulder or butt

Loin

Ham (or leg)

Picnic ham or picnic shoulder and hock

Ribs

Bacon

Sautéed Medallions of Pork with Lemon and Parsley

Makes 4 servings • **Time:** 15 minutes

Like chicken, medallions of pork are so thin that they cook through in the time it takes to brown them. Here's a basic recipe on which to build. (You can also use pork medallions in recipes for boneless chicken breasts or cutlets, pages 58–61.) Add a tablespoon or two of drained capers with the lemon juice if you like.

> 1 (1- to 1¼-pound) pork tenderloin
>
> ¼ cup olive oil
>
> Flour for dredging, liberally seasoned with salt and pepper
>
> ½ cup dry white wine
>
> Juice of 1 lemon
>
> Minced fresh parsley leaves for garnish
>
> 1 lemon, quartered

1 Cut the tenderloin into ½-inch-thick slices (it will be easier if you freeze the meat for about 30 minutes before cutting). Pound them gently (use a flat rolling pin, the back of a skillet, or a similar object) between two sheets of waxed paper to make them a bit thinner.

2 In a large skillet over medium heat, heat the olive oil; set the seasoned flour in a shallow bowl near the stove.

3 When the oil is good and hot (a pinch of flour will sizzle), dredge the medallions, one at a time, in the flour, then place them in the skillet. Cook them over heat high enough to make the oil bubble; don't crowd. Set the oven to 200°F.

4 Turn the pieces as soon as they're browned, then cook the other side; total cooking time should be 5 minutes or less, so adjust heat accordingly. As the meat is done, remove it to an ovenproof platter and place the platter in the oven.

5 When all the pork is finished, pour off the fat from the pan. Return the skillet to the stove and add the wine, over medium-high heat. Cook, stirring, until the wine is just about evaporated. Add the lemon juice, stir, and pour this sauce (there won't be more than a few tablespoons) over the meat. Garnish and serve, passing lemon quarters at the table.

Preparation Tip: Pounding meat isn't hard and helps make the meat even more tender. Remember to pound each of the pork medallions to an even thickness, so they cook at the same rate.

Roast Pork with Garlic and Rosemary

Makes 6 or more servings
Time: 1 1/2 to 2 hours, largely unattended

This is basic roast pork, the kind of dish that drives you wild and makes you eat more than you want to. Serve with very light side dishes.

> Salt and freshly ground black pepper to taste
>
> 2 tablespoons minced fresh rosemary leaves or 1 teaspoon dried rosemary
>
> 1/4 teaspoon cayenne (optional)
>
> 1 tablespoon sugar
>
> 1 teaspoon minced garlic
>
> 1 (3- to 4-pound) pork loin roast, bone-in, or 1 (2- to 3-pound) boneless roast, or a similar-size portion of fresh ham
>
> 1 1/2 cups dry white wine or chicken broth, approximately
>
> 1 tablespoon butter (optional)

1 Preheat the oven to 450°F. Mix a liberal amount of salt and pepper together with the rosemary, cayenne, sugar, and garlic, and rub it all over the roast. Place the meat in a roasting pan (use a rack if the roast is boneless, but don't bother if the bone is still in) and put in the oven. Roast, undisturbed, for 15 minutes.

2 Open the oven and pour about 1/2 cup of wine or stock over the roast; lower the heat to 325°F. Continue to roast, adding about 1/4 cup of liquid every 15 minutes or so. If the liquid accumulates on the bottom of the pan, use it to baste; if not, add more.

3 Start checking the roast after 1 1/4 hours of total cooking time (it's likely to take about 1 1/2 hours). When it is done—an instant-read thermometer will register 145° to 150°F—remove it to a warm platter. Put the roasting pan on the stove over one or two burners set to medium-high. If there is a great deal of liquid in it, reduce it to about 3/4 cup, scraping the bottom of the pan with a wooden spoon to release any brown bits that have accumulated. If the pan is dry, add 1 cup of liquid and follow the same process. When the sauce has reduced some, stir in the butter if you like, slice the roast, and serve it with the sauce.

Shopping Tip: The generally preferred cut of pork for oven-roasting is the loin. A boneless roast is easier to carve, but leaving the bone in usually results in moister meat—the added bulk and protection of the bone gives you more flexibility in timing—and always results in more flavorful meat. Other good cuts for roasting: the shoulder, butt, and (fresh) ham.

Preparation Tip: If you want a more garlicky flavor, cut a clove of garlic into tiny slivers and, using a thin-bladed knife, insert them into the roast all over. You can do this 1 or 2 days in advance; if you do, rub the roast all over with salt, too, and keep refrigerated, covered loosely with a towel or piece of waxed paper.

Basic Grilled or Broiled Lamb Chops

Makes 4 servings
Time: 15 minutes, plus time to preheat the grill

Like a simple strip sirloin steak, the lamb chop is a terrific convenience food—filling, fast, and, even without additions, flavorful. If you can get butcher-like service at your meat counter, or visit a butcher, ask for double-rib chops, which are easier to cook to medium-rare, exactly how they should be. You can also pan-grill these in a skillet; see Pan-Grilled Steak, page 81.

> 4 double-rib or large shoulder chops or 8 rib or loin chops
>
> Salt and freshly ground black pepper to taste
>
> 1 clove garlic (optional)
>
> Lemon wedges

1 Start a charcoal or wood fire or preheat a gas grill or broiler; the fire should be moderately hot for double chops, very hot for single chops. Sprinkle the meat with salt and pepper. If you like, cut the clove of garlic in half and rub it over the meat.

2 Grill or broil the chops, 3 or 4 inches from the heat source, until they are nicely browned on both sides. If they are single chops, allow no more than 2 or 3 minutes per side. With double chops, there is a greater margin for error, but cooking time will most likely still be less than 10 minutes. Serve with lemon wedges.

Shopping Tip: Lamb rib chops are the most tender and least fatty. Loin chops are similar. Both rib and loin chops should be cooked rare to medium-rare. The far less expensive shoulder chops are equally flavorful, but you have to discard a bit more fat and do a bit more chewing. Cook shoulder chops a little longer, until just about medium.

LAMB CUTS

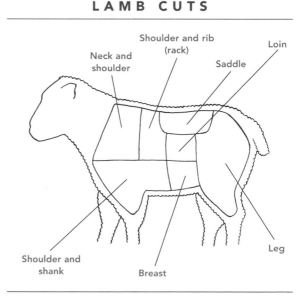

The Basics of Lamb

The most flavorful of all of our domesticated meats, lamb—like the best beef—needs little more than salt but can stand up to whatever flavors you add to it. Unlike beef, however, this can be said for almost all lamb, regardless of which cut you buy and where you buy it.

In fact, thanks to an odd combination of factors, lamb is the closest to "natural" meat you can buy in the supermarket, which is at least in part why it has such intense flavor. I'm more comfortable buying lamb than any other meat in a supermarket.

Furthermore, because lamb is so small (a whole lamb usually weighs well under a hundred—and often half that—pounds, compared to several hundred for pig and close to half a ton for steer), many cuts contain several muscles, meaning you get a variety of different tastes and textures, an unusual pleasure.

Most lamb is best rare, but not quite as rare as beef. However, it also can be quite delicious medium, and even well done—it has the flavor and juiciness to handle it. What's wonderful about leg of lamb, with or without the bone, is that its odd shape means that if the thick center is cooked to rare the thinner edges are well done. So, for once, you can satisfy everyone.

Here are the basic cuts of lamb and the best preparations for them:

Shoulder Fatty and flavorful. *Best cooking options:* roasts (must be tied), chops (chewy and juicy), and stews. Good at every stage beyond medium-rare.

Shank/Breast Bony cuts that take long, slow cooking. *Best cooking options:* braised; the breast can be cut into ribs, parboiled and grilled.

Rib and Loin Prime cuts, always expensive. *Best cooking options:* roasts (rack of lamb), chops (grilled or broiled). The boneless loin can be cut into medallions and sautéed. Cook rare- to medium-rare, about 125°F.

Leg A great cut, whether whole, half, or boned (butterflied). *Best cooking options:* Usually roasted; also grilled, especially when boned. Cook rare to well-done; good at any stage.

Grilled Skewered Lamb Chunks

Makes 4 to 6 servings
Time: 20 minutes, plus time to preheat the grill

Chunks of lamb shoulder make for moister shish kebab and more margin for error in cooking; pieces cut from the leg are leaner but easier to overcook and drier if cooked beyond the rare stage. But because it is leaner, the leg is easily cut into beautiful chunks that brown quickly without rendering a lot of fat, the cause of flare-ups on the grill. The choice is yours.

2 pounds boneless shoulder or leg of lamb, trimmed of all excess fat and cut into 2-inch chunks

3 bell peppers (any color but green), stemmed, peeled if desired, seeded, and cut into 1½-inch squares

1 large or 2 medium onions, quartered and separated into layers

About 16 cherry tomatoes (optional)

1 tablespoon olive oil

Salt and freshly ground black pepper to taste

½ cup freshly squeezed lemon juice

2 cloves garlic, roughly chopped

6 pita breads

Lemon wedges

1   Start a charcoal or wood fire or preheat a gas grill or broiler; the fire should be moderately hot, and, in the broiler, the rack should be a good 6 inches from the heat source.

2   Thread the lamb onto three skewers and the vegetables onto three others.

3   Brush lightly with olive oil and season liberally with salt and pepper. Mix together the lemon juice and garlic and brush a little of this mixture onto the meat and vegetables.

4   Grill or broil, turning the skewers as each side browns and taking care to avoid flare-ups; total cooking time should be from 12 to 15 minutes for medium-rare meat. The meat will become slightly more done after you remove it from the grill, so take this into account. Brush frequently with the lemon-garlic mixture.

5   Serve each of the skewers with a bread (you can wrap the bread around the meat and vegetables to pull them from the skewer) and a couple of lemon wedges.

Preparation Tip: Use 12-inch metal skewers, if you have them, to thread the meat and vegetables. Wood skewers are more convenient but remember to soak them in cold water (at least 15 minutes) before using to prevent them from burning.

Cooking Tip: Although alternating pieces of meat and vegetables on the same skewer is attractive, they may cook at different rates, so it makes more sense to make separate skewers of each. If you do want to mix meat and veggies on skewers, cut the vegetables a little smaller, to make sure they're tender by the time the meat is cooked.

Lamb Shanks with White Beans

Makes 4 servings
Time: 2 hours or more, plus soaking time

Lamb and white beans is one of the most comforting combinations I know. This dish can easily serve eight people if no one is too determined to fill up on meat. A great way to finish these: Cook the lamb as directed here, take it all off the bone and shred it, then stir it back into the beans. Then top with bread crumbs and run under the broiler until they brown lightly.

1 pound dried white beans (such as Great Northern, cannellini, navy)

4 cloves garlic, crushed

1 cup cored and chopped tomatoes (canned are fine; drain them first)

1 bay leaf

1 tablespoon minced fresh sage leaves or 1 teaspoon dried sage; or 1 teaspoon fresh thyme leaves or $1/2$ teaspoon dried thyme

4 lamb shanks, $3/4$ to 1 pound each

Salt and freshly ground black pepper to taste

$1/2$ cup red wine or water

$1/2$ cup Quickest Chicken Stock (page 17) or store-bought chicken, beef, or vegetable broth, or water

Minced fresh parsley or sage leaves or thyme sprigs for garnish

1　Place the beans in a large, deep pot with water to cover. Turn the heat to high and bring to a boil; skim the foam if necessary. Turn the heat down so the beans simmer, then add the garlic, tomatoes, bay leaf, and about a third of the herb. In 1 hour or more, when they are tender but not mushy, turn off the heat.

2　Meanwhile, preheat the oven to 350°F. Rub the lamb shanks with a third of the herb along with some salt and pepper, and place them in a roasting pan. Pour the wine and the stock or water around them and cover tightly with aluminum foil. Bake until the shanks are completely tender (a toothpick inserted into the meaty part will meet little resistance on its way in or out), about $1^1/2$ to 2 hours.

3　Remove the shanks to a plate, spoon off as much fat from the pan juices as is possible, and pour the remaining liquid into the still-warm beans. (Do not wash the roasting pan.) Simmer until most of the liquid is absorbed, 10 to 15 minutes; the beans should be quite soft. (The recipe can be prepared a day or two in advance up to this point; cool, place in a covered container, and refrigerate.)

4　Check the seasoning and spoon the beans into the roasting pan. Nestle the lamb shanks among them, sprinkle with the remaining sage, and return the pan to the oven, uncovered this time, for 15 minutes or so, or until hot. Garnish and serve.

Cooking Tip: Lamb shanks can be cooked in advance; up to a day or two if you refrigerate them, up to a week or two if you freeze them. Skim excess fat from the top before reheating.

Roast Leg of Lamb

Makes at least 6 servings
Time: About 1¹/₂ hours, largely unattended

This most basic of leg of lamb is mildly flavored. See the wonderfully strong-flavored variation as an option.

> 1 leg of lamb, about 5 to 7 pounds, preferably at room temperature
>
> 1 teaspoon salt
>
> 1 teaspoon freshly ground black pepper
>
> 2 pounds waxy red or white potatoes, peeled and cut into 1¹/₂-inch chunks
>
> 4 carrots, peeled and cut into 1¹/₂-inch chunks
>
> 2 onions, quartered
>
> ¹/₂ cup Quickest Chicken Stock (page 17) or store-bought chicken, beef, or vegetable broth, or water, plus more as needed

1 Preheat the oven to 425°F. Remove as much of the surface fat as possible from the lamb; rub the meat all over with salt and pepper. Place it in a roasting pan and scatter the vegetables around it; moisten with ¹/₂ cup of the stock or water.

2 Roast the lamb for 30 minutes, then turn the heat down to 350°F. Check the vegetables; if they're dry, add another ¹/₂ cup of liquid. After about 1 hour of roasting, check the internal temperature of the lamb with an instant-read thermometer. Continue to check every 10 minutes, adding a little more liquid if necessary. When it reaches 130°F for medium-rare (125°F for very rare)—check it in several places—it is done (total cooking time will be less than 1¹/₂ hours). Let it rest for a few minutes before carving (see illustrations on the following page for carving instructions). Serve with the vegetables and pan juices.

Roast Leg of Lamb with Garlic and Coriander Seeds: Include or omit the vegetables as you like. Mix the salt and pepper with 2 tablespoons of crushed coriander seeds (put them in a plastic bag and pound gently with a rolling pin, rubber mallet, or like object) and 1 teaspoon minced garlic. Use a thin-bladed knife to cut some small slits in the lamb and push a bit of the spices into them; rub the lamb all over with the remaining spices. If you have the time, let the lamb sit, for an hour or more (refrigerate if it will be much longer). Roast as in Step 2, omitting liquid if you choose to omit the vegetables. This roast is better cooked closer to medium than to rare—about 135°F.

The Basics of Leg of Lamb

Leg of lamb is one of the great roasts for a crowd of six people or so—even with minimal seasoning, its flavor and juice power a meal. With lots of herbs and spices, it's the greatest, and the ideal excuse to break out that good bottle of red wine you've been hoarding.

You can buy the leg with the shank, but it's a better buy without, because the shank doesn't take that well to roasting, and so adds a pound of not-great meat to the price. It also necessitates a longer roasting pan, which you may not have.

You can also buy half-legs of lamb; the butt half is preferable. Plan on cooking times for a 3- to 4-pound half-leg to be about two-thirds of what they are for a whole leg.

CARVING LEG OF LAMB

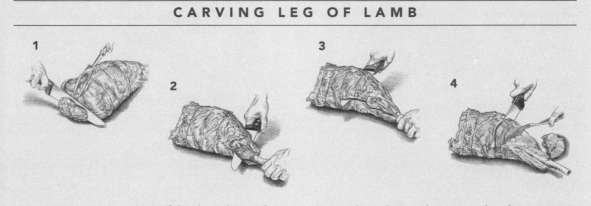

(Step 1) To carve a leg of lamb, take a slice or two off the thick end and set aside. (Steps 2–3) Make a long slice parallel to the cutting board as close to the bone as is possible. (Step 4) Cut thin slices from the top of the leg.

Meat Loaf

Makes 6 to 8 servings
Time: About 1 hour, largely unattended

I like free-form meat loaf more than the kind cooked in a loaf pan, for a couple of reasons—it browns on three sides rather than just one, and the fat can run off, rather than become trapped between pan and meat. It's easy to shape meat loaf by hand, and it will retain virtually any shape you give it.

$^1/_2$ cup plain bread crumbs,
preferably fresh (see Preparation Tip)

$^1/_2$ cup milk

2 pounds mixed ground meats:
beef, pork, veal, or lamb

1 egg, lightly beaten

$^1/_2$ cup freshly grated Parmesan cheese

$^1/_4$ cup minced fresh parsley leaves

$^1/_2$ teaspoon minced garlic

1 small onion, minced

1 small carrot, peeled and minced

1 teaspoon minced fresh sage leaves
or pinch crumbled dried sage leaves

Salt and freshly ground black pepper
to taste

3 slices bacon (optional, but good,
especially if ground meat is very lean)

1 Preheat the oven to 350°F. Soak the bread crumbs in the milk until the milk is absorbed, about 5 minutes.

2 Mix together all ingredients except bacon. Shape the meat into a loaf on a baking sheet or pan large enough to leave space around the loaf; top with bacon if you like. Bake 45 to 60 minutes, basting occasionally with rendered pan juices. When done, meat loaf will be lightly browned and firm, and an instant-read thermometer inserted into the center of a meat loaf reads 160°F.

Preparation Tips: You can make meat loaf from all beef, all pork, or all veal—but a combination of any of these (you can even throw in some lamb) is even better, making the flavor much more complex.

To make your own fresh bread crumbs, put 3 or 4 slices of slightly stale bread in a food processor. Process until fairly fine. Freeze extra in a sealed container.

---

6 | Grains and Beans

In the past 20 years, our consumption of rice has tripled, and our consumption of pasta (another form of grain, after all) has multiplied by a factor of more than ten. But many grains, like barley and wild rice, rank among the oldest foods eaten by our species and deserve a place on today's tables. Most grains are versatile, and are fast and easy to prepare, though each requires slightly different treatment.

Beans, a term used for beans, peas, split peas, lentils, and other dried legumes, may never be chic, but they have become standard fare in the last 10 years. Not surprising, since they are, generally speaking, a low-fat, no-cholesterol, low-calorie source of fiber and protein. In addition, they're cheap, easily stored, and almost never go bad. Because they are dried, their shelf life is more or less unlimited. Still, it makes sense to find fresh dried beans, those from the most recent harvest: They're likely to contain more nutrients, and they certainly cook more quickly.

Finally, they bring variety to the table at any time of year, especially in winter, when good fresh vegetables are hard to find. Although there are literally hundreds of varieties of dried beans, virtually all of them can be treated in the same way.

In this chapter you'll find cooking information on rice—both plain and a little fancier, in the form of the Italian dish, risotto. You'll also find flavorful bean recipes, and best of all bean and rice combinations like Black Beans and Rice, Spanish-Style (Moors and Christians).

Long-Grain Rice

Makes 4 servings • **Time:** About 20 minutes

Cooking rice is easy. As a general rule, you can combine it with one and a half to two times as much water and cook until the water is absorbed, or cook it like pasta (see Simple Precooked Grains, page 106). Just be sure to use gentle heat once the water comes to a boil.

1¹/₂ cups long-grain rice

2¹/₄ cups Quickest Chicken Stock (page 17) or store-bought chicken broth, or water

1 teaspoon salt, or to taste

1 Combine all ingredients in a medium saucepan and turn the heat to medium-high. Bring to a boil.

2 Turn the heat to medium-low and cover. Cook for 15 minutes, or until the water is absorbed and the rice is tender. At this point:

- If the water is not absorbed but the rice is tender, uncover and raise the heat a bit. Cook, stirring (you can add a little butter or oil if you like to prevent sticking), until the liquid evaporates.

- If the water is not absorbed and the rice is not yet tender, re-cover and check in 3 minutes.

- If the water is absorbed and the rice is not yet tender, add a few tablespoons of hot or boiling liquid, re-cover, and check in 3 minutes.

Short- or Medium-Grain Rice

Makes 4 servings • **Time:** About 45 minutes

This method takes more time, but is very easy and reliable, and produces rice that keeps well in the pot. It produces sticky, clumpy rice that is easy to eat with chopsticks and nice and chewy. Try it with Stir-Fried Chicken with Broccoli or Cauliflower (page 68).

1¹/₂ cups short- or medium-grain rice, well rinsed and drained

2¹/₂ cups water

1 teaspoon salt, or to taste

1 Combine all ingredients in a medium saucepan and let sit for about 30 minutes. The rice will absorb much of the water.

2 Cover the pan, place it over high heat, and bring to a boil. Turn the heat to medium-low and cook, undisturbed, for 15 minutes.

3 Turn off the heat. The rice will be done in 10 minutes, or will hold for up to 1 hour.

Fast-Cooked Short- or Medium-Grain Rice:
This is considerably faster because you don't need to soak the rice first: Combine all ingredients in a small saucepan and turn the heat to high. When the water starts boiling, turn the heat down to medium-high. In 8 to 12 minutes small craters will appear on the surface of the rice, indicating that the water is almost all absorbed. Cover the pot, turn the heat to low, and cook until tender, about 5 more minutes. Serve immediately or let the rice sit for up to 1 hour before serving.

The Basics of Rice

There are essentially two kinds of rice: long and short grain. There are many varieties, and different ways in which the grain is treated.

Long-grain rice, handled correctly, cooks in separate, firm, dry kernels, a tendency that can be enhanced by cooking the rice in butter or oil before adding liquid. Basmati, jasmine, and most other aromatic rices are long grain.

Short-grain (and so-called medium-grain) rice cooks up soft, moist, and a little sticky, because its outer layer softens readily and absorbs more liquid—and also more flavor—than long-grain rice. This tendency can be downplayed by cooking the rice gently, or enhanced by stirring the rice during cooking, as in risotto, a technique that allows more of the starch to leach out, making a creamy rice dish.

Know that all rice grows with a husk. Inside the husk, which is removed, is a layer of bran. Brown rice is rice with an intact bran layer. It takes longer to cook, because it takes longer for the water to penetrate the bran layer and soften the starch; it never becomes soft. Wild rice is not a rice but a grass; nevertheless, it is treated like a grain. (See Simple Precooked Grains, page 106.)

Rice Pilaf

Makes 4 servings • **Time:** About 30 minutes

There are many definitions of pilaf, but two are common to all: The rice must be briefly cooked in oil or butter before adding liquid, and the liquid must be flavorful. The oil or butter may be flavored with vegetables, herbs, or spices; the liquid may be anything from lobster stock to yogurt; and other foods may be added to the pot.

2 tablespoons butter or oil

1 cup chopped onion

1½ cups long-grain rice

Salt and freshly ground black pepper

2½ cups Quickest Chicken Stock (page 17) or store-bought chicken, beef, or vegetable broth, or water, heated to the boiling point

Minced fresh parsley leaves for garnish

1 Place the butter or oil in a large, deep skillet that can later be covered and turn the heat to medium-high. When the butter melts or the oil is hot, add the onion. Cook, stirring, until the onion softens but does not begin to brown, 5 to 8 minutes.

2 Add the rice all at once, turn the heat to medium, and stir until the rice is glossy and completely coated with oil or butter, 2 or 3 minutes. Season well, then turn the heat down to low and add the liquid, all at once. Cover the pan.

3 Cook for 15 minutes, then check the rice. When the rice is tender and the liquid is absorbed, it's done. If not, cook for 2 or 3 minutes and check again. Check the seasoning, garnish, and serve immediately.

Pilaf with Onions, Raisins, and Pine Nuts: In Step 2, stir in ½ cup raisins or dried currants and ¼ cup pine nuts along with the rice. Finish as above.

Classic Risotto

Makes 4 to 6 servings • **Time:** 45 minutes

Risotto is a wonderfully rich, creamy, and satisfying rice dish that can be a first or main course. It's not difficult to cook but you need patience to make sure the liquid in which you cook the rice is absorbed slowly.

True *risotto alla Milanese* contains saffron, a wonderful but not essential addition. You can add almost anything you like to a risotto: different combinations of herbs and spices; cooked vegetables, meats, or fish; quick-cooking raw vegetables, meats, or fish; even leftovers. Use the following recipe as a springboard to learn how to incorporate different flavors.

> 4 to 6 cups Quickest Chicken Stock (page 17) or store-bought chicken, beef, or vegetable broth, or water
>
> 1/2 teaspoon saffron threads (optional)
>
> 2 tablespoons butter or extra-virgin olive oil, plus 2 tablespoons butter, softened (optional)
>
> 1 medium onion, minced
>
> 1 1/2 cups Arborio or other short- or medium-grain rice
>
> Salt and freshly ground black pepper to taste
>
> 1/2 cup dry white wine
>
> 1/2 cup freshly grated Parmesan cheese, or to taste

1 Warm the liquid in a medium saucepan over medium heat, crumble the saffron into it, and leave the heat on.

2 Place 2 tablespoons of butter or oil in a large saucepan or skillet, preferably non-stick, and turn the heat to medium. When it's hot, add the onion and cook, stirring occasionally, until it softens, 3 to 5 minutes.

3 Add the rice and stir until it is coated with butter. Add a little salt and pepper, then the white wine. Stir and let the liquid bubble away.

4 Begin to add the warmed stock, 1/2 cup or so at a time, stirring after each addition and every minute or so. When the stock is just about evaporated, add more. The mixture should be neither soupy nor dry. Keep the heat medium to medium-high, and stir frequently (constant stirring is not necessary).

5 Begin tasting the rice 20 minutes after you add it; you want it to be tender but with still a tiny bit of crunch. (Do not overcook.) It could take as long as 30 minutes to reach this stage. When it does, add the softened butter and Parmesan. Check the seasoning, adjust if necessary, and serve immediately.

Shopping Tip: Arborio rice is preferable but not essential. You can use other short-grained rice imported from Italy or Spain or ordinary short- or medium-grain rice to make risotto.

Simple Precooked Grains

Makes 4 servings

Time: 15 minutes to more than 1 hour; depends on the grain

This is a general method that works well for just about any grain: It is the best technique for brown rice, pearled barley, and wild rice, but it works with plain white rice, too.

>   At least 6 cups water
>
>   1½ cups any grain listed in the box below, rinsed

1 Bring at least 6 cups water to a boil in a medium-to-large pot; salt it. Stir in the grain and adjust the heat so that the water boils, but not furiously.

2 Cook, stirring occasionally, until the grain is tender. This will take about 7 or 8 minutes with some white rice, and as long as 1 hour or more for some brown rice, unpearled barley, and other unhulled grains. Add additional boiling water if necessary to keep grains covered.

3 Pour the grain into a strainer; plunge the strainer into ice-cold water to stop the cooking. Drain again. Reheat within 1 hour or refrigerate for later use.

The Basics of Cooking Grains

Because grains are dried foods, they must be rehydrated and cooked at the same time. The time this takes depends on the nature of the grain, how dry it is (older grains are drier than newer ones), how much of its outer coating remains (brown rice has a hull; white rice does not), whether it has been milled ("rolling" or "cutting" oats exposes more surface area), and whether it has been precooked.

But you can cook most grains by the method above, which does not require either precise timing or guesswork about the quantity of water that must be added. Rather, it enables you to cook the grain as you would pasta, by tasting it until it is done. Once the grain is tender and you have drained it, you may serve it immediately, set it aside and reheat it later, or drain it and store it in the refrigerator to be reheated in a day or two.

Below are some basic grains that cook well using this method. Cooking time listed is an average per 1 cup of grain:

Long-grain white rice: 15 minutes

Brown rice: 45 minutes

Pearled barley: 20 minutes

Wild rice: 45 minutes

Precooked Grains with Butter or Oil

Makes 4 servings • **Time:** 10 minutes or more

Once you've cooked grains with the method at left, reheating them is a snap. At the same time, you can add a variety of different flavorings to them.

> 3 tablespoons olive oil, butter, or a combination
>
> 3 to 4 cups Simple Precooked Grains (page 106)
>
> Salt and freshly ground black pepper to taste
>
> Minced fresh parsley leaves for garnish

1 Place the oil and/or butter in a large skillet, preferably non-stick, and turn the heat to medium. When the oil is hot or the butter melted, add the grains. Cook, stirring occasionally, until heated through, about 10 minutes.

2 Season with salt and pepper, garnish, and serve.

Precooked Grains with Garlic, Onions, or Mushrooms: In Step 1, cook 1 tablespoon minced garlic, $1/2$ cup chopped onion, or 1 cup trimmed and chopped mushrooms (or a combination of the three) in the butter or oil, stirring occasionally, until softened. Add the grains and finish as above.

Three Ideas for Precooked Grains

1. Stir in any minced herb or cooked vegetable during the last minute of cooking.

2. Add dried fruit such as raisins or minced apricots along with the grains.

3. Add to soups at the last minute.

Classic Beans

Time: 30 minutes to 2 hours, largely unattended

It's best to precook beans whenever you can because, unfortunately, precise timing is nearly impossible. So allow enough time unless you've cooked beans from the same batch before and can predict cooking time. Typical white, black, or red beans are done in an hour or so, but may take longer; chickpeas almost always take more than 2 hours.

Most beans double or triple their bulk during cooking; that is, a cup of dried beans yields at least two cups of cooked beans. As a side dish, you'd figure $1/2$ to 1 full cup of cooked beans per person; as a main dish, somewhat more. So 1 cup of dried beans will safely serve four people as a side dish when done.

Any quantity dried beans, washed and picked over (see The Basics of Buying and Preparing Beans, page 109)

Salt to taste

1 Place the beans in a large pot with water to cover. Turn the heat to high and bring to a boil; skim the foam if necessary. Turn the heat down so the beans simmer. Cover loosely.

2 Cook, stirring occasionally, until the beans begin to become tender; add about 1 teaspoon salt per $1/2$ pound of beans, or to taste.

3 Continue to cook, stirring gently to avoid breaking the beans, until they are as tender as you like; add additional water if necessary. Drain and serve, or use in other recipes, or store covered, in their cooking liquid, in the refrigerator (3 days) or freezer (3 months).

Cooking Tips: Beans are always cooked in liquid, and that liquid is usually water, but beans cooked in meat or vegetable stock or broth are especially delicious and take no more work.

You can deal with the gassiness beans produce in several ways: ignore it; eat beans more often so you develop a tolerance; cook beans with the commercial product Beano; or try this—boil the beans in abundant water, cook for 2 minutes, then turn off the heat. Soak for at least 1 hour, then rinse the beans and cook as usual in fresh water.

Faster Beans: You can speed the cooking process a little bit by thinking ahead. Soak the beans for at least 6 hours in water to cover, drain, then cook in fresh water. Or boil the beans for 2 minutes in water to cover, then soak them for 2 hours in that water, drain, then cook in fresh water. Either of these techniques usually reduces cooking time by 25 to 50 percent, or 15 to 30 minutes.

Four Additions to Classic Beans

1. Cook with bay leaf, a couple of cloves, some peppercorns, thyme sprigs, parsley leaves and/or stems, chile powder, or other herbs and spices. Remove the bay leaf before serving.

2. Cook an unpeeled onion, a carrot, a celery stalk, and/or three or four cloves of garlic.

3. Cook in Quickest Chicken Stock (page 17) or store-bought chicken, beef, or vegetable broth.

4. Cook a few slices of diced bacon (or pancetta) until crisp; remove, then reheat the beans in the rendered bacon fat. Garnish with the bacon.

The Basics of Buying and Preparing Beans

Generally, beans should look consistent, and have deep, somewhat glossy color; faded, dry-looking beans are likely to be older, and avoid wrinkled ones or a batch with a high percentage of cracked or broken beans.

Store beans in covered containers or thick plastic bags in a dry place.

Sort through the beans just before soaking or cooking: Put the beans in a pot and fill it with water, then swish the whole thing around while looking into the pot. Remove any beans that are discolored, shriveled, or broken and remove any pebbles or other stray matter. Then dump the beans into a colander and rinse for a minute or so.

Although beans take longer to cook than other foods, many can simmer away on a back burner, with only an occasional stir, and soften completely in as little as an hour (far less for lentils and split peas). To speed cooking, soak them before cooking (see Faster Beans, page 108). Or use a pressure cooker (see Pressure-Cooked Beans, page 110).

Two alternatives cut time even more: The first is to buy canned pre-cooked beans. You open the can, drain and rinse the beans, and proceed. Elapsed time: a minute. Disadvantage: They're not as good as beans you prepare yourself. The alternative is to freeze cooked beans. Instead of cooking a cup of dried beans, cook a couple of cups, or more. Freeze the remainder in individual containers, in the bean cooking liquid. Defrost in the refrigerator or microwave and proceed. Frozen beans keep perfectly for months. Disadvantage: You must think ahead!

Pressure-Cooked Beans

Makes 4 servings • **Time:** About 30 minutes

Although a pressure cooker is not usually thought of as an essential tool, using it is really the only way to reliably cook most dried beans in less than an hour, and usually in less than half that time, presoaked or not. Timing is imprecise, though, so open the device and check the progress, usually two or three times.

1¹/₂ cups dried beans, any type except quick-cooking beans like lentils, washed and picked over (see The Bean Lexicon, page 111)

6 cups water, plus more if necessary

1 tablespoon any oil

1 teaspoon salt

1 Combine all ingredients in a pressure cooker and lock on the lid. Turn the heat to high.

2 Bring to high pressure, then adjust the heat so that it is just high enough to maintain pressure. Cook 10 to 25 minutes (the shorter time for small or quite fresh beans, the longer for larger or very dry beans).

3 Cool the pressure cooker by running cold water over the top. When the pressure is down, carefully remove the top and taste a bean. If it is done, store the beans in their liquid or drain and serve, or use in any recipe for cooked beans. If the beans are tender but not quite soft, add more water if necessary, and cook without the lid for a few minutes. If they are not yet tender, repeat Steps 1 and 2, cooking for 5 to 10 minutes at a time.

The Basics of Pressure Cookers

New-model pressure cookers are easy to use and completely safe and they can help you make beans, soups, stews, and grain dishes in less time.

Pressure-cooked beans are done in 15 to 20 minutes—without presoaking. You can use virtually any recipe using dried beans in the pressure cooker; just don't fill the pot more than half full, because very "foamy" beans can clog the relief valve.

Pressure cookers also work well for soups, stews, and pot roasts, with cooking times of about half that of normal (not counting initial browning and bringing the pot up to pressure). Sauté vegetables or brown meats right in the pressure cooker, using it as you would any other pot, before adding liquid.

When making a soup, stew, or other dish that combines tough meat with vegetables, cook in two stages. First cook the meat under pressure until it is nearly done. Add the vegetables during the final 5 to 10 minutes of cooking; if you add them at the beginning they will turn to mush before the meat is tender.

The Bean Lexicon

Most beans are interchangeable in recipes, but there will be differences. Generally, it's safe to substitute white beans for other white beans, and red for red. Other than that, I'd try to stick to the bean listed in a recipe. Here are some common beans.

Bean	Appearance	Use	Cooking Time
Black (Turtle bean)	Medium-sized (up to 1/2 inch long), round to almost square, deep black with a white line and interior.	Multipurpose, among the most valuable and best-tasting beans. Especially good in soup (page 15).	Can be quite long, up to 2 hours, but usually 1 hour or less. Good candidate for the pressure cooker.
Black-Eyed Pea (Cow pea)	Ivory in color, with a black spot; kidney-shaped and small, no more than 1/2 inch long.	Southern dishes, often with meat; Southern Beans and Rice (page 116).	20 (these are often very fresh) to 45 minutes.
Cannellini	Looks like a white kidney bean, which it is sometimes called.	As for other white beans.	Up to 1 hour.
Chickpea (Garbanzo)	Deep beige, round, but with lumps and lines; 1/4 to 1/2 inch in diameter.	With pasta, in casseroles and salads, by itself.	Often as long as 2 hours, sometimes less. Good for the pressure cooker.
Great Northern	Large (up to 1 inch long), oval, and white. One of the most common white beans.	All-purpose.	Usually 1 hour or so.
Kidney	Reddish brown, up to 1 inch long, kidney-shaped.	Chili, beans and rice, puree, refried beans, baked beans—virtually all-purpose.	A good hour, or more.
Lentil	There are three major kinds: common green (or brown), which are round disks about 1/8 inch in diameter; red, which are smaller, bright orange, quick-cooking, and have a tendency to fall apart; and French (not always from France), or Le Puy, a tiny, dark-green French variety, which takes the longest to cook and has the best flavor.	In salads, soups, and simple side dishes. Very useful.	From 20 minutes (red) to 40 minutes (Le Puy). Rarely longer.
Navy (Pea bean)	Small round bean, white, about 1/4 inch in diameter.	The most basic of white beans. Great for puree, baked beans, and simple uses. Mild-flavored.	About 45 minutes.
Pink (Red)	Its name tells you its color. A small, slightly ovate bean essentially interchangeable with the pinto.	Beans and rice, refried beans, puree, chili.	About 45 minutes.
Pinto	From beige to rust, usually mottled; about 1/2 inch long, oval-shaped.	Beans and rice, refried beans, puree, chili.	About 45 minutes.

White Beans, Tuscan-Style

Makes 4 servings
Time: 1 to 2 hours, largely unattended

The classic, simple, and always delicious beans of Tuscany. Great olive oil makes a big difference here. Add some cooked sausage and sautéed red bell peppers to make this into a simple main course.

About ¹/₂ pound dried white beans (cannellini, navy, or Great Northern washed and picked over; see The Basics of Buying and Preparing Beans, page 109)

20 fresh sage leaves or 1 tablespoon dried sage

Salt and freshly ground black pepper to taste

2 teaspoons minced garlic

2 tablespoons extra-virgin olive oil

1 Place the beans in a pot with water to cover. Turn the heat to high and bring to a boil. Add the sage; adjust the heat so the beans simmer. Cover loosely.

2 Cook, stirring occasionally, until the beans begin to soften; add about ¹/₂ teaspoon salt and some pepper. Continue to cook until the beans are very tender; add additional water if the beans dry out.

3 Drain the cooking liquid if necessary, then add the garlic, along with some more salt and pepper if necessary. Stir in the olive oil and serve.

Chili non Carne

Makes 4 servings
Time: About 2 hours, largely unattended

Chili can be quite simple or more complicated. Although some chili purists insist that
chili should be made with meat and no beans,
I like bean-based chili. All chili contains chile
powder or, even more basic, a combination of
ground chiles, cumin, and oregano.

> 2 cups pinto, kidney, or other beans,
> washed and picked over (see The Bean
> Lexicon, page 111)
>
> 1 whole onion, unpeeled, plus 1 small
> onion, minced
>
> Salt and freshly ground black pepper
> to taste
>
> 1 cup bean cooking liquid, Quickest
> Chicken Stock (page 17) or store-bought
> chicken, beef, or vegetable broth,
> or water
>
> 1 fresh or dried hot chile, seeded,
> stemmed, and minced, or to taste
> (optional)
>
> 1 teaspoon ground cumin, or to taste
> (optional)
>
> 1 teaspoon minced fresh oregano
> leaves or ¹/₂ teaspoon dried oregano
> (optional)
>
> 1 tablespoon chile powder (optional),
> if you prefer it to the combination of
> pepper, cumin, and oregano above
>
> 1 tablespoon minced garlic
>
> Minced cilantro leaves for garnish

1 Place the beans in a large pot with water to
cover. Turn the heat to high and bring to a boil; skim
the foam if necessary. Add the whole onion. Turn the
heat down so the beans simmer and cover loosely.

2 When the beans begin to soften, season
with salt and pepper. Continue to cook, stirring
occasionally, until the beans are quite tender
but still intact, 1 to 2 hours; add additional water
if necessary.

3 Drain the beans, reserving the cooking liquid
if you choose to use it. Discard the whole onion
and add all the remaining ingredients except
cilantro. Turn the heat to medium and bring to a
boil. Cover and turn the heat to low.

4 Cook, stirring occasionally and adding more
liquid if necessary, until the beans are very tender
and the flavors have mellowed, about 15 minutes.
Adjust seasoning as necessary and garnish with
cilantro. Serve with rice, crackers, or tortilla chips,
and bottled hot sauce, such as Tabasco.

Chili con Carne: While the beans are cooking,
place 1 tablespoon canola or other neutral oil
in a large skillet and turn the heat to medium.
Add 1 pound hand-chopped or ground beef,
pork, turkey, or chicken and cook, stirring,
until the meat has lost its color. Season the
meat with salt, pepper, and about 2 teaspoons chile powder, or to taste. Stir it into
the beans along with the other ingredients.

Baked Beans

Makes 4 servings

Time: At least 4 hours, largely unattended

These are traditional baked beans and as such are fairly minimalist. The pork or bacon adds a lot of flavor but you can do without it.

1 pound cannellini, navy, or other white beans

$1/2$ pound salt pork or slab bacon (optional; see Shopping Tip, page 116)

$1/2$ cup molasses, or to taste

2 teaspoons ground mustard or 2 tablespoons prepared mustard, or to taste

Salt and freshly ground black pepper to taste

1 Cook the beans as in Classic Beans (page 108), but only until they begin to become tender, about 30 minutes.

2 Preheat the oven to 300°F. Cube or slice the salt pork or bacon and place it in the bottom of a bean pot or other deep-sided ovenproof covered pot, such as a Dutch oven. Drain the beans, then mix them with the molasses and mustard. Pour them over the meat. Gently add enough boiling water to cover the beans by about an inch. Add salt and pepper.

3 Bake, uncovered, for about 3 hours, checking occasionally and adding more water if necessary. At the end of 3 hours, taste and adjust seasoning; you may add more salt, sweetener, or mustard.

4 When the beans are very tender, scoop the meat up from the bottom and lay it on top of the beans; raise the heat to 400°F. Cook until the pork browns a bit and the beans are very bubbly, about 10 minutes. (You may repeat this process several times, scooping the meat to the top and browning it; each repetition darkens the color of the dish and adds flavor.) Serve hot.

Vegetarian Baked Beans: Substitute 2 tablespoons butter or neutral oil (such as canola) and 1 large or 2 medium onions, quartered, for the meat. Add 2 cups peeled, seeded, and chopped tomatoes (canned are fine; don't bother to drain) along with the molasses and mustard. Cook as above.

Black Beans and Rice, Spanish-Style

Makes 4 to 6 servings
Time: 30 minutes with precooked beans

Rice and beans are one of the most important of all culinary marriages. They are cheap, provide good protein and carbohydrates, and don't take a lot of work to make them delicious.

Moors and Christians, the common name for this dish, and the beans, peas, and rice dish called Hoppin' John (see Southern Beans and Rice, next page) are just two favorites, but you can also simply take any well-seasoned bean dish and serve it with any well-prepared rice. (The name, Moors and Christians, by the way, comes from the seventh-century rule of devoutly Christian Spain by the Muslim Moors.)

2 tablespoons extra-virgin olive oil

1 medium onion, finely chopped

1 red or yellow bell pepper, stemmed, peeled if desired, and chopped

Salt and freshly ground black pepper to taste

1 tablespoon minced garlic

3 cups drained cooked or canned black beans

1 cup chopped tomatoes (canned are fine; don't bother to drain), optional

1 cup bean cooking liquid, or chicken, beef, or vegetable broth, or water

1/2 cup minced fresh parsley leaves

Rice Pilaf (page 104)

1 Place the oil in a large, deep skillet and turn the heat to medium. A minute later, add the onion and bell pepper. Season with salt and pepper and cook, stirring, until the pepper is soft, 8 to 10 minutes. Stir in the garlic, the beans, the optional tomatoes, and the liquid.

2 Turn the heat to medium-high and cook, stirring, until the beans are hot and most of the liquid is evaporated, 10 to 20 minutes. Stir in most of the parsley.

3 Arrange the pilaf on a platter, in a ring if you like. Spoon the beans over the rice or into the center of the ring, or pass them separately. Garnish with the remaining parsley and serve.

Southern Beans and Rice

Makes 4 to 6 servings
Time: $1^{1}/_{2}$ to 2 hours, largely unattended

Bacon, peas, and rice—southern staples—comprise Hoppin' John, our best indigenous rice and bean dish.

> 1 cup black-eyed or other dried peas, washed and picked over (see The Bean Lexicon, page 111)
>
> $^{1}/_{4}$ pound slab bacon or 1 smoked ham hock
>
> 1 large onion, chopped
>
> 1 (4-inch) sprig fresh rosemary, 2 sprigs fresh thyme, or $^{1}/_{2}$ teaspoon dried rosemary or thyme
>
> Salt and freshly ground black pepper to taste
>
> $1^{1}/_{2}$ cups long-grain rice

1 Place the peas in a medium pot with the bacon or ham hock, onion, herb, and water to cover by at least 2 inches. Bring to a boil over medium-high heat.

2 Turn the heat down to medium and cook, skimming any foam that arises, until the peas are tender, 1 to $1^{1}/_{2}$ hours. Remove the meat and reduce the liquid to about 3 cups; as the liquid is reducing, cut the meat into chunks, removing extremely fatty pieces if you like. Return it to the pot.

3 Taste the cooking liquid and add salt and pepper if needed. Remove the rosemary or thyme sprigs, if used. Stir in the rice and cook, covered, until the rice is done and the liquid is absorbed, 15 to 20 minutes. This can sit for 15 to 20 minutes before serving.

Shopping Tip: Beans and many stews were traditionally cooked with a piece of fatty pork for flavor (and nutrition; there was a time, believe it or not, when many people had trouble getting enough fat in their diet). Salt pork, slab bacon, and ham hocks are all good for this use.

---

7 | Vegetables

The typical supermarket produce section has grown enormously in recent years. Where there was once spinach, there are now kale, bok choy, and half a dozen other greens for cooking; where there were all-purpose potatoes, there are now Yukon gold, little red, long white, and more. On any given day the choices are staggering.

Fortunately, cooking vegetables is easy. Because although they are very distinctive—it would be much easier to mistake beef for lamb than it would be to mistake zucchini for broccoli—most of them can be handled in very similar ways. Few vegetables cannot be simmered or steamed to tenderness and then lightly dressed, with something as simple as lemon juice, vinaigrette, or that old standby, butter. And few vegetables cannot be cooked in a little olive oil, either over high heat so that they become crisp, or with some liquid, covered, over lower heat, so that they become meltingly tender.

But each vegetable is better suited to some techniques than others. Vegetables usually must be tenderized if they are to be considered cooked, and there are different ways to accomplish this. To some extent, the correct cooking technique depends upon shape. You would not use a sauté pan to cook a whole potato, or a whole head of broccoli; but cut either into small bits and the skillet becomes a fine alternative to boiling or steaming. And there are other factors that determine the best cooking method for a given vegetable. Broccoli, for example, should not be roasted dry; its relatively low moisture content would ensure that the result was tough unless extraordinary measures were taken. A baking potato, however, contains enough moisture of its own to be cooked with dry heat.

You can cook almost any vegetable by immersing it in enough boiling water to cover it, until crisp and tender, and in most cases that's the easiest method. But most vegetables can also be steamed, and steaming has its advantages: It's quicker (you don't have to wait for a large pot of water to boil), and the vegetable has less of a chance of becoming waterlogged. There are disadvantages, too: If you're not attentive, the pot can boil dry, and since steaming is done under a cover, it's a little more difficult to track the cooking progress.

Precooked Vegetables in Butter or Oil

This technique will not work for every vegetable, such as those with super-high water content like zucchini. But it can be used with the vast majority, and has real advantages. It allows you to prepare the vegetable (up to a day or two in advance) so that it can later be finished within 5 minutes of when you want to serve it. You can start and finish the vegetable as you're bringing other dishes to the table, or just before.

This method is also applicable to "leftover" simmered or steamed vegetables; just make sure to rinse them with boiling water to remove any prior seasoning if necessary.

The process is simple:

1 Prepare the vegetable for cooking.

2 Steam or simmer individual vegetables in salted boiling water to cover until it is tender.

3 Drain it, then drop it into ice-cold water.

4 Drain it again.

5 Set aside or cover and refrigerate for a day or two.

When you're ready to eat:

1 Turn the heat under a skillet to medium. Add enough butter or olive oil—usually 1 or 2 tablespoons—to cover the bottom of the skillet. (Alternatively, bring a pot of water to a boil.)

2 Add the vegetables to the pan, turn the heat to medium-high, and cook, stirring, until hot, just a couple of minutes (or submerge in the boiling water until hot, a minute or so). Season and serve.

Three Ideas for Precooked Vegetables

1. Add minced onion, shallot, or garlic to the butter or oil. Cook for about 1 minute before adding the main vegetable.

2. Add herbs or spices to the vegetable as it heats. Parsley is always appropriate, but most fresh herbs combine nicely with simply cooked vegetables. Ginger, curry powder, dried red chiles, and other spices can all add flavor to a variety of vegetables.

3. Sauce the vegetable with béchamel (page 31), or top it with grated Parmesan or other cheese, then run it under the broiler—carefully, so as not to burn the top—until hot.

The Basics of Buying Vegetables

There are some general rules for buying vegetables.

- Never buy a vegetable with obvious damage—bruises, exceptionally soft spots, holes, and so on.
- Look for vegetables that are firm.
- Look for lots of green, or whatever the primary color of the vegetable happens to be (purple for eggplant, red for tomato); brown generally speaking, is a color you want to avoid (yellow is too, to some extent).

It pays to wash almost every vegetable before you go any further (the exceptions, such as onions—which are peeled—are obvious). A soft brush is very useful for potatoes you don't want to peel, cucumbers with little spines, and other tasks. Greens and other vegetables should be washed as described on page 2.

Information about peeling, slicing, dicing, and otherwise preparing vegetables, accompany each vegetable recipe. One special way, slicing into thin matchstick pieces—good for salads and sautées—is shown below.

MAKING JULIENNE CUTS

1

2

(Step 1) To julienne any vegetable, cut a piece off each end so it will stand straight. Then cut thin slices using a knife or a mandoline.

(Step 2) Cut the thin slices into matchsticks. If you want tiny cubes, stack the matchsticks and cut across them.

Roasted, Broiled, or Grilled Asparagus

Makes 4 servings

Time: 30 minutes, plus time to preheat the grill

If you're grilling or roasting meat or fish, it's easy to cook the asparagus the same way. And they're great when browned. Thick asparagus should really be peeled before cooking; thin asparagus need not be.

> 1½ to 2 pounds asparagus, trimmed and peeled (see illustration)
>
> 1 to 2 tablespoons extra-virgin olive oil
>
> Salt to taste
>
> Lemon wedges

1 Preheat the oven to 450°F, preheat the broiler or a gas grill, or start a charcoal or wood fire. If you're roasting or broiling, place the asparagus in a roasting pan and drizzle with 1 or 2 tablespoons of oil; sprinkle with salt. If you're grilling, brush the asparagus with oil and sprinkle with salt. Place the asparagus in the oven, under the broiler, or on the grill.

2 Roast or grill, turning the spears once or twice, just until the thick part of the stalks can be pierced with a knife, 10 to 15 minutes. Broiling time will be shorter, 5 to 10 minutes total. Serve immediately, with lemon wedges.

PREPARING ASPARAGUS

Snap off the bottom of each stalk; they will usually separate naturally right where the woody part ends.

All but the thinnest asparagus are best when peeled.

The Basics of Asparagus

Spears rising from the earth in early spring, year after year—no wonder asparagus is the favorite of so many home gardeners. These days, we can buy it year-round (it's always spring somewhere), but the best asparagus is local asparagus, sold from February in the South through May or June in the North.

Classically, asparagus is steamed, but it doesn't much matter how you cook the stalks, as long as you leave them just a little crisp—not so crisp that they crunch when you bite them, but not so soggy that they begin to fall apart. Some people eat asparagus with a knife and fork, but using your fingers is considered polite, even among sticklers.

Buying and storing Any color asparagus is good; we usually see green, but white and purple are common in Europe and occasionally make it to our markets. If you buy super-thin stalks, they don't need to be peeled. But big, fat stalks are great to eat, too. Don't buy shriveled spears, or damaged ones (and don't buy canned or frozen asparagus). Store, wrapped loosely in plastic, in the refrigerator. Use as soon as possible.

Preparing Snap off the bottom of each stem; it will naturally break (more or less) where the woody part ends and tender part begins. Unless the asparagus are pencil-thin (or unless you're pressed for time), it's best, although not essential, to peel them from the base up to the beginning of the flower (the layered end of the stalk).

Best cooking methods Steaming is basic, but you can cook asparagus, especially thin ones, any way you like; you can even roast them.

When is it done? Asparagus are done when you can easily insert a skewer or thin-bladed knife into the thickest part of the stalk. Undercooked asparagus are crisp; overcooked asparagus are mushy.

Simmered, Steamed, or Microwaved Broccoli

Makes 4 servings • **Time:** 20 minutes

The thick stalks of broccoli are always worth peeling and it usually makes sense to start cooking them 1 or 2 minutes before the much more tender florets.

1 to 1½ pounds broccoli trimmed and cut up

1 To simmer the broccoli, bring a large pot of water to a boil; salt it. Place the stalk sections in the water and cook for 2 minutes. Add the florets and continue to cook for 2 to 6 minutes longer, until the pieces are bright green and tender.

2 To steam the broccoli, place the stalk sections in a steamer above an inch or two of salted water. Cover and cook about 2 minutes. Add the florets and continue to cook for 2 to 6 minutes longer, until the pieces are bright green and tender.

3 To microwave the broccoli, place the stalk sections on a microwave-proof plate or in a shallow bowl with about 2 tablespoons of salted water; cover with a lid or plastic wrap. Microwave on high for 2 minutes; shake the container and add the florets. Continue to microwave on high for 1-minute intervals, shaking and checking the broccoli, until it is bright green and tender.

4 Serve hot broccoli with butter, vinaigrette (page 3), or freshly squeezed lemon juice. Or drain it, drop it into a bowl of ice water to stop the cooking, drain again, place in a covered container, and refrigerate for up to 2 days. Then follow the directions for Precooked Vegetables in Butter or Oil (page 118).

Cooking Tip: To steam, you can use a special pot designed for steaming, or the common and convenient basket of interlocking metal leaves that will convert almost any saucepan into a steamer. Or, if necessary, you can simply arrange four metal chopsticks, or an upside-down ramekin, to build a little platform on the bottom of a pot; steam the vegetables on a heatproof plate resting on this platform.

The Basics of Broccoli and Cauliflower

Broccoli and cauliflower are members of the massive cabbage family. And although they look different, broccoli and cauliflower are essentially interchangeable in recipes.

Broccoli keeps well, is nutrition- and flavor-packed, and like cauliflower is good raw or lightly or fully cooked; see Precooked Vegetables in Butter or Oil, page 118.

Buying and storing These grow best in cool weather, are shipped nationwide from western states throughout the winter, and are available from local sources all over the country—with the exception of the Sun Belt—from April through November or even later. Fresh broccoli and cauliflower are vastly superior to frozen. Look for tight heads, with no yellowing (broccoli) or browning (cauliflower). Store in a loose plastic bag in the vegetable bin, and cook as quickly as you can.

Preparing For broccoli, strip the stalk of leaves, if any (these can be cooked along with the tops and eaten, if you like). Remove the bottom inch of the stalk, or wherever it has dried out. Peel the tough outer skin of the broccoli stalk as best you can: a paring knife or vegetable peeler will both do the job. If you like, cut the stalk into equal-length pieces and break the head into florets. Cauliflower can be cooked whole or broken into florets.

Best cooking methods Simmering, steaming, or microwaving all work fine; broccoli is good when precooked by one of these methods and then reheated. Regardless of the method, it often makes sense to cook the stalks longer than the florets; just start them 1 or 2 minutes earlier. Broccoli also makes a good soup (see Cream of Broccoli Soup, page 12), and stir-fry dish (see Stir-Fried Chicken with Broccoli or Cauliflower, page 68).

When is it done? It's a matter of taste. When bright green, broccoli is still crisp and quite chewy, and some people like it that way; cook it another couple of minutes and it becomes tender; overcook it and it becomes mushy and begins to fall apart. Cauliflower doesn't give the same visual tips, but it goes through the same stages. Cook it until a skewer or thin-bladed knife can easily pierce the stalk.

Quick-Braised Carrots with Butter

Makes 4 servings • **Time:** About 20 minutes

Best with butter, but still delicious when made with oil. You can cut back on the oil, if you like. Simply cooked carrots are good spiked with spices. Try adding fresh ginger or ground cardamom, cinnamon, cumin, or coriander.

1 pound carrots, peeled and cut into ¼-inch-thick slices

2 tablespoons butter or 1 tablespoon canola or other neutral oil

¼ cup water

1 teaspoon sugar or 1 tablespoon maple syrup

Salt and freshly ground black pepper to taste

Minced fresh parsley, mint, chervil, or cilantro leaves for garnish

1 Place the carrots, butter or oil, water, sugar, salt, and pepper in a medium saucepan over high heat; bring to a boil and cover. Turn the heat to medium-low and cook for 5 minutes.

2 Uncover and raise the heat a bit. Cook, stirring occasionally, until the liquid has evaporated and the carrots are cooking in butter or oil. Lower the heat and continue to cook, stirring occasionally, until tender, a couple of minutes longer.

3 Taste and adjust the seasoning if necessary, then garnish and serve.

The Basics of Carrots

Carrots are great eaten raw, in soups or stews, or as a simply cooked vegetable.

Buying and storing   Carrots keep so well that even bagged carrots are usually quite good. Officially, the season is late summer through early winter, but carrots are available year-round. Don't buy them if they're flabby or growing new leaves.

Preparing   Among the easiest vegetables to prepare. Peel with a vegetable peeler (make long strokes), then trim off both ends.

Best cooking methods   Steaming, simmering, braising. You can also use carrots in the recipe for Mashed Potatoes (page 132) and Roasted Root Vegetables (page 138).

When is it done?   When tender but not soft. Taste and you'll know.

DICING A CARROT

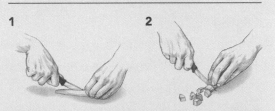

1   2

(Step 1) To dice a carrot, cut it in half lengthwise, then into quarters or, if necessary, smaller sections. **(Step 2)** Cut across the sections, as small as you like.

Steamed Corn

Makes 4 servings • **Time:** 20 minutes or less

Keep corn cool, shuck it at the last minute, cook it just long enough to heat it up, and you'll get the most out of it.

> 8 ears fresh corn, shucked
> Salt and freshly ground black pepper to taste
> Butter (optional)

1 Place the corn in a large pot with an inch or two of salted water; it's okay if some of the corn sits in the water and some above it. Cover and cook over high heat until it is just hot, 10 minutes or less (if the water is already boiling when you add the corn, or if you have a powerful stove, the cooking time could be as little as 3 minutes).

2 Serve the corn with salt, pepper, and, if you like, butter.

PREPARING CORN

The "silk" must always be removed from corn before cooking. You can remove the husk, or simply peel it back and take out the silk, then fold the husk back over the corn. This works well for grilling; for steaming or boiling, remove the husk entirely.

Use a sharp knife to scrape kernels from the cob.

The Basics of Corn

Buying and storing   Decide which corn on the cob you like best: Big ears or little, young, pale (even white) corn, or deep-yellow corn. You're better off buying corn at a farmstand than at a supermarket, if you have the option. Refrigerate corn, still in its husk; it will not go bad, but will decline in sweetness as it ages. Frozen corn is a good substitute for cooking, though of course there's no substitute for fresh corn on the cob.

Preparing   Shuck corn just before cooking it. For use in recipes, scrape the kernels from the cob with a knife.

Best cooking methods   Steaming, roasting, grilling; the kernels can be used in stir-fries, stews, soups, or mixed vegetable dishes.

When is it done?   When it's hot; there's no point in cooking it any further.

Sautéed Mushrooms with Garlic

Makes 4 servings • **Time:** About 20 minutes

These are best served at room temperature. Stir in some other herbs—such as chives, chervil, and/or tarragon—and 1 or 2 teaspoons of good vinegar along with the parsley if you like.

> ¹/₂ cup extra-virgin olive oil
>
> About 1 pound mushrooms, preferably an assortment, cleaned, trimmed, and sliced
>
> Salt and freshly ground black pepper to taste
>
> ¹/₄ cup dry white wine
>
> 1 teaspoon minced garlic
>
> 2 tablespoons chopped fresh parsley leaves

1 Place the olive oil in a large, deep skillet over medium heat. When it is hot, add the mushrooms, then some salt and pepper. Cook, stirring occasionally, until tender, 10 to 15 minutes.

2 Add the wine and let it bubble away for just 1 minute or so longer. Turn the heat to low. Add the garlic and parsley, stir, and cook for 1 minute. Turn off the heat and allow the mushrooms to sit in this mixture for 1 hour or so before serving.

PEELING GARLIC

If you're peeling more than a few cloves, drop them in boiling water for a few seconds and the peels will slip right off. To peel without parboiling, crush the cloves lightly with the side of a large knife.

The peels will come off easily.

MINCING GARLIC

There are many techniques to mince garlic, but the easiest is to peel, crush, and then chop (or thinly slice) the cloves.

Then use a rocking motion of the knife to cut across the pieces repeatedly; the knife must be sharp.

The Basics of Mushrooms

You can start out cooking with the simple button mushrooms, but many mushrooms can be used interchangeably, so once you feel comfortable with mushrooms, try combining them. Here are some facts about a few basic options:

Button The common white-to-tan cultivated mushroom. Much improved when cooked with some reconstituted dried porcini, or with some fresh shiitakes.

Cremini/Portobello The second is merely a giant version of the first. Both are domesticated brown mushrooms, and have much better flavor than button mushrooms. Portobellos are wonderful grilled.

Shiitake The best domesticated mushroom, now sold in most supermarkets. Great flavor. Also sold dried (the Chinese black mushroom is shiitake and is usually very inexpensive).

Porcini (dried) Sold at upscale markets and many Italian shops. Buy them in bulk, a couple of ounces at a time. (Tiny packages are a rip-off). They keep forever, and improve the taste of other mushrooms. Soak a small handful in hot water for 10 minutes, and combine with fresh mushrooms in any recipe; the soaking liquid is good added to sauces.

Buying and storing Don't buy drying, damaged, shriveled up, or slimy mushrooms. Buy them in bulk instead of buying prepackaged mushrooms. Store fresh mushrooms, loosely wrapped in waxed paper (not plastic), in the refrigerator; they often keep upward of a week.

Preparing Rinsing the mushrooms as lightly as you can, try to get dirt out of hidden crevices. Cut off any hard or dried-out spots—usually just the end of the stem. The stems of most mushrooms are perfectly edible, but those of shiitake should be discarded or reserved for stock. Clean the stems well, cut them in half if they're large (as are those of portobellos), and cook them with the caps.

Best cooking methods Sautéing and grilling. Wonderful in soups and omelets. You can also simmer or steam mushrooms for about 5 minutes, which will firm them up a bit; then dress them with olive oil and freshly squeezed lemon juice; or slice them, raw, and serve with olive oil, freshly squeezed lemon juice, and thinly sliced Parmesan.

When is it done? When tender.

Marinated Roasted, Grilled, or Broiled Peppers

Makes 4 servings
Time: About 1 hour, plus marinating time and time to preheat grill

There are many techniques for "roasting" peppers; all work. These are the three easiest and neatest. Roasted peppers are delicious in sandwiches, salads, and with meat, fish, and other vegetable dishes. They are also terrific on their own, with crackers, anchovies, or bread.

> 4 red or yellow bell peppers, rinsed
>
> 1/4 cup extra-virgin olive oil
>
> 1 clove garlic, crushed
>
> 1 tablespoon balsamic, sherry, or other flavorful vinegar
>
> Salt and freshly ground black pepper to taste
>
> Minced fresh basil, oregano, or parsley leaves for garnish

1 **To roast:** Preheat the oven to 500°F. Put the peppers in a roasting pan and place in the oven, with the rack set near the top. Roast, shaking the pan frequently, until the peppers shrivel and collapse, 30 to 40 minutes. Proceed to Step 2.

To grill: Start a charcoal or wood fire or preheat a gas grill; the fire should be quite hot. Place the peppers on the grill (cover the grill if possible) and cook, turning occasionally, and taking care not to let the peppers burn too badly (some blackening is not only okay, it's desirable), until the peppers collapse, 10 to 20 minutes total. Proceed to Step 2.

To broil: Preheat the broiler. Place the peppers in a roasting pan and set under the broiler, about 4 inches from the heat source. Broil, turning as each side browns and taking care not to let the peppers burn too badly (some blackening is not only okay, it's desirable), until the peppers shrivel and collapse, 10 to 20 minutes total. Proceed to Step 2.

2 Place the hot peppers in a bowl and cover with plastic wrap. Let cool, then peel, discarding skins, seeds, and stems.

3 Combine the oil, garlic, vinegar, salt, and pepper and marinate the peppers in this mixture, from 1 to 24 hours. Serve at room temperature, garnished with minced herb.

PREPARING PEPPERS

(Step 1) To core a pepper, first cut around the stem. **(Step 2)** Then pull the core out; rinse to remove remaining seeds. **(Step 3)** Alternatively, cut the pepper in half, break out the core, and scrape out the seeds.

The Basics of Peppers

Here we're talking about sweet, or bell peppers (as opposed to hot, which are best called chiles to avoid confusion). When it comes to sweet peppers, color is far more important than shape. Actually, there's only one color that really matters: green. Green peppers may be "mature," but they are not ripe, at least not if ripeness implies the peak of flavor. Where a green pepper is sharp, almost acrid, and likely as not to cause indigestion, the same pepper picked a week or two later, when red, yellow, or orange, will have mellowed considerably. Red peppers are usually more expensive than green, and not always available. Note: Purple peppers are green peppers in disguise; the purple color fades to muddy green as they cook, and the flavor is usually bitter.

Buying and storing Yellow and orange peppers seem to be mellowest, but they're usually expensive, so red is the common first choice, green a distant last. Avoid peppers with soft spots or bruises, or those that feel very full—since you buy them by weight, there's no need to pay for lots of seeds. Store peppers, unwrapped, in the vegetable bin, for a week or so.

Preparing Peppers should be cored and stemmed before cooking unless you're roasting or grilling them whole. If you plan to cut the peppers into strips, or dice them, just start by cutting them in half; remove the cap and seed mass with your fingers. Alternatively, you can cut a circle around the cap and pull it off, along with most of the seeds; rinse out the remaining seeds.

Best cooking methods Roasting, grilling, broiling, sautéing.

When is it done? When roasting or grilling, blackened and collapsed. In a pan, when very tender and soft; taste one.

Baked Potatoes

Makes 4 servings • Time: $1^1/_2$ hours

A good baked potato is a cornerstone of cooking—it's easy and satisfying. If you're in a hurry, you can crank up the oven to 450°F and cut the cooking time to under an hour, but the potato will not be as nicely mealy, and the skin not as pleasantly chewy. Don't resort to the microwave unless you want a potato that is more steamed than baked.

4 large baking potatoes, such as Idaho or Russet, well scrubbed and trimmed

1 Preheat the oven to 350°F. Poke a hole or two in each potato. Place them in the oven and bake for about $1^1/_4$ hours, or until you can easily poke a thin-bladed knife into them.

2 Serve immediately, with salt, pepper, butter, sour cream, and chives, or other toppings.

The Basics of Potatoes

Starchy potatoes, often called Idaho or Russet, make the best baked and mashed potatoes and good French fries.

All-purpose potatoes have a moderate amount of starch—too much to make great boiled potatoes, but they make good mashed potatoes, French fries, and baked potatoes. Yukon gold potatoes are the closest thing to a true "all-purpose."

Low-starch or "new" potatoes (although any potato can be new—it means freshly dug), may be red- or white-skinned, are usually thin-skinned, and are sometimes quite "waxy." They make the best boiling potatoes, are great roasted, and are decent for other uses.

Buying and storing Smooth, nicely shaped potatoes are easier to peel and clean. All potatoes should be firm when you buy them. Look out for potatoes with mold or soft spots, sprouts, or green spots. Store potatoes in a cool, dark place but not in the refrigerator (low-starch potatoes can be refrigerated, however).

Preparing Wash. Peel if needed, removing "eyes," or dark or green spots.

Best cooking methods All.

When is it done? Starchy potatoes: when mealy. Low-starch potatoes: when tender.

Other recipes in which you can use potatoes: Mashed Potatoes, French fries, Roasted Root Vegetables (page 138).

Baked Sweet Potatoes

Makes 4 servings • **Time:** About 1 hour

You must bake sweet potatoes in a baking pan, because they tend to drip their syrupy juice, which clings to everything.

> 4 sweet potatoes
> Butter

1 Preheat the oven to 425°F. Line a baking pan with aluminum foil and place the potatoes in it.

2 Pierce each of the potatoes a few times with a skewer or thin-bladed knife. Bake, shaking the pan once or twice, for about 1 hour, or until the potatoes are very soft and tender. Serve with butter.

The Basics of Sweet Potatoes

Not yams, which are—popular nomenclature to the contrary—a different tuber. These are the familiar bright orange-fleshed tubers (more exotic varieties have rose, purple, yellow, or white flesh) of fall and winter. Brilliant baked, they are also good handled in many of the same ways you would treat white potatoes and winter squash—fried, mashed, or roasted.

Buying and storing Like potatoes—firm, undamaged tubers. Store, like potatoes, in the dark, in a cool place, but not for as long—just a couple of weeks.

Preparing Peel if necessary.

Best cooking methods Baking, by far. Cooking in liquid is also good. You can also use sweet potatoes in Mashed Potatoes recipe, page 132.

When is it done? When very tender and mealy. (It flakes or breaks apart easily.)

Mashed Potatoes

Makes 4 servings • **Time:** About 40 minutes

So much fuss has been made about mashed potatoes in recent years that you'd think they were difficult to make; nothing could be further from the truth. If you like your mashed potatoes lumpy, mash them with a fork or potato masher; if you like them creamy, use a food mill or ricer. And if you like them with the peel, just scrub them well before cooking. This same technique can be used for mashing almost any other vegetable, but especially root vegetables, like carrots, turnips, parsnips, sweet potatoes, and beets.

2 pounds baking potatoes,
such as Idaho or Russet,
peeled and cut into quarters

3 tablespoons butter

³/₄ cup milk, gently warmed

Salt and freshly ground black pepper
to taste

1 Boil the potatoes in a pot with salted water to cover, until soft; this will take about 30 minutes. Do not overcook or poke them too often to check doneness, or they will absorb too much water.

2 When the potatoes are done, drain them, then mash them well or put them through a food mill. Return them to the pot over very low heat and stir in the butter and—gradually—the milk, beating with a wooden spoon until smooth and creamy. Season with salt and pepper as necessary. Serve immediately, keep warm, or reheat in a microwave.

Preparation Tip: An old-fashioned potato masher still works well for mashed potatoes, but if you like a really smooth pile of spuds, buy a ricer (found in cookware stores), which does a perfect job.

French Fries

Makes 4 servings • **Time: 40 minutes**

Making French fries at home is neither difficult nor especially messy. And these are likely to be the best fries you've ever had. For European flair, try dipping them into Mayonnaise (or Garlic Mayonnaise), page 7, instead of ketchup.

4 large or 6 medium baking potatoes, such as Idaho or Russet, peeled

Vegetable oil as needed

Salt to taste

1 Cut the potatoes into any shape you like. Rinse in a few changes of water, then soak in ice water while you heat the oil.

2 Place the vegetable oil to a depth of at least 3 inches in a large, deep saucepan over medium-high heat. Heat it to a temperature of 325°F.

3 Drain the potatoes and dry them well; drop them, a handful at a time, into the oil. After the first addition, turn the heat to high. Once they are all in, turn the heat to medium. Fry the potatoes in one batch, stirring occasionally, for about 10 minutes, or until the majority of them have begun to brown. Turn the heat to low (or turn it off if you're going to wait to fry them again) and drain the potatoes on paper towels or a paper bag; they will be pale and soggy. If you like, you can allow them to rest here for up to 1 hour before proceeding.

4 Raise the heat to high and bring the oil to 375°F. Put the potatoes back in the oil and cook, stirring now and then, until brown and crisp, just a couple of minutes. Drain on paper towels or paper bags, season with salt, and serve immediately.

Three Flavorings for French Fries

Note: To thoroughly coat fries with a dry condiment such as chile powder, toss them together in a paper bag while the fries are still hot.

1. Spicy mustard.
2. Chile powder.
3. Three kinds of ground pepper: black, Szechwan, and a pinch of cayenne.

Boiled, Steamed, or Microwaved Spinach

Makes 4 servings • **Time:** 20 minutes

I prefer to boil spinach—it takes less than 1 minute from the time the spinach hits the water until it is done. But you can also steam or microwave it successfully.

> 10 to 16 ounces spinach, trimmed and well washed (see next page)

1 To boil the spinach, bring a large pot of water to a boil; salt it. Place the spinach in the water and cook for about 1 minute, or until it is bright green and tender.

2 To steam the spinach, place it in covered saucepan with about 1 tablespoon of water (or with the water that clings to its leaves after washing). Cook about 4 minutes, until the spinach is bright green and tender.

3 To microwave the spinach, place in a microwave-proof plate or shallow bowl with just the water that clings to its leaves after washing; add salt and cover with a lid or plastic wrap. Microwave on high for 1 minute, shake the container, and continue to microwave at 1-minute intervals, just until it wilts.

4 Serve hot spinach with butter. Or drain it, drop it into a bowl of ice water to stop the cooking, drain again, place in a covered container, and refrigerate for up to 2 days. Then cook it according to the directions for Precooked Vegetables in Butter or Oil (page 118).

Creamed Spinach: Cool the cooked spinach; squeeze excess moisture from it and chop it. Place 1/2 cup cream in a small saucepan, turn the heat to medium, and cook for 5 minutes. Turn the heat to low and add the spinach, 2 tablespoons of butter, a pinch of freshly grated nutmeg, salt, and pepper. Simmer, stirring occasionally, until the mixture is creamy and very soft, about 10 minutes. Serve hot.

Five Quick Toppings for Simply Cooked Spinach

1. Extra-virgin olive oil.
2. Freshly squeezed lemon or lime juice.
3. Soy sauce.
4. Worcestershire sauce.
5. Vinegar, especially balsamic, rice, or sherry.

The Basics of Spinach and Other Dark Leafy Greens

Dark, leafy greens are nutritious and cook quickly. They can be cooked simply or added for flavor to soups, grain and bean dishes.

Buying and storing Spinach leaves must be plump; any wilting or yellowing is a bad sign. Store it, loosely wrapped in plastic, in the vegetable bin, but use it as fast as you can. It will keep for a few days. Sold year-round, in season locally in cool but not cold or hot weather. The large, relatively tough, super-crinkly leaves of packaged spinach cannot compare with the tender, flat-leafed variety grown by local farmers and gardeners. When it is young, with stems $1/8$ inch in diameter or less, it wilts in a flash and requires almost no trimming.

Preparing Wash well, in several changes of water; it's sandy. Remove very thick stems, but leave thinner ones on; they'll be fine. Don't chop before cooking, or you'll lose too many little pieces to the cooking water.

Best cooking methods Quick simmering (drop into boiling water, then remove). Or steaming or sautéing. In any case, don't overcook. Leftover spinach makes an ideal omelet filling

When is it done? As soon as it wilts.

Collards, dandelion, kale, mustard and turnip greens—there are many, many varieties—are all strong-tasting. You can prepare and cook them just like spinach, though some, especially thick-stemmed kale, will take longer.

Dark greens don't disappear into the background when seasoned, so it's important to choose flavorings that offset the greens' intrinsic bitterness. Fortunately, there are many: the list begins with acidic liquids, such as lemon, lime, or other citrus, and vinegar, but continues with soy sauce, garlic, ginger, chiles (or simply Tabasco), olives, anchovies, and so on.

Steaming and simmering work for these greens, and if their stems are less than $1/8$ inch thick, greens can be sautéed without any precooking. Braising works well also, and since the greens absorb the flavors of the braising liquid, this is a wonderful technique.

Sautéed Summer Squash or Zucchini

Makes 4 servings • **Time:** 15 to 45 minutes

Salting grated summer squash enables you to brown it quickly, but it isn't essential.

> About 2 pounds summer squash or zucchini, the smaller the better
>
> 1 tablespoon salt (optional)
>
> 3 to 4 tablespoons olive or other oil
>
> 1 clove garlic, smashed (optional)
>
> Freshly ground black pepper to taste
>
> Minced fresh mint, parsley, or basil leaves for garnish

1 Coarsely grate the squash by hand or with the grating disk of a food processor. If time allows, place grated squash in a colander and salt it liberally—use 1 tablespoon or more of salt. Toss to blend and let drain for at least 30 minutes. Rinse quickly and dry by wringing in a towel.

2 When you're ready to cook, place the oil in a large non-stick skillet and turn the heat to medium-high; add the garlic if you choose to do so. When the oil is hot, toss the squash in the oil, sprinkle with pepper, and raise the heat to high. Cook, stirring frequently, until the squash is browned, about 10 minutes. Garnish and serve hot.

The Basics of Summer Squash and Zucchini

Bought (or picked) young, these can be firm and flavorful, but as they age and grow bigger they become watery.

Buying and storing There are many varieties, including yellow summer squash and the ubiquitous green zucchini, but the same rules hold for all: Buy the firmest specimens you can find, which will usually—though not always—be the smallest. If they're at all soft, dented, or bruised, move on. Store in the vegetable bin, but use as fast as you can.

Preparing If the squash is at all flabby, and you have a bit of time, cut it into chunks, put it in a colander, and sprinkle lightly with salt. Let sit for about a half hour, then rinse and dry. It will be much crisper. (This same technique will work for cucumber.)

Best cooking methods Sautéing (especially after salting), grilling, roasting.

When is it done? When tender; cooked too long it will fall apart.

Sautéed Eggplant

Makes 4 servings
Time: About 30 minutes, longer if you salt the eggplant

It takes a while to cook eggplant on top of the stove, but the result is creamy, flavorful cubes that are like no other vegetable.

> 2 medium or 1 large eggplant
> (1 1/2 to 2 pounds total)
>
> Salt (optional)
>
> 1/3 cup olive oil, more or less
>
> 2 teaspoons minced garlic
>
> Freshly ground black pepper to taste
>
> Minced fresh parsley leaves for garnish

1 Peel the eggplant if the skin is thick or the eggplant is less than perfectly firm. Cut it into 1/2 inch cubes and salt it if you like.

2 Place the olive oil and all but 1/2 teaspoon of the garlic in a large, deep skillet, preferably non-stick, over medium heat. Two minutes later, add the eggplant. Stir and toss almost constantly until, after 5 or 10 minutes, the eggplant begins to release some of the oil it has absorbed.

3 Continue cooking, stirring frequently, until the eggplant is very tender, about 30 minutes (this can vary greatly). About 5 minutes before it is done, add the remaining garlic.

4 Season with pepper and additional salt if necessary; garnish and serve.

The Basics of Eggplant

Eggplant comes in all sizes and colors; the smaller varieties, usually sold in Asian markets, are best.

Buying and storing Eggplant must be firm; like cucumber. Long, narrow eggplant is preferable to big, fleshy eggplant, which usually contain more seeds and become softer more readily. Store eggplant in the refrigerator, and use it as soon as you can; although the outside will not look much different, the inside will become soft and bitter within a few days.

Preparing Eggplant need not be peeled unless the skin is very thick. It's usually worth salting larger eggplant, a process that draws out excess moisture and bitterness. Trim off the ends, then cut it into slices from 1/2 to 1 inch thick. Or cut it into chunks. Sprinkle liberally with coarse salt, then let drain in a colander for 30 minutes, or up to 2 hours. Rinse and squeeze dry between paper or cloth towels.

Best cooking methods Many, especially grilling, broiling, roasting, and sautéing.

When is it done? When tender and almost creamy.

Roasted Root Vegetables

Makes 4 servings • **Time:** 1 hour or more

This is a dish that defines contemporary cooking: It's low in fat, high in flavor, gets lots of vegetables into you, is easy—and it's roasted. You can combine almost any vegetables you want, but I think carrots, onions, and garlic (unpeeled—you peel each clove before you eat it) are essential to the mix. Experiment and see what you like.

4 tablespoons extra-virgin olive oil, butter, or a mixture

1$\frac{1}{2}$ to 2 pounds mixed root vegetables, such as carrots, potatoes, sweet potatoes, parsnips, turnips, shallots (leave whole), and onions, peeled and cut into 1$\frac{1}{2}$- to 2-inch chunks

Several sprigs fresh thyme or about 1 tablespoon fresh rosemary leaves (optional)

Salt and freshly ground black pepper to taste

1 head garlic, broken into cloves

Minced fresh parsley leaves for garnish

1 Preheat the oven to 425°F. Place the olive oil or butter in a large roasting pan on top of the stove and turn the heat to low. When the butter melts or the oil is hot, add all the vegetables (except the garlic), along with the thyme or rosemary. Sprinkle them with salt and pepper and cook them briefly, shaking and stirring so that everything is coated with oil or butter. Place the pan in the oven.

2 Cook for 30 minutes, opening the oven and shaking the pan once or twice during that period. Add the garlic and stir the vegetables up; at this point they should be starting to brown. If they are not, raise the oven temperature to 450°F.

3 Continue to cook, stirring and shaking every 10 minutes or so, until the vegetables are tender and nicely browned, at least another half hour. If the vegetables soften before they brown, just run them under the broiler for 1 or 2 minutes. If they brown before they soften, add a few tablespoons of water to the pan and turn the heat down to 350°F.

4 Garnish and serve hot or at room temperature.

Preparation Tip: To cook several vegetables at once, prepare them so they all soften at about the same time. Vegetables of similar textures—potatoes and turnips, or broccoli and cauliflower—take about the same amount of time if you cut them into pieces of similar size. For vegetables with different cooking times—eggplant, for example, cooks more slowly than zucchini—make larger chunks of fast-cooking vegetables, smaller ones of slow cookers.

---

8 | Fruit Desserts and Pies

Like vegetables, fruit now has a greatly increased presence in the supermarket compared to just 10 years ago. In apple season, there may be six or eight varieties; the same is true of plums. There are fruits we never heard of, and many we still don't know what to do with. You could eat a different fruit every day for a month.

It's still safe to say, however, that the best fresh fruit is grown locally. In other words, eat oranges in January and peaches in July and you'll be eating good fruit. Eat them where they're ripe and you'll be eating great fruit.

Of course this isn't always possible, so it pays to know the characteristics of your favorites. Some (pineapple, for example, and certain melons), barely ripen once removed from the vine—it isn't worth buying these unless they are already ripe. Most, however, continue to ripen, although in some instances refrigeration can retard that ripening. In many instances, ripening can also be hastened by placing it in a sealed paper bag.

There are many simple desserts that play on the natural flavors and textures of fruits. Depending on your mood and the season, you can finish a meal with a simply elegant poached pear or a luscious berry pie.

Fruit pies, in particular, are a joy of summer and autumn. I keep thickener to a minimum—

there's nothing wrong with a little fruit juice on the plate—and I taste as I sweeten, to use just the right amount of sugar. IQF (individually quick frozen) fruit, packed in plastic bags with no added ingredients, can be quite good, although it tends to become watery as it thaws. If you increase both sugar and thickener a little when using it, this frozen fruit can make your winter desserts a reminder of the past summer.

Pies may require a little more time and practice than other recipes, but the rewards are great and the recipes quite basic: You start with flour and water, and add butter for the dough, and all that's left is the filling, which is usually pretty easy. Although technique for pastry-making must be learned, if you can roll out a Play-Doh pie, you can make a real one. As with any simple food, the quality of the pastry is determined by the quality of your ingredients, so aim for the freshest or highest quality you can, particularly of the staples—butter, flour, sugar, and eggs.

Baked Apples

Makes 4 servings • **Time:** About 1 hour

A simple and healthy dessert, satisfying at its most basic and special when embellished. Best served with a little sweet or sour cream or yogurt.

4 large round apples, preferably Cortland or Rome

About 1 cup water, sweet white wine, or apple juice

About 8 teaspoons sugar

① Preheat the oven to 350°F.

② Core the apples (see illustrations below) and peel the top half of each, leaving the stem end intact. Place in a baking dish with about $1/2$ inch of liquid on the bottom. Put about 1 teaspoon of sugar in the cavities of each apple, and sprinkle another teaspoon or so of sugar on top.

③ Bake open end up, uncovered, until the apples are very tender, about an hour. Cool and serve warm, or at room temperature, or refrigerate (it's best to bring the apples back to room temperature before serving).

Five Ideas for Baked Apples

1. Mix the sugar with 1 teaspoon or more ground cinnamon and/or other spices.

2. Cream the sugar with 2 tablespoons unsalted butter before adding it.

3. Substitute maple syrup, honey, or brown sugar for the white sugar.

4. Add about $1/2$ cup chopped nuts, shredded coconut, raisins, and/or chopped figs or dates to sugar for filling.

5. Fill cavities of apples with jam about 10 minutes before the end of cooking.

PEELING AND CORING AN APPLE

You can core an apple either of two ways. For baked apples, use a melon baller and dig into the flower (non-stem) end, taking out a little at a time until the core has been removed.

For other uses, simply cut the apple in quarters and remove the core with a melon baller or a paring knife.

The Basics of Apples

The best time and place to buy apples is in the fall. Save softer specimens for recipes in which you want the apples to fall apart—like pies—and firmer ones for those where it's important that they hold their shape, such as baked apples. Here are some good varieties for cooking (and eating):

Apple Type	Description	Use
Braeburn	Very sweet	Good for cooking; sometimes a little too sweet for eating
Cortland	Good all-purpose apple	Great for eating or cooking; makes wonderful baked apples
Empire	Decent flavor, keeps well	Good winter/spring eating and cooking apple
Granny Smith	Super-crisp, mildly tart, super keeper	Holds its shape well during cooking
McIntosh	Sweet, crisp when very fresh, becomes mushy quickly	Excellent for sauce, good all-purpose
Rome	Great flavor, soft texture	Best for sauce and pies

Buying and storing Firmness is key; mushy apples are fit only for cooking. Apples can be kept in your refrigerator (or garage, if it's cool), for weeks, especially if they're "keeping" apples like Empires.

Preparing Start at the stem or flower end and working in latitudinal strips; a U-shaped peeler is best.

For coring, you can remove the core and leave the apple whole by digging into the stem end with a sturdy melon baller and removing it; this leaves the blossom end intact, a nice presentation for baked apples. Or, you can quarter the apple and dig out each piece of the core with a paring knife (see illustration).

Apples brown quickly once peeled. To prevent this, drop them into acidulated water (one part lemon juice to about ten parts water) or white wine, or toss with lemon juice.

Other recipes in which you can use apples: Pears Poached in Red Wine, page 142; Traditional Apple Pie (Double Crust) and its variation, page 152.

Pears Poached in Red Wine

Makes 4 servings
Time: Overnight, largely unattended

A light, simple, and classic dessert. Use not-quite-fully-ripe Bosc pears if possible.

4 Bosc pears, ripe but not mushy

1½ cups water

1½ cups red wine

¾ cup sugar

1 lemon, sliced

1 cinnamon stick

1 Peel the pears; use a melon baller to remove the core from the blossom end, but leave the stem on.

2 In a medium saucepan, bring the water, wine, and sugar to a boil. Turn the heat to medium-low and add the lemon, cinnamon stick, and pears. Cover the pan and simmer until the pears are very tender, at least 20 minutes.

3 Remove the pears to a bowl and continue to cook the sauce, over medium-high heat, until it reduces by about half and becomes syrupy. Strain the syrup over the pears and refrigerate overnight.

4 Serve the chilled pears whole, with a little of the syrup poured over them.

The Basics of Pears

Catching a pear at the peak of its ripeness is a trick, so a perfectly ripe but less-than-prime variety like the Anjou is preferable to an unripe Comice—even though a perfect Comice is a near-perfect fruit.

There are countless varieties of pears. It pays to distinguish among them, even though we're usually offered only the first two or three listed here.

Pear Type	Description
Anjou	Green to greenish red, and broad. Texture can be a little gritty; flavor never spectacular. Good for poaching.
Bartlett	Green with red, an early pear that ripens in summer.
Bosc	The narrow yellow-to-brown pear. More aromatic than the Anjou, with equally good texture.
Comice	Short, green tending toward brown. The best pear commercially available, very fragrant, with fantastic texture.
Seckel	Small yellow-to-brown pear. Great, spicy flavor. Texture is not the best, but always worth biting into.

Buying and storing Pears do ripen on the kitchen counter, so there's little or no reason to eat unripe pears just because that's all the supermarket sells. A pear is ripe when the "shoulders" feel quite tender and the body yields to soft pressure.

Preparing Peel a pear with a vegetable peeler. You can core it by cutting it into quarters and scooping out the core with a paring knife, but it's easier to cut the pear in half, then dig out each half of the core with a melon baller or spoon; if you like, you can also dig out the core from the blossom (bottom) end with a melon baller, leaving the pear intact. (The latter method is best when you're going to poach the pear.)

Another recipe in which you can use pears is the Fruit Crisp, page 146.

Sautéed Bananas

Makes 4 servings • Time: 15 minutes

A fast and easy dessert, and one for which you will almost always have the ingredients on hand.

> 4 bananas, ripe but not too soft
>
> 3 tablespoons unsalted butter
>
> Flour for dredging
>
> 2 tablespoons sugar, plus more to pass at the table
>
> Freshly squeezed lemon juice

1 Peel the bananas, cut them in half crosswise, then lengthwise, so that each banana has been made into 4 pieces. Place the butter in a large, deep skillet over medium-high heat.

2 Dredge the banana pieces lightly in the flour, shaking them to remove the excess. When the butter foam subsides, add the pieces to the skillet. Cook, turning frequently, until they are golden and beginning to brown, about 10 minutes. Sprinkle with the 2 tablespoons sugar and cook 1 minute more.

3 Serve, passing additional sugar and lemon juice.

Sautéed Apples: Apples don't take well to flour (they're simply too moist to become crisp), so just cut them into thin slices and brown them quickly in butter, sprinkling with sugar and cinnamon as they cook. Delicious with sour cream or ice cream.

The Basics of Bananas

Next to the apple, the banana is our most common and useful fruit, and probably the most widely eaten fruit in the world. We don't cook it much, which is unfortunate, because even sweet, or dessert bananas, make great desserts.

There are four hundred varieties of bananas, but until recently we were only offered one. Nowadays you might see red bananas, little yellow bananas, or other oddities from time to time; all are worth sampling.

Buying and storing Bananas may be bought green or ripe; although personal tastes vary, they are generally considered to be at their peak when deep yellow and spotted with brown, with no traces of green remaining.

Another recipe in which you can use bananas is the Summer Fruit Compote, page 145.

Summer Fruit Compote

Makes 4 to 6 servings • **Time:** 20 minutes

A quick compote that is a delicious way to make a variety of fresh, flavorful fruit into something special without heating up your kitchen too much.

> ¹/₂ cup sugar, plus more if needed
>
> ¹/₂ cup water
>
> ¹/₄ cup minced fresh mint leaves
>
> About 1¹/₂ pounds mixed ripe fruit: berries, peeled and pitted peaches, peeled bananas, pitted plums or cherries, chunks of melon or pineapple, etc.
>
> Pinch salt
>
> 1 teaspoon vanilla extract
>
> A few tablespoons freshly squeezed lemon juice, plus more if needed

1 Mix the sugar, water, and mint in a small saucepan and turn the heat to medium. Bring to a boil, stir to dissolve the sugar, and cool. Strain and set aside.

2 Puree about half the fruit; cut the rest into bite-sized pieces or slices if necessary; mix the puree with the remaining fruit. Add the salt, vanilla, sugar syrup, and a few tablespoons of lemon juice. Taste and add more lemon juice or sugar as needed. Serve immediately or refrigerate for a couple of hours before serving.

Easy Compote with Dried Fruits

Makes 6 to 8 servings
Time: 3 to 24 hours, depending on the fruit

In the dead of winter when you're hungry for the taste of good fruit, this treat will surely satisfy. And it's practically effortless. Serve with yogurt or fresh or sour cream, if you like.

> 2 pounds assorted dried fruit: apricots, pears, peaches, prunes, raisins, etc.
>
> 1/2 pound blanched almonds, halved or slivered (optional)
>
> 2 cups orange juice, preferably freshly squeezed, or water
>
> 1 teaspoon ground cinnamon

1 Mix all ingredients together; add enough water to cover the fruit by an inch or two. If your house is cool, simply cover and put aside; if it is warm, refrigerate.

2 Stir every few hours and serve when fruit is tender, at least 4 hours. Or, when fruit is tender, drain it, cover, and refrigerate.

Fruit Crisp

Makes 6 to 8 servings • **Time:** About 1 hour

You can top fruit with almost any pastry before baking, but if I had to pick a favorite it would be the crisp, because I love the way its sweet, crunchy granola-like topping works with fruit, especially soft, tart fruit such as blueberries, or apples spiked with lemon.

6 cups peeled, cored, sliced apples
or other fruit

1 teaspoon ground cinnamon

Juice of 1/2 lemon

2/3 cup brown sugar, or to taste

5 tablespoons cold unsalted butter,
cut into bits, plus butter for greasing
the pan

1/2 cup rolled oats

1/2 cup all-purpose flour

1/4 cup shredded unsweetened coconut
(optional)

1/4 cup chopped nuts (optional)

Dash salt

1 Preheat the oven to 400°F. Toss the fruit with half the cinnamon, the lemon juice, and 1 tablespoon of the sugar, and spread it in a lightly buttered 8-inch square or 9-inch round baking pan.

2 Combine all the other ingredients—including the remaining cinnamon and sugar—in the container of a food processor and pulse a few times, then process a few seconds more until everything is well incorporated but not uniform. (To mix the ingredients by hand, soften the butter slightly, toss together the dry ingredients, then work in the butter with your fingertips, a pastry blender, or a fork.)

3 Spread the topping over the apples and bake 30 to 40 minutes, until the topping is browned and the apples are tender. Serve hot, warm, or at room temperature.

Preparation Tip: You can make this crisp with apples, pears, stone fruits, berries, or a combination. Start with 6 cups of fruit, somewhere between 2 and 3 pounds. If you use more watery fruits, such as berries, toss them with 1 or 2 tablespoons of flour or cornstarch before cooking. If you use very tart fruits, increase the sugar.

Fruit Cobbler

Makes 6 to 8 servings • **Time:** About 1 hour

My friend John Willoughby found this recipe, with its easy-to-make pastry topping, at a southern boardinghouse about 15 years ago. I've since made it dozens of times, and it's always been a hit. I love this with blueberries, but you can make it with any fruit you like.

> 4 to 6 cups blueberries or other fruit, washed and well dried
>
> 1 cup sugar, or to taste
>
> 8 tablespoons (1 stick) cold unsalted butter, cut into chunks, plus some for greasing the pan
>
> $1/2$ cup all-purpose flour
>
> $1/2$ teaspoon baking powder
>
> Pinch salt
>
> 1 large egg
>
> $1/2$ teaspoon vanilla extract

1 Preheat the oven to 375°F. Toss the fruit with half the sugar, and spread it in a lightly buttered 8-inch square or 9-inch round baking pan.

2 Combine the flour, baking powder, salt, and $1/2$ cup sugar in the container of a food processor and pulse once or twice. Add the butter and process for 10 seconds, until the mixture is well blended. By hand, beat in the egg and vanilla.

3 Drop this mixture onto the fruit by tablespoonfuls; do not spread it out. Bake until golden yellow and just starting to brown, 35 to 45 minutes. Serve immediately.

Preparation Tip: The food processor makes fast work of dough, but it's imperative that the butter be cold, or the dough will become too tough. You want the same result as you do when making dough by hand: tiny bits of butter surrounded with flour; if the butter is too tiny, or too warm, the outcome is kind of a sticky paste. When working by hand, you can always refrigerate the dough, right in the middle of cutting in the butter, if it starts to get greasy. But in the food processor, the only thing to do is keep the butter cold and the processing time as short as possible.

Blueberry and Other Berry Pies (Single Crust)

Makes about 8 servings
Time: About 1¹/₂ hours, plus cooling time

There are variations on this standard, but it is the model for all berry pies. I like to minimize the spices and other flavorings, emphasizing the flavor of the berries. Be sure to refrigerate the dough until it's cold before trying to roll it out.

5 cups blueberries, picked over, briefly rinsed, and lightly dried

¹/₂ to 1 cup sugar, depending on your taste and the sweetness of the berries, plus a little for the top of the pie

2 tablespoons cornstarch or 3 tablespoons instant tapioca

Pinch salt

¹/₄ teaspoon ground cinnamon

Pinch ground allspice or nutmeg

1 tablespoon freshly squeezed lemon juice

1 teaspoon minced lemon zest (optional)

1 recipe Flaky Pie Crust (page 150), fitted into a 9-inch pie pan and refrigerated

2 tablespoons unsalted butter, cut into bits

1 Gently toss the blueberries with the sugar, thickener, salt, and spices. Stir in the lemon juice and optional zest and pile into the rolled-out shell, making the pile a little higher in the center than at the sides. Dot with butter. Decorate the edges of the crust with a fork or your fingers, using any of the methods illustrated on page 153. Refrigerate while you preheat the oven to 450°F.

2 Place the pie on a baking sheet and place in the oven; bake for 10 minutes. Reduce the heat to 350°F and bake another 40 to 50 minutes, or until the shell is golden brown and the fruit cooked. Do not underbake. Cool on a rack before serving warm or at room temperature.

Shopping Tip: Though I would argue that making a crust is almost as easy as buying one, to guarantee a successful pie-making experience, start with a store-bought crust, refrigerated preferred. The best will contain flour, butter, sugar, water, salt, and maybe baking powder. Those with margarine will not be good.

Blackberry or Raspberry Pie: Combine these berries with each other, or with blueberries. Be gentle in washing and drying the fragile berries, and increase the amount of either thickener by 1 tablespoon.

Strawberry Pie: Hull strawberries; slice in half or leave whole. Use 3 tablespoons of cornstarch or 4 tablespoons of instant tapioca for thickener. Omit the lemon juice and zest.

The Basics of Berries

There are hundreds of types of berries, but these are the most popular. You can use any of these in Summer Fruit Compote (page 145), or in Blueberry and Other Berry Pies (page 148).

Blueberries Sweet enough to eat raw, whole, and out of hand, sturdy enough to store, and even freezes well. The closest thing to an all-purpose berry.

Buying and storing Avoid mushy or dried up blueberries. You want them firm and plump. Size has little impact on flavor; don't fall for the "tiny berries are best" line. The best berries taste best, and you can always sample one or two before buying.

Preparing Pick over and remove stems. You can also mix these with strawberries to make Strawberry Shortcakes, page 175.

Blackberries and Raspberries These fragile berries cover a wide range of colors; blackberries keep best, but all are at their peak right after picking.

Buying and storing Expensive, largely because they are so perishable. Look carefully for mold, which is quite common in store-bought berries. When you get them home, don't store; eat.

Preparing Wash and dry very gently if at all; I do not wash wild berries as long as I'm sure of the source.

Strawberries They are just too fragile, and too precious, to mess around with much. Eat them plain, with cream, in shortcake or jam, or in lightly cooked pies. Local ones are always best.

Buying and storing Buy only those that taste good, and as many as you will eat (or turn into jam) in the next 24 hours. Do not refrigerate.

Preparing Pick off the leaves with your fingers, or cut them off with a paring knife, or use a paring knife or small melon baller to dig out the stem and small core (which is not all that distasteful, but is relatively tough) at the same time. Wash and dry.

Flaky Pie Crust

For any single-crust pie, 8 to 10 inches in diameter
Time: About 45 minutes, including resting time

I like to add a little sugar to any dessert pie shell. Many crusts are bland and tasteless, and sugar changes that. In addition, it aids in browning. I also add a scant amount of flour initially, which gives you the leeway to add flour liberally during rolling.

1¹/₈ cups (about 5 ounces) all-purpose flour, plus some for dusting work surface

¹/₂ teaspoon salt

1 teaspoon sugar

8 tablespoons (1 stick) cold unsalted butter, cut into about 8 pieces

About 3 tablespoons ice water, plus more if necessary

1 Combine the flour, salt, and sugar in the container of a food processor; pulse once or twice. Add the butter and turn on the machine; process until the butter and flour are blended and the mixture looks like cornmeal, about 10 seconds.

2 Place the mixture in a bowl and sprinkle 3 tablespoons of water over it. Use a wooden spoon or a rubber spatula to gradually gather the mixture into a ball; if the mixture seems dry, add another ¹/₂ tablespoon ice water. When you can make the mixture into a ball with your hands, do so. Wrap in plastic, flatten into a small disk, and freeze the dough for 10 minutes (or refrigerate for 30 minutes); this will

ease rolling. (You can also refrigerate the dough for a day or two, or freeze it almost indefinitely.)

3 You can roll the dough between two sheets of plastic wrap, usually quite successfully; sprinkle both sides of it with a little more flour, then proceed. Or sprinkle a countertop or large board with flour. Unwrap the dough and place it on the work surface; sprinkle its top with flour. If the dough is hard, let it rest for a few minutes; it should give a little when you press your fingers into it.

4 Roll with light pressure, from the center out. (If the dough seems very sticky at first, add flour liberally; but if it becomes sticky only after you roll it for a few minutes, return it to the refrigerator for 10 minutes before proceeding.) Continue to roll, adding small amounts of flour as necessary, rotating the dough occasionally, and turning it over once or twice during the process. (Use ragged edges of dough to repair any tears, adding a drop of water while you press the patch into place.) When the dough is about 10 inches in diameter (it will be less than ¹/₄ inch thick), place your pie plate upside down over it to check the size.

5 Move the dough into the pie plate by draping it over the rolling pin or by folding it into quarters, then moving it into the plate and unfolding it. When the dough is in the plate, press it firmly into the bottom, sides, and junction of bottom and sides. Trim the excess dough to about ¹/₂ inch all around, then tuck it under itself around the edge of the plate. Decorate the edges with a fork or your fingers, using any of the methods illustrated on page 153. Freeze the dough for 10 minutes (or refrigerate it for 30 minutes).

6 When you're ready to bake, prick it all over the top with a fork.

Preparation Tip: It's easiest to mix pie crusts in the food processor, but if you want to mix by hand, cut cold butter into bits and rub it and the flour very quickly between your fingers, picking it up, rubbing it, and dropping it. If the mixture begins to feel greasy, refrigerate it for a few minutes before proceeding.

Baking Tip: When you bake a filled pie, place the pie plate on a baking sheet. Not only does this prevent spills from falling to the bottom of your oven and burning, it aids in the browning of the bottom crust.

Sweetened, Enriched Pie Crust: Use this when you want a more flavorful crust. Follow the Flaky Pie Crust recipe (page 150), using 2 tablespoons sugar and 1 egg yolk, adding the yolk along with the water.

Pie Shell for a Two-Crust Pie: Increase flour to 2 1/4 cups, salt to 1 teaspoon, sugar to 2 teaspoons, butter to 16 tablespoons, water to 6 tablespoons.

Prebaked Flaky Pie Crust

For any single-crust pie, 8 to 10 inches in diameter
Time: About 30 minutes

Prebaking—also called "blind baking"—ensures that the crust cooks thoroughly, which produces the best flavor and color, and also controls shrinking, a problem with many crusts. This is most applicable to custard pies. Custard filling would curdle if baked as long as the crust would need to become crisp and brown, so the crust should be baked in advance. See Custard Pie and Pumpkin Pie, page 156.

1 recipe Flaky Pie Crust (page 150), refrigerated or frozen and pricked all over with a fork at 1/2-inch intervals

Unsalted butter as needed

1   Preheat the oven to 425°F. Tear off a piece of foil large enough to fit over the entire crust when folded in half; fold it. Smear butter on one side of the foil, then press it into the crust. Weight the foil with a pile of dried beans or rice (these can be reused for this same purpose), pie weights, anything that will sit flat on the surface.

2   Bake 12 minutes. Remove from the oven, reduce the heat to 350°F, and carefully remove the weight and foil.

3   Bake another 10 to 15 minutes, or until the crust is a beautiful shade of brown. Remove and cool on a rack.

Traditional Apple Pie (Double Crust)

Makes about 8 servings
Time: About 1^1/$_2$ hours, plus cooling time

I usually don't thicken the filling for a simple apple pie, but if you want to make sure the juices don't run, add 1^1/$_2$ tablespoons cornstarch or 2 tablespoons instant tapioca when you toss the apples with the spices.

^{1}/$_4$ cup brown sugar

^{1}/$_4$ cup white sugar, or more if you would like a very sweet pie, plus a little for the top of the pie

^{1}/$_2$ teaspoon ground cinnamon

^{1}/$_8$ teaspoon freshly grated nutmeg

Pinch salt

5 or 6 Cortland, McIntosh, or other good cooking apples

1 tablespoon freshly squeezed lemon juice

1^1/$_2$ tablespoons cornstarch or 2 tablespoons instant tapioca (optional)

1 recipe Pie Shell for a Two-Crust Pie (page 151), bottom crust fitted into a 9-inch pie pan, top crust transferred to a rimless baking sheet, both refrigerated

2 tablespoons unsalted butter, cut into bits

Milk as needed

1 Toss together the sugars, spices, and salt. Peel and core the apples and cut them into ^{1}/$_2$- to ^{3}/$_4$-inch-thick slices. Toss the apples and lemon juice with the dry ingredients, adding the cornstarch or tapioca if you want a less runny pie.

2 Pile the apples into the rolled-out bottom crust, making the pile a little higher in the center than at the sides. Dot with butter. Cover with the top crust. Decorate the edges with a fork or your fingers, see Fluting a Pie Crust on the following page. Refrigerate while you preheat the oven to 450°F.

3 Place the pie on a cookie sheet and brush the top lightly with milk; sprinkle with sugar. Use a sharp paring knife to cut two or three 2-inch-long vent holes in the top crust; this will allow steam to escape. Place in the oven and bake for 10 minutes. Reduce the heat to 350°F and bake another 40 to 50 minutes, or until the pie is golden brown. Do not underbake. Cool on a rack before serving warm or at room temperature.

Dutch Apple Pie: Add 2 tablespoons cornstarch or 3 tablespoons instant tapioca to the mixture. Proceed as above, making sure to cut a large vent hole in the center of the top crust. About 30 minutes into the baking time, pour ^{1}/$_2$ cup heavy cream into the vent hole and finish baking as above.

Five Additions to Apple Pie

1. Chopped nuts, $1/2$ to 1 cup.

2. Any appealing spice, generally in small amounts, such as minced fresh or crystallized ginger, allspice, or cloves.

3. Bourbon or rum sprinkled over the top, about 2 tablespoons.

4. Cranberries, left whole, about 1 cup (increase the amount of sugar slightly).

5. Dried fruit, such as raisins or dried cranberries, $1/2$ to 1 cup.

FLUTING A PIE CRUST

Method 1   Method 2   Method 3

You can flute the edges of a pie crust in a variety of different ways. Three of the easiest are: **Method 1:** Pinch the dough between the side of your forefinger and your thumb; **Method 2:** Press a knuckle from one side into the space made by your thumb and forefinger on the other; **Method 3:** Press down with the tines of a fork along the edges of the dough.

Free-Form Tart with Fruit

Makes about 8 servings • **Time:** About 45 minutes

The simplest of all tarts, essentially a sweet fruit pizza. Even including time for making the dough, you can whip one of these up in less than an hour. Best served with ice cream.

1 recipe Sweetened, Enriched Pie Crust (page 151), not yet rolled out

2 cups raspberries or other berries, picked over, washed, and dried

2 tablespoons unsalted butter, melted

2 tablespoons confectioners' sugar

1 Preheat the oven to 425°F. Roll the crust out and place it directly on a baking sheet. One of the beauties of this tart is that the crust need not be perfectly round, or any special size; just roll it out to a very rough 9- or 10-inch circle.

2 Cover the round with the fruit, leaving about a 1¹/₂-inch border all around. Fold up the edges of the crust around the fruit, pinching them together. Don't try to cover all of the fruit, just the outer rim of it.

3 Brush the exposed dough with most of the butter, and brush a little onto the fruit as well. Bake until the crust is golden brown and the fruit bubbly, 20 to 30 minutes.

4 Remove from the oven and cool on a rack; serve warm, dusted with confectioners' sugar.

Five Ideas for Free-Form Tarts

1. Use pitted, peeled, and sliced soft fruit (peaches, plums, nectarines, mangoes, etc.).

2. Use peeled, cored, and very thinly sliced (¹/₈ inch or less) apples or pears.

3. Place a layer of crushed almonds or walnuts under the fruit.

4. Brush the fruit with a combination of 2 tablespoons honey and 1 tablespoon melted butter.

5. Toss the fruit with 1 teaspoon or more ground cinnamon before placing it on the crust.

The Basics of Tarts

Tarts are European-style pies, open-faced, made with a rich, sweet crust (not unlike Sweetened, Enriched Pie Crust, page 151) and filled with fruit, pastry cream, and/or nuts. The typical fillings are a little more complex than those used in American pies, but still quite easy. Almost any tart can be made richer by adding pastry cream as a base, but I usually don't bother.

Not surprisingly, you bake tarts in a tart pan instead of a pie pan. The difference is shape—in tarts, the sides of the crust are perpendicular to the bottom, as in a cake pan. These straight sides give tart pans an advantage: They are often made with perfectly flat bottoms and removable sides; when the tart is done, you can lift out the bottom and place the beautiful tart on a serving dish. This makes presentation lovely and cutting extremely easy. For these reasons, I recommend using two-piece tart pans.

Fruit tarts are often glazed with strained jam, which is then heated and thinned with liqueur or other flavorful liquid. I sometimes skip this step, because it is largely cosmetic—the tart is already flavorful and sweet enough—but it's a nice touch, and easily done. Try it once and decide for yourself.

Custard Pie

Makes about 8 servings • **Time:** About $1^1/_2$ hours

In order to keep your crust from getting soggy and your custard from overcooking, bake the crust while you prepare the custard, then combine both while hot. Remove the pie from the oven before it solidifies completely.

1 Flaky Pie Crust (page 150)

$2^1/_2$ cups half-and-half, light cream, or whole milk

4 eggs

$^1/_2$ cup sugar

1 teaspoon vanilla extract

$^1/_4$ teaspoon freshly grated nutmeg

Pinch salt

$^1/_2$ teaspoon ground cinnamon

1 Prepare pie crust dough. Follow steps 1 and 2 of Prebaked Flaky Pie Crust (page 151) to begin baking. While the crust is in the oven, start the filling. When the crust is done, transfer the crust to a baking sheet, and turn the oven to 325°F.

2 For the filling: Combine the half-and-half with the eggs in a bowl and beat until well blended. Add the remaining ingredients except for the cinnamon. Transfer to a medium saucepan and warm over medium-low heat, stirring occasionally, until hot to the touch; do not boil.

3 Pour the egg mixture into the still-hot crust and sprinkle with the cinnamon. Bake about 30 minutes, until the mixture shakes like Jell-O but is still quite moist. Cool on a rack and serve warm or at room temperature.

Good To Know

Pumpkin Pie

Makes about 8 servings • **Time:** About $1^1/_2$ hours

A variation on Custard Pie, with lots of added spice and, of course, pumpkin.

1 Flaky Pie Crust (page 150)

3 eggs

$^3/_4$ cup sugar

$^1/_2$ teaspoon ground cinnamon

$^1/_8$ teaspoon freshly grated nutmeg

$^1/_2$ teaspoon ground ginger

Pinch ground cloves

Pinch salt

2 cups canned or fresh pumpkin puree or cooked

2 cups half-and-half, light cream, or whole milk

1 Prepare pie crust dough. Follow steps 1 and 2 of Prebaked Flaky Pie Crust (page 151) to begin baking. While the crust is in the oven, start the filling. When the crust is done, transfer the crust to a baking sheet, and turn the oven to 325°F.

2 For the filling: Beat the eggs with the sugar, then add the spices and salt. Stir in the pumpkin puree and then the half-and-half. Warm this mixture in a medium saucepan over medium-low heat, stirring occasionally, until hot to the touch; do not boil.

3 Pour the mixture into the still-hot crust and bake 30 to 40 minutes, until the mixture shakes like Jell-O but is still quite moist. Cool on a rack and serve warm or at room temperature.

9 | Cookies and Cakes

Cookies and brownies are our most commonly made desserts, not only because they have a great combination of flavor and texture but because they are incomparably easy to prepare. Cakes are another story: They may be little more than sweet and eggy quick breads, or as complicated as anything else in cooking.

Leavening is an essential component of all cookies and cakes; it's what makes them rise. This may be accomplished by using beaten eggs or egg whites, whose incorporated air makes them so sturdy that they can support other ingredients—such as flour and fat—during the baking process; with yeast, which produces bubbles when combined with flour and liquid, causing the dough to rise; or by combining baking soda or baking powder with liquid, heat, and/or acidic ingredients, which also produces gas. Because yeast takes extra time, and its flavor is most closely associated with that of bread, we usually leaven desserts using eggs, baking soda, or baking powder, singly or in combination.

Besides leavening, all cookies and cakes contain fat. And though good olive oil can make a good cookie or cake, it's a different animal. What's absolutely true is that good baking uses neither margarine nor shortening. Period.

When you cream butter for cookies or cakes, you use an electric mixer (or a fork), and the butter is much easier to work if it is slightly softened. If you plan ahead by an hour or so, this presents no problems. If, however, you decide to make cookies or a cake on the spur of the moment, you will want to soften the butter more quickly. To do that, cut the butter into small cubes (say, sixteen cubes for a stick of butter), or microwave on the lowest power for 10-second intervals, removing the butter well before it actually begins to melt.

A word about sifting: Flour, once an inconsistent product, is now so fine that sifting is usually unnecessary. Nor is it necessary when mixing flour with other dry ingredients, such as sugar, salt, or baking powder, although it's worth whisking those ingredients together with a fork or whisk just to eliminate any lumps that might exist.

From this chapter, you'll pick up how make a range of favorites, from a batch of chocolate chip cookies to a simple frosted layer cake.

Classic Chocolate Chip Cookies

Makes 3 to 4 dozen • **Time:** About 30 minutes

This simple drop cookie recipe makes a typically chewy chocolate chip cookie, one with a little height. Add 2 tablespoons milk or water to the batter if you want a flatter, crisper cookie.

1/2 pound (2 sticks) unsalted butter, softened

3/4 cup white sugar

3/4 cup brown sugar

2 eggs

2 cups (9 ounces) all-purpose flour

1/2 teaspoon baking soda

1/2 teaspoon salt

1 teaspoon vanilla extract

2 cups chocolate chips

1 Preheat the oven to 375°F.

2 Use an electric mixer to cream together the butter and sugars; add the eggs one at a time and beat until well blended.

3 Combine the flour, baking soda, and salt in a bowl and add them to the batter by hand, stirring to blend. Stir in the vanilla and then the chocolate chips. Drop by teaspoons or tablespoons onto ungreased baking sheets and bake until lightly browned, about 10 minutes. Cool for about 2 minutes on the sheets before using a spatula to transfer the cookies to a rack to finish cooling. Store in a covered container at room temperature for no more than a day or two.

Baking Tip: Turn the baking sheets back to front about halfway through the baking time; if you're cooking more than one sheet at the same time, rotate them top to bottom as well.

Chunky Cookies: To the finished batter, you can add a cup or two of almost anything you like in place of chocolate chips: M&Ms (or other similar candy); or roughly chopped walnuts, pecans, or cashews; slivered almonds; raisins; coconut; dried cherries; or a combination of the above.

Oatmeal Cookies

Makes 3 to 4 dozen • **Time:** About 30 minutes

These can be made with raisins, chopped dried fruit (cranberries and cherries are good), chocolate chips, or coconut—the batter can handle up to 1½ cups of any of these, or a combination. Stir them into the batter along with the dry ingredients.

> 8 tablespoons (1 stick) unsalted butter, softened
>
> ½ cup white sugar
>
> ½ cup brown sugar
>
> 2 eggs
>
> 1½ cups (about 7 ounces) all-purpose flour
>
> 2 cups rolled oats (not the instant kind)
>
> ½ teaspoon ground cinnamon
>
> Pinch salt
>
> 2 teaspoons baking powder
>
> ½ cup milk
>
> ½ teaspoon vanilla or almond extract

1 Preheat the oven to 375°F.

2 Use an electric mixer to cream together the butter and sugars; add the eggs one at a time and beat until well blended.

3 Combine the flour, oats, cinnamon, salt, and baking powder in a bowl. Alternating with the milk, add the dry ingredients to the batter by hand, a little a time, stirring to blend. Stir in the vanilla or almond extract. Drop by teaspoons or tablespoons onto ungreased baking sheets and bake until lightly browned, 12 to 15 minutes. Cool for about 2 minutes on the sheets before using a spatula to transfer the cookies to a rack to finish cooling. Store in a covered container at room temperature for no more than a day or two.

Refrigerator (Rolled) Cookies

Makes at least 3 dozen
Time: 30 minutes, plus time to chill

Refrigerator cookies—also called rolled cookies, because they can be rolled out and cut with a lightly floured cookie cutter (or that old standby, a glass)—must be made in advance. You can make the dough days ahead and bake them whenever you get the urge. These are ideal for cookie-cutter cookies because refrigerating a stiff cookie dough makes it easy to roll out. Or, you can shape the dough into logs and slice it thinly before baking.

$^1/_2$ pound (2 sticks) unsalted butter, softened, plus some for greasing the baking sheets

1 cup sugar

1 egg

3 cups (about 14 ounces) all-purpose flour, plus some for dusting the work surface

Pinch salt

1 teaspoon baking powder

1 tablespoon milk

1 teaspoon vanilla extract

1 Use an electric mixer to cream the butter and sugar together until light; beat in the egg.

2 Combine the flour, salt, and baking powder in a bowl. Mix the dry ingredients into the butter-sugar mixture, adding a little milk at a time as necessary. Stir in the vanilla.

3 Shape the dough into a disk (for rolled cookies) or a log (for sliced cookies), and refrigerate for at least 2 hours, or as long as 2 days (or wrap very well, and freeze indefinitely).

4 Preheat the oven to 400°F. Cut the dough disk in half. Lightly flour a work surface and a rolling pin and roll gently until about $^1/_8$ inch thick, adding flour as necessary and turning the dough to prevent sticking. Cut with any cookie cutter. (To slice, simply cut slices from the log, about $^1/_8$ inch thick.)

5 Bake on lightly greased baking sheets until the edges are lightly brown and the center set, 6 to 10 minutes. Let rest on the sheets for a minute or two before removing with a spatula and cooling on a rack. Store in a covered container at room temperature for no more than a day or two.

Preparation Tip: You can freeze the dough, and need not defrost it before baking, as long as you're happy to slice it instead of rolling and cutting it into shapes.

Baking Tips: Generally, rolled cookies are more crumbly and less chewy than drop cookies. But if you want them on the chewy side, underbake them just a little bit, removing them from the oven while the center is still a little soft.

To glaze cookies, drizzle or spread them with a mixture of 1 cup confectioners' sugar and just enough milk or cream to make a thin paste—about $^1/_3$ cup. Or decorate before baking with sprinkles or other tiny candies.

Lighter Rolled Cookies: In Step 1, add $1/2$ cup additional white (or brown) sugar and beat 2 eggs into creamed butter and sugar. In Step 2, add $1/2$ teaspoon baking soda to the dry ingredients (including the baking powder); add $1/4$ cup of milk to the batter along with the flour mixture.

Peanut Butter Cookies: In Step 1, cream $1/2$ to $3/4$ cup peanut butter with the butter-sugar mixture. You can use smooth or crunchy peanut butter, as you like. You can also add about $1/2$ cup chopped peanuts (try those with salt for an interesting change), along with the vanilla, in Step 2.

Five Ideas for Rolled Cookies

1. Stir 1 tablespoon grated lemon or orange zest into the flour mixture before combining with the butter-sugar mixture (omit the vanilla). Add 2 tablespoons poppy seeds as well, if you like.

2. Add 1 cup dried unsweetened coconut to the butter-sugar mixture, alternating with the flour.

3. Add 1 cup chopped walnuts, pecans, almonds, or hazelnuts to the batter along with the vanilla. Or add $1/2$ cup nuts and $1/2$ cup raisins or chopped dried fruit.

4. Replace some or all of the white sugar with brown sugar.

5. Dust cookies with mixture of 2 tablespoons white sugar and 1 teaspoon ground cinnamon just before baking.

Brownies

Makes 1 to 2 dozen • **Time:** 30 to 40 minutes

These are chewy and dense, dominated by chocolate and nothing else. (I prefer brownies without nuts.) If you like cakier brownies, add ¹/₂ teaspoon baking powder to the flour.

2 ounces unsweetened chocolate, roughly chopped

8 tablespoons (1 stick) unsalted butter, softened, plus a little for the greasing pan

1 cup sugar

2 eggs

¹/₂ cup all-purpose flour

Pinch salt

¹/₂ teaspoon vanilla extract

1 Preheat the oven to 350°F. Grease an 8-inch square baking pan, or line it with aluminum foil and grease the foil.

2 Combine the chocolate and butter in a small saucepan over very low heat, stirring occasionally. When the chocolate is just about melted, remove from the heat and continue to stir until the mixture is smooth.

3 Transfer the mixture to a bowl and stir in the sugar. Then beat in the eggs, one at a time. Gently stir in the flour, salt, and vanilla. Pour and scrape into the prepared pan and bake 20 to 25 minutes, or until just barely set in the middle. It's better to underbake brownies than to overbake them. Cool on a rack before cutting. Store, covered and at room temperature, for no more than a day.

Baking Tip: If you like very soft brownies, remove them from the oven when the center first sets; a toothpick inserted into the middle will still bring a few crumbs out with it, although it will not actually be wet.

Five Ideas for Brownies

1. Add ¹/₂ to 1 cup chopped nuts to the batter; toast the nuts first for even better flavor.

2. Add ¹/₂ to 1 cup chocolate chips to the batter.

3. Add ¹/₂ cup mashed bananas or dried fruit, especially dried cherries, into the prepared batter.

4. Add 2 tablespoons instant espresso powder with the vanilla.

5. Top with Vanilla Butter Cream Frosting (pages 168).

Gabrielle's Lemon Squares

Makes 1 to 2 dozen squares • **Time:** About 1 hour

Gabrielle Hamilton, who taught me this simple recipe, once cooked at my daughter's summer camp, and is the talented chef at New York City's Prune restaurant. These two-step squares are sweet-tart and moist. **Line the pan with aluminum foil, then grease it, to ease bar removal and cleanup.**

8 tablespoons (1 stick) unsalted butter, softened, plus a little for greasing the pan

1¼ cups sugar

1 cup all-purpose flour, plus 2 tablespoons (about 5 ounces)

2 eggs

2 tablespoons freshly squeezed lemon juice

½ teaspoon baking soda

Grated or minced zest of 1 lemon

Confectioners' sugar

1   Preheat the oven to 350°F. Grease an 8-inch square baking pan.

2   Use an electric mixer to cream the butter with the ¼ cup of sugar. Stir in the cup of flour. This mixture will be quite dry; press into the greased pan and bake for 15 minutes, no longer. Remove from the oven and cool slightly.

3   Beat together the eggs, lemon juice, baking soda, remaining sugar and flour, and lemon zest. Pour over the crust and bake until firm on the edges but still a little soft in the middle, another 20 minutes. Cool, then sprinkle with confectioners' sugar. Cut into squares and serve. Store, covered and refrigerated, for up to 2 days.

Preparation Tip: Use a light touch with the zester or grater to get only the lemon zest. You want to leave behind the white part of rind, which can be bitter.

Quick Coffee Cake

Makes at least 8 servings • **Time:** About 1 hour

This is an easy-to-make, satisfying cake. It is essentially an enriched biscuit batter, so it cooks faster than other cakes.

8 tablespoons (1 stick) cold unsalted butter, plus some for greasing the pan

2 cups all-purpose flour, plus 3 tablespoons (about 10 ounces)

1¼ cups sugar

2 teaspoons ground cinnamon

1 cup chopped walnuts or pecans

2 teaspoons baking powder

½ teaspoon salt

1 egg

¾ cup milk

1 Preheat the oven to 375°F. Grease a 9-inch square baking pan. For the streusel topping, combine 3 tablespoons of flour, ¾ cup of sugar, 1 teaspoon of cinnamon, and 3 tablespoons of butter with the nuts. Set aside.

2 Combine remaining 2 cups of flour, the baking powder, salt, and the remaining ½ cup of sugar, 1 teaspoon of cinnamon, and 5 tablespoons of the butter, cut into bits, in a bowl (you can use an electric mixer for this; use low speed). Mix well with a fork until all of the flour is coated with some of the butter.

3 Still on low speed, beat the egg into the butter-flour mixture, then the milk until blended. Pour half the batter into the prepared pan and sprinkle over it about half the streusel mixture. Add the remaining batter, then the remaining streusel. Bake for about 30 minutes, or until a toothpick inserted in the center comes out clean. Cool on a rack for at least 15 minutes before cutting. Best served warm, but not bad a day or two later, reheated.

The Basics of Cakes

Use high-quality butter, eggs, chocolate, nuts, and extracts for the best cakes. Stale (or worse, rancid) ingredients will ruin the results of your labor. Use the right bakeware, too. The difference between an 8-inch and a 9-inch cake pan can affect the baking time and height and texture of your cake.

When baking cakes, butter the entire pan, and flour it lightly as well: Smear the butter all over, dust with flour, then tap out the excess flour. To be sure you don't leave part of the delicate batter behind, it pays, too, to line the pan with parchment or waxed paper. With multiple pans, during baking, rotate and switch the pans to even out their baking time in hotter and cooler parts of the oven.

Pound Cake

Makes at least 8 servings • **Time:** About $1^1/_2$ hours

Really, this should be called "half-pound" cake, because the proportions are about half of the classic, which makes two loaves, or one huge one. The idea is the same: roughly equal amounts (by weight) of flour, eggs, butter, and sugar. It remains a delight, especially toasted with butter.

> $1/_2$ pound (2 sticks) unsalted butter, softened, plus some for greasing the pan
>
> 2 cups (9 ounces) cake or all-purpose flour
>
> 1 teaspoon baking powder
>
> Pinch salt
>
> $1/_2$ teaspoon freshly grated nutmeg (optional but very nice)
>
> 1 cup sugar
>
> 5 eggs, separated
>
> 2 teaspoons vanilla extract

1 Preheat the oven to 350°F. Butter a 9 × 5-inch loaf pan. Combine the flour, baking powder, salt, and nutmeg in a bowl and set aside.

2 Use an electric mixer to cream the butter until it is smooth. Add about half the sugar and beat until it is well blended, then add the remaining sugar. Beat until the mixture is light in color and fluffy in texture, scraping down the sides of the mixing bowl if necessary. Beat in the egg yolks, one at a time.

3 Mix in the dry ingredients by hand just until smooth; do not overmix, and do not beat. Add the vanilla and stir until blended. Beat the egg whites until they hold soft peaks; fold them in gently but thoroughly.

4 Turn into the loaf pan and bake for about $1^1/_4$ hours, or until a toothpick inserted into the top comes out clean. Let the cake rest in the pan for 5 minutes before inverting onto a rack. Remove the pan, then turn the cake right side up. Cool before slicing. Store at room temperature, covered with waxed paper, for a day or two; you can gain a couple more days by wrapping in plastic, but at some loss of texture.

Shopping Tip: It's worth using cake flour here for extra tenderness, but if you don't have it, all-purpose flour will give you fine results.

Baking Tip: To ease the cake out of the pan, gently run a thin knife all the way around the inside edge. Press the knife against the pan, not against the cake, to avoid damaging the sides of the cake.

Golden Layer Cake

Makes at least 10 servings • **Time:** About 1 hour

This tender, delicate cake takes either white or chocolate butter cream frosting beautifully, and can be given the subtle flavor of vanilla or the bolder flavor of orange. You can also fill the cake with your favorite jam, such as seedless raspberry or apricot. This recipe also makes wonderful cupcakes—see the variation.

10 tablespoons (1¼ sticks) unsalted butter, softened, plus some for greasing the pans and the paper

2 cups (about 9 ounces) cake or all-purpose flour, plus some for dusting the pans

1¼ cups sugar

4 eggs or 8 yolks

1 teaspoon vanilla extract or 1 tablespoon grated or minced orange zest

¼ teaspoon almond extract

2½ teaspoons baking powder

¼ teaspoon salt

¾ cup milk

1 Preheat the oven to 350°F. Butter the bottom and sides of two (9-inch) or three (8-inch) layer cake pans; cover the bottom with a circle of waxed or parchment paper, butter the paper, and sift flour over the pans; invert to remove the excess flour.

2 Use an electric mixer to cream the butter until smooth, then gradually add the sugar. Beat until light, 3 or 4 minutes. Beat in the eggs or yolks, one at a time, then the vanilla or orange zest and the almond extract. Combine the flour, baking powder, and salt; add to the egg mixture by hand, a little at a time, alternating with the milk. Stir just until smooth.

3 Turn the batter into the pans and bake for about 25 minutes, or until a toothpick inserted into the center of the cakes comes out clean. Cool on a rack for 5 minutes, then invert onto a rack and complete cooling. Finish with one of the frostings on page 168. Store, covered with waxed paper and at room temperature, for no more than a day.

Golden Cupcakes: Liberally butter two muffin tins. Place cupcake papers in each of the compartments; fill almost to the brim. Bake at 350°F for 20 to 25 minutes. Cool on a rack, then use any frosting to top the cupcakes while still in the tins. Remove and serve in the papers.

Chocolate Layer Cake

Makes at least 10 servings • **Time:** About 1 hour

This is a simple layer cake everyone will love; not much more difficult than a mix but far more delicious.

8 tablespoons (1 stick) unsalted butter, softened, plus some for greasing the pans and the paper

2 cups (9 ounces) cake or all-purpose flour, plus some for dusting the pans

3 ounces unsweetened chocolate, roughly chopped

1 cup sugar

2 eggs, separated

1 teaspoon vanilla extract

2 teaspoons baking powder

1/2 teaspoon baking soda

1/2 teaspoon salt

1 1/4 cups milk

1 Preheat the oven to 350°F. Butter the bottom and sides of two (9-inch) layer cake pans; cover the bottom with a circle of waxed or parchment paper, butter the paper, and sift flour over the pans; invert to remove the excess flour.

2 Melt the chocolate in a small saucepan or double boiler. If over a saucepan, cook over very low heat, stirring occasionally; if in a double boiler, cook over hot (not boiling) water, stirring occasionally. When the chocolate is just about melted, remove from the heat and continue to stir until the mixture is smooth.

3 Use an electric mixer to cream the butter until smooth, then gradually add the sugar. Beat until light and fluffy, 3 or 4 minutes. Beat in the egg yolks, one at a time, then the vanilla, and finally the chocolate. Mix together the flour, baking powder, baking soda, and salt in a bowl and add them to the chocolate mixture by hand, a little at a time, alternating with the milk. Stir until smooth, no longer.

4 Beat the egg whites until they hold soft peaks. Use your hand or a rubber spatula to fold them gently but thoroughly into the batter. Turn it into the cake pans and bake for about 30 minutes, or until a toothpick inserted into the center of the cakes comes out clean. Cool on a rack for 5 minutes, then invert onto a rack and complete cooling. Finish with one of the frostings on page 168. Store, covered with waxed paper and at room temperature, for no more than a day.

Cooking Tip: Chocolate should be warmed gently, over very low heat or in a double boiler over hot (not boiling) water. Chop the chocolate first, so that it melts evenly, reducing the risk of burning it. Stir frequently, keeping the heat very low. You can also melt chocolate in the microwave: Place in a container and microwave on medium, checking every minute and stirring once the chocolate starts to melt. If you burn chocolate—it will become unappealingly grainy instead of smooth—start again.

Chocolate Cupcakes: Use this batter, and see Golden Cupcakes, page 166, for directions.

Vanilla Butter Cream Frosting

Makes enough frosting and filling for 1 (9-inch) layer cake, or 2 dozen cupcakes
Time: 10 minutes

The simplest and best frosting you can make. Cream is better than milk here, but you can use milk if you like.

> 8 tablespoons (1 stick) unsalted butter, softened
>
> 4 cups confectioners' sugar
>
> 6 tablespoons cream or milk, plus a little more if needed
>
> 2 teaspoons vanilla extract

1 Use a fork or electric mixer to cream the butter. Gradually work in the sugar, alternating with the cream and beating well after each addition.

2 Stir in the vanilla. If the frosting is too thick to spread, add a little more cream, a teaspoon at a time. If it is too thin, refrigerate; it will thicken as the butter hardens.

Chocolate Butter Cream Frosting: Add 2 ounces melted and cooled unsweetened chocolate to the mixture after adding about half of the sugar.

Dark Chocolate Glaze

Makes enough to cover 1 (9-inch) layer cake
Time: 10 minutes

If you fill your cake with jam or butter cream frosting, and you love dark chocolate, this is the perfect finish for your cake. It's bittersweet and rich, and very intense. Apply it while it's hot, with an oiled spatula, on a chilled cake; it will solidify perfectly and almost instantly.

> 3/4 cup top-quality unsweetened cocoa powder
>
> 1/2 cup heavy cream
>
> 6 tablespoons (3/4 stick) unsalted butter, cut into bits
>
> 3/4 cup confectioners' sugar
>
> Tiny pinch salt
>
> 1/2 teaspoon vanilla extract

1 Mix together the cocoa, cream, butter, confectioners' sugar, and salt in a small saucepan. Cook over low heat until combined and thickened, 5 to 10 minutes.

2 Stir in the vanilla and use immediately.

10 | Breads and Breakfast

Bread—especially the home-baked variety—is not only a healthy part of a good diet, it's something everyone loves. Mixers, food processors, and bread machines have made it easier than ever to produce bread at home.

Great bread contains at least four elements: flour, leavener, water, and salt. In yeast breads, the basic leavener is yeast. In quick breads—so named because there is no rising time involved—the leavener is usually baking powder. Whether quick or yeast, breads can contain a variety of other ingredients too, of course, from butter, eggs, and milk to fruits, nuts, sweeteners, and whole grains.

There are two important non-food ingredients that go into bread as well: energy (this need not be yours, or much of it), and time. Quick breads, biscuits, muffins, and other baked goods leavened with baking powder or soda only take an hour or so, but the best yeast bread takes the better part of a day to make. Fortunately, most of that time is unattended.

Bread is basic morning food, too, but there is no denying that a luxurious breakfast of eggs, pancakes, or something even more complex, along with breakfast meat, is a treat that many people look forward to all week. And the preparation of it need not be especially time-consuming. Given that ingredients for most breakfasts are limited, here you'll find several pages devoted to that all-important ingredient: The Egg.

Fastest Yeast Bread

Makes 1 loaf • **Time:** 1¹/₂ hours, largely unattended

This does not have the great crust, crumb, and flavor of slow-rising breads, but you can start it at 5:30 and be eating it warm at 7. Add 1 tablespoon or so of minced fresh herbs—such as parsley, dill, or sage—for variety. If you have two ovens, allow the bread to rise in one that has been turned on for just 2 minutes, then turned off again, while you preheat the other.

> 3 cups (about 14 ounces) bread or all-purpose flour, plus more as needed
>
> 2 teaspoons instant yeast
>
> 1 teaspoon salt
>
> 1 cup warm water (1¹/₄ cups if you omit the olive oil), plus more if necessary
>
> ¹/₄ cup olive oil (optional)
>
> Coarse salt to taste (optional)

1 Combine the flour, yeast, and salt in a bowl or food processor. Add the water all at once, stirring with a wooden spoon or with the machine on; add the olive oil and continue to mix, for a minute or two longer by hand, about 30 seconds total with the food processor. Add water by the tablespoon if necessary, until a ball forms.

2 Shape the dough into a boule, or flat round loaf (see illustrations below), adding only enough flour to allow you to handle the dough. Place dough on baking sheet or pizza peel. Let rise in the warmest place in your kitchen, covered, while you preheat the oven to 425°F.

3 Brush the loaf with water, sprinkle it with coarse salt if you like, and bake on a sheet or slide onto a stone for 15 minutes. Lower the heat to 350°F and continue baking until done—the crust will be golden and crisp—about 30 to 45 minutes more.

SHAPING A ROUND LOAF (BOULE)

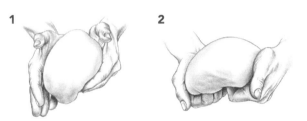

(Step 1) To make a round loaf or "boule," shape the dough into a ball. **(Step 2)** Working around the ball, continually tuck the dough toward the center of the bottom, stretching the top slightly and creating surface tension. Pinch together the seam created at the bottom of the dough.

The Basics of Yeast Bread

Making the Dough First, hand-kneading is optional. Heavy-duty standing mixers do a good job, but the food processor is ideal because it allows you to maximize the water-to-flour ratio, and good yeast dough is wet, usually too wet to handle comfortably. If you flour your hands and the work surface lightly after making the dough, you'll have no trouble handling the dough from then on.

You can rush the rising of bread by doubling the amount of yeast, or by letting it rise in a warm (no more than 150°F) oven, but if you have the time, you might consider a schedule like this: Mix the dough in the morning, let it rise at room temperature until noon or early afternoon, then shape it (or deflate the dough and allow it to rise again) and let it rest for another hour or more before baking. Contrary to older recipe directions, there are no precise rising times; dough is really quite flexible.

You can also mix dough at night and refrigerate it, allowing it to rise slowly for a day or even more; you can hurry the rise as mentioned above, and, in a pinch, you can even skip rising: Make the dough, shape it, let it rest while you preheat the oven, and bake it.

Baking Bread Start with a hot oven and turn the heat down about halfway through the baking. Most bread is done when it makes a hollow sound when you thump it, or when an instant-read thermometer inserted into the center of the loaf reads 210°F.

Storing Bread You can store unbaked dough, well wrapped in aluminum foil or plastic, in the freezer for a couple of weeks. You can also store baked bread, wrapped in waxed paper—plastic makes the crust soggy—on the counter for up to 4 or 5 days. Baked bread can also be frozen; in this instance aluminum foil or heavy plastic bags are fine, because you'll need to recrisp the bread anyway. Unwrap, then place thawed or unthawed bread in a preheated 350°F oven for 5 to 15 minutes, until thawed and crisp.

Pizza

Makes 1 large or 2 or more small pizzas
Time: About 3 hours, largely unattended

This is a classic that's fun to make, even if it takes practice to master. (If you want, try it first with store-bought pizza dough.) Other toppings to try: fresh basil; pitted oil-cured black olives; and lightly cooked sausage, bacon, or (uncooked) salami.

> 1 recipe Pizza Dough (at right)
>
> 2 tablespoons extra-virgin olive oil, approximately
>
> 2 cups Easy Tomato Sauce (page 27), or any other tomato sauce
>
> 2 cups freshly grated mozzarella cheese
>
> Salt and freshly ground black pepper to taste

1 Preheat the oven to 500°F; make sure the oven is thoroughly preheated.

2 Knead the dough ball lightly, form it into a ball, and divide it into as many equal pieces as you like; roll each piece into a ball. Place each ball on lightly floured surface, sprinkle with a little more flour, and cover with plastic wrap or a towel. Let rest until they puff slightly, about 20 minutes.

3 Roll or lightly press each dough ball into a flat round, lightly flouring the work surface and the dough as necessary (do not use more flour than you need to). Let the rounds sit for a few minutes; this will relax the dough and make it easier to roll out. Roll or pat out the dough on a lightly oiled baking sheet or floured pizza peel. Roll the dough as thinly as you like.

4 Drizzle the rounds with the olive oil, then top them with the sauce and cheese; sprinkle with salt and pepper. Place the baking sheet in the oven or slide the pizza directly onto the stones and bake until the crust is crisp and the cheese melted, usually 8 to 12 minutes.

Best From Scratch

Pizza Dough

Makes 1 large or 2 or more small pizzas
Time: At least 1 hour, largely unattended

This is the simplest, most basic pizza dough you can make. Knead it with a mixer (use the dough hook), or by hand, but I like the food processor best. Olive oil makes a smoother, more flavorful dough and a slightly cracklier crust.

> 1 teaspoon instant or rapid-rise yeast
>
> 3 cups (about 14 ounces) all-purpose or bread flour, plus more as needed
>
> 2 teaspoons coarse kosher or sea salt, plus extra for sprinkling
>
> 1 to 1¼ cups water
>
> 2 tablespoons plus 1 teaspoon olive oil

1 Combine the yeast, flour, and 2 teaspoons salt in the container of a food processor. Turn the machine on and add 1 cup water and the 2 tablespoons of oil through the feed tube.

2 Process for about 30 seconds, adding more water, a little at a time, until the mixture forms a

ball and is slightly sticky to the touch. If it is dry, add another tablespoon or two of water and process for another 10 seconds. (If the mixture is too sticky, add flour, a tablespoon at a time.)

3 Turn the dough onto a floured work surface and knead by hand a few seconds to form a smooth, round dough ball. Grease a bowl with the remaining olive oil, and place the dough in it. Cover with plastic wrap or a damp cloth and let rise in warm, draft-free area until the dough doubles in size, 1 to 2 hours. You can cut this rising time short if you are in a hurry, or you can let the dough rise more slowly, in the refrigerator, for up to 6 or 8 hours.

4 Proceed with Pizza recipe on page 172, or wrap the dough tightly in plastic wrap and freeze for up to a month. Defrost in a covered bowl in the refrigerator or at room temperature.

Preparation Tip: When stretching the dough, as soon as it shows resistance—it returns to its former shape and size—stop. Try again in a few minutes. This may take 20 to 30 minutes, resting between each attempt.

Cooking Tip: Pizza can be cooked on a flat baking sheet (or one with a small lip), but it cooks best on a pizza stone. With the stone, a peel—a broad sheet of wood or metal with a handle—is important. You can sprinkle flour or cornmeal on the peel, roll the dough out on the peel and slide it right onto the pizza stone.

SHAPING PIZZA

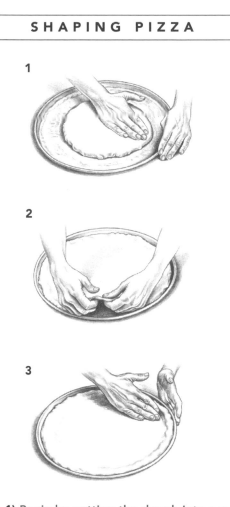

1

2

3

(Step 1) Begin by patting the dough into a round disk (or a rectangle as you prefer). Let the dough relax for a few minutes before continuing. **(Step 2)** Stretch the dough by pulling and patting it, adding flour (or use olive oil) as necessary. If you allow the dough to rest every now and then the gluten will relax and the dough will be less resistant to stretching. **(Step 3)** When you have stretched the dough out to the edges of the pan, it is ready.

Yogurt or Buttermilk Biscuits

Makes 10 or more biscuits • **Time:** 20 to 30 minutes

These are the best, especially (I think) when made with yogurt. When made correctly—and you can do it the first time, I swear—they're sweet, slightly sour, crisp, and tender. Oh, and very, very fast. If you don't have yogurt or buttermilk here; use the Baking Powder Biscuits variation.

> 2 cups (about 9 ounces) all-purpose or cake flour, plus more as needed
>
> 1 scant teaspoon salt
>
> 3 teaspoons baking powder
>
> 1 teaspoon baking soda
>
> 2 to 5 tablespoons cold butter (more is better)
>
> $7/8$ cup plain yogurt or buttermilk

1 Preheat the oven to 450°F.

2 Mix the dry ingredients together in a bowl or food processor. Cut the butter into bits and either pulse it in the food processor (the easiest) or pick up a bit of the dry ingredients, rub them with the butter between your fingers, and drop them again. All the butter should be thoroughly blended before proceeding.

3 Use a large spoon to stir in the yogurt or buttermilk, just until the mixture forms a ball. Turn the dough out onto a lightly floured surface and knead it ten times; no more. If it is very sticky, add a little flour, but very little; don't worry if it sticks a bit to your hands.

4 Press into a $3/4$-inch-thick rectangle and cut into 2-inch rounds with a biscuit cutter or glass. Place the rounds on an ungreased baking sheet. Gently reshape the leftover dough and cut again; this recipe will produce 10 to 14 biscuits.

5 Bake 7 to 9 minutes, or until the biscuits are a beautiful golden brown. Serve within 15 minutes for them to be at their best.

Baking Powder Biscuits: Use 4 teaspoons baking powder and sweet milk in place of yogurt or buttermilk. Proceed as above.

Cheese Biscuits: Stir in $1/2$ cup grated Cheddar, Gruyère, Fontina, blue, or Parmesan cheese and $1/4$ teaspoon cayenne (optional) along with the yogurt or milk. Lightly grease the baking sheet and proceed as above. This will make 14 to 16 biscuits.

Drop ("Emergency") Biscuits: These cut 5 minutes off the prep time. Increase the yogurt or milk to 1 cup and drop tablespoons of the dough onto a greased baking sheet. Bake as above.

Strawberry Shortcakes

Makes 12 shortcakes, enough for 12 people
Time: About 40 minutes from scratch, less with already-made biscuits

These are real strawberry shortcakes—buttery biscuits with strawberries and cream. Strawberries treated in this manner—trimmed, sliced, and "juiced up" with a bit of sugar—are great even without a biscuit. Try them with ice cream, on pancakes, or with some store-bought cookies.

1 recipe Drop ("Emergency") Biscuits (page 174), with 2 tablespoons sugar added to the dry ingredients

2 pints (1 quart) ripe strawberries

2 tablespoons sugar

2 cups heavy cream, preferably not ultra-pasteurized

1/2 teaspoon vanilla extract

1 Make the biscuits and bake them. Let them cool on a rack when they're done; you don't want to eat them hot.

2 Meanwhile, wash, hull, and slice the strawberries. Toss them with 1 tablespoon of sugar and let sit while you whip the cream.

3 Whip the cream until it holds soft peaks, then whip 1 minute more, incorporating the remaining sugar and the vanilla.

4 Split the biscuits and fill them with cream and strawberries. Serve immediately.

Classic Muffins

Makes 8 large or 12 medium muffins
Time: About 40 minutes

Fast, easy, and almost infinitely variable (there isn't a single quick-bread batter that cannot be baked as muffins, or vice versa), muffins have somehow become the domain of doughnut shops. But baking at home gives you control over fat content and quality of ingredients, and introduces you to one of life's great luxuries: the fresh-from-the-oven muffin. I do not like very sweet muffins, so I have kept the sugar to a minimum.

> 3 tablespoons melted butter or canola or other neutral oil, plus some for greasing the muffin tin
>
> 2 cups (about 9 ounces) all-purpose flour
>
> 1/4 cup sugar, or to taste
>
> 1/2 teaspoon salt
>
> 3 teaspoons baking powder
>
> 1 egg
>
> 1 cup milk, plus more if needed

1. Preheat the oven to 400°F. Grease a standard 12-compartment muffin tin.

2. Mix together the dry ingredients in a bowl. Beat together the egg, milk, and butter or oil. Make a well in the center of the dry ingredients and pour the wet ingredients into it. Using a large spoon or rubber spatula, combine the ingredients swiftly, stirring and folding rather than beating, and stopping as soon as all the dry ingredients are moistened. The batter should be lumpy, not smooth, and thick but quite moist; add a little more milk or other liquid if necessary.

3. Spoon the batter into the muffin tins, filling them about two-thirds full and handling the batter as little as possible. (If you prefer bigger muffins, fill the cups almost to the top. Pour 1/4 cup water into those cups left empty.) Bake 20 to 30 minutes, or until the muffins are nicely browned and a toothpick inserted into the center of one of them comes out clean. Remove from the oven and let rest for 5 minutes before taking them out of the tin. Serve warm.

Banana-Nut Muffins: This is good with half bran or whole wheat flour. Add $1/2$ cup roughly chopped walnuts, pecans, or cashews to the dry ingredients. Substitute 1 cup mashed very ripe banana for $3/4$ cup of the milk. Use honey or maple syrup in place of sugar if possible.

Bran Muffins: Substitute 1 cup oat or wheat bran for 1 cup of the all-purpose flour (you can use whole wheat flour for the remainder if you like). Use 2 eggs and honey, molasses, or maple syrup for sweetener. Add $1/2$ cup raisins to the prepared batter if you like.

Blueberry or Cranberry Muffins: Add 1 teaspoon ground cinnamon to the dry ingredients; increase sugar to $1/2$ cup. Stir 1 cup fresh blueberries or cranberries into the batter at the last minute. You can also use frozen blueberries or cranberries here; do not defrost them first. Blueberry muffins are good with $1/2$ teaspoon lemon zest added to the batter along with the wet ingredients. Cranberry muffins are excellent with $1/2$ cup chopped nuts and/or 1 tablespoon minced orange zest added to the prepared batter.

Spice Muffins: Add 1 teaspoon ground cinnamon, $1/2$ teaspoon each ground allspice and ground ginger, and 1 pinch ground cloves and mace or nutmeg to the dry ingredients; use 1 cup whole wheat flour in place of 1 cup all-purpose flour. Add $1/2$ cup raisins or currants to the prepared batter if you like.

Savory Muffins: Cut sugar back to 1 tablespoon. Add up to 1 cup of minced cooked bacon, minced ham, or shredded cheese—alone or in combination—to the batter just before baking.

Corn Bread

Makes about 6 servings • **Time:** About 45 minutes

With the possible exception of brownies, there is no other baked good than corn bread that packs so much flavor, and can be used in so many situations, with so little work. When you memorize this recipe—and personalize it—you will have the batter made before the oven is preheated, and produce it without thinking. This batter can also be made into muffins.

1¼ cups buttermilk, milk, or yogurt (or 1¼ cups milk and 1 tablespoon white vinegar—see Step 2 at right), plus more as needed

2 tablespoons butter, olive oil, lard, or bacon drippings

1½ cups (about 7 ounces) medium-grind cornmeal

½ cup all-purpose flour

1½ teaspoons baking powder

1 teaspoon salt

1 tablespoon sugar, plus more if you like sweet corn bread

1 large egg

1 Preheat the oven to 375°F.

2 If you are using buttermilk, milk, or yogurt, ignore this step. If you want to use soured milk (a good substitute for buttermilk), warm the milk gently—1 minute in the microwave is sufficient, just enough to take the chill off—and add the vinegar. Let it rest while you prepare the other ingredients.

3 Place the fat in a medium ovenproof skillet or in an 8-inch square metal baking pan over medium heat; heat until good and hot, about 2 minutes, then turn off the heat. Meanwhile, combine the dry ingredients in a bowl. Mix the egg into the buttermilk, milk, yogurt, or soured milk. Stir the liquid mixture into the dry ingredients, combining well; if it seems too dry, add another tablespoon or two of milk. Pour the batter into the preheated fat, smooth out the top if necessary, and place in the oven.

4 Bake about 30 minutes, until the top is lightly browned and the sides have pulled away from the pan; a toothpick inserted into the center will come out clean. Serve hot or warm.

Preparation Tip: You can make corn bread with sweet milk or buttermilk, yogurt, or soured milk; the major difference is taste, although buttermilk (or soured milk) makes a somewhat lighter bread.

Lighter, Richer Corn Bread: Use 4 tablespoons of butter (do not use other fat). Increase sugar to $1/4$ cup. Use 2 eggs; stir their yolks into the milk, as above, and beat the whites until stiff but not dry, then gently stir them into the prepared batter after yolks and milk have been incorporated. Bake as directed.

Bacon Corn Bread: Before beginning, sauté $1/2$ cup minced bacon in 1 tablespoon canola or other neutral oil, bacon fat, or lard until crisp. Remove the bacon with a slotted spoon, leaving the fat behind. Keep the fat hot, and prepare the batter as above. Stir the bacon into the prepared batter and bake as directed.

Five Quick Additions to Corn Bread

1. Chile powder or cumin, about 1 tablespoon.
2. Fresh or creamed corn, about 1 cup.
3. Minced or pickled jalapeños to taste.
4. Grated cheese, typically Cheddar, about 1 cup.
5. Minced herbs, especially cilantro or fresh parsley, about 2 tablespoons.

Weekday Morning Scrambled Eggs

Makes 2 servings • **Time:** 10 minutes

You can make good scrambled eggs in a hurry as long as you do not overcook them. Adding a little extra liquid helps prevent overcooking. (If that liquid is cream, of course, it also lends a luxurious texture.)

1 tablespoon butter or olive oil

4 eggs

Salt and freshly ground black pepper to taste

1 to 2 tablespoons milk, cream, or water (optional)

1 Place a medium skillet, preferably non-stick, over medium heat for about 1 minute. Add the butter and swirl it around the pan. Meanwhile, crack the eggs into a bowl and beat them, just until the yolks and whites are combined. Season with salt and pepper and beat in milk, cream, or water if you like.

2 Add the eggs to the skillet and turn the heat to medium-low. Cook, stirring, frequently, just until the eggs have lost their runny quality, 2 to 4 minutes; do not overcook. Serve immediately.

Four Additions to Scrambled Eggs

You can add almost anything you want to the beaten uncooked eggs before scrambling.

1. Sautéed mushrooms or onions or other cooked vegetables, or raw tomatoes or scallions, cut into small dice, about $1/2$ cup.

2. Chopped fresh herbs, 1 teaspoon (stronger herbs) to 1 tablespoon (milder ones). For scrambled eggs with herbs, add about $1/2$ teaspoon tarragon, 1 teaspoon chervil, and 1 tablespoon each parsley and chives, all chopped.

3. Sour cream, cream cheese (cut into bits), or goat cheese, about $1/3$ cup.

4. Chopped salami or other smoked meats, about $1/2$ cup.

Hard-Boiled Eggs

Makes 1 serving per egg • **Time:** About 15 minutes

Good to know for breakfast or for use in other recipes such as Classic American Potato Salad (page 6). Much better when it's ever so slightly undercooked, so the yolk is still moist.

1 Use a pin or needle to poke a hole in the broad end of each egg. Place each egg on a spoon, ladle, skimmer, or other tool and lower it into a small saucepan of gently boiling water; do not crowd.

2 Cook for 10 to 15 minutes; the shorter time guarantees a fully cooked white, and leaves some of the yolk a little underdone, which I prefer. Any time longer than 12 minutes will give you the standard hard-boiled egg (if you want to be doubly sure the egg is cooked through, increase the time to 15 minutes).

3 To remove the shell, plunge into cold running water for 30 seconds (if you want to eat the egg while hot) to 2 minutes (if you want to make shell removal as easy as possible and don't care whether the egg cools off). Remove the peel gently.

The Basics of Eggs

No other ingredient has the power to transform itself or other dishes as does the egg, perhaps the most important food in our kitchens. It plays both a leading or supporting role, and many of our favorite foods—not just breakfasts, of course, but desserts and baked goods of all types—would be unrecognizable without the egg. The egg is also a nutritional miracle, containing all nine essential amino acids and a host of vitamins.

If egg intake concerns you, there is a simple measure you can take to make almost any egg-based dish with less fat and cholesterol: Substitute some egg whites for some whole eggs, in a proportion of about two to one. For example, instead of using 4 eggs in a given recipe, use 3 eggs and 2 whites, or 2 eggs and 4 whites.

A note about egg size: Large eggs weigh 24 ounces per dozen, or about 2 ounces each; extra-large eggs weigh 27 ounces per dozen, or about 2.25 ounces each. They may be substituted freely for each other in these or any other recipes, with the possible exception of those baking recipes that use more than 6 eggs, in which case you should always use large eggs.

Fried Eggs

Makes 2 servings • **Time:** 10 minutes

Fried eggs can be tough and rubbery or nearly as delicate as poached eggs. The key to keeping the whites tender and the yolk undercooked is low heat. Follow these instructions carefully once or twice and you'll never have trouble making fried eggs again. You can use the smaller amount of butter listed here with only a minor sacrifice in flavor.

1 teaspoon to 1 tablespoon butter
2 eggs
Salt and freshly ground black pepper
to taste

1 Place a medium skillet, preferably non-stick, over medium heat for about 1 minute. Add the butter and swirl it around the pan. When its foam subsides, about a minute later, crack the eggs into the skillet. As soon as the whites lose their translucence—this only takes a minute—turn the heat to low and season with salt and pepper.

2 Cook until the whites are completely firm; the last place for this to happen is just around the yolk. If the egg has set up high, rather than spread out thin, there are two techniques to encourage it to finish cooking: The first is to cut right through the uncooked parts with a small knife; this allows some of the still-liquid white to sink through the cooked white and hit the surface of the pan, where it will cook immediately. The second is to cover the skillet for a minute or two longer to encourage the white to finish cooking. When the eggs are cooked, remove them from the pan and eat immediately.

Five Ideas for Fried Eggs

1. As the butter or oil heats, season it with a few leaves of fresh herbs or a smashed clove of garlic.

2. Cook bacon in the skillet, then use its rendered fat to fry the eggs.

3. As the white sets, use a butter knife to fold its edges over the yolk, making a little package and further protecting the yolk from overcooking.

4. Add Worcestershire sauce or other liquid seasoning such as soy or hot sauce to the white before it sets.

5. Cook 1/2-inch-thick tomato slices alongside the eggs (increase the amount of butter slightly).

The Basics of Bacon

Eggs and bacon are a classic combination, and of course bacon goes beyond the breakfast table. Here's how to cook it:

Figure three or four slices as a serving. Doneness is a matter of taste; I like bacon cooked but still chewy, but many people prefer it crisp, almost burned. Always drain on paper towels before eating.

Sautéing You see what's going on, which is an advantage, and can regulate the heat accordingly. But it requires the most attention, and inevitably messes up the stove. Start the bacon in a large, deep skillet over medium-high heat. When it begins to sizzle, separate the slices if you haven't done so already and regulate the heat so that the slices brown evenly without burning, turning frequently. Total time will be 10 to 20 minutes, longer for large quantities.

Microwaving The best method for three to six slices, although the microwave will smell if you don't clean it thoroughly afterward (on the other hand, you might enjoy the aroma). Place the bacon on a triple layer of paper towels on a microwave-safe plate, and cover with a double layer of towels. Microwave on high for 2 minutes, then check; move the pieces around a little and continue to microwave for 1-minute intervals until done. Total time will depend on the power of your microwave, but will be less than 5 minutes.

Roasting Slow, but easy and reliable, especially for large quantities. Preheat the oven to 450°F. Place the bacon in a roasting pan large enough to hold it in one layer (this may be a very large pan) and slide it into the oven. Check after 10 minutes; separate the slices if necessary. Continue to roast, turning occasionally, pouring off excess fat, and checking every 5 minutes or so; total time will be 30 minutes or so. If you like, brown under the broiler at the last minute.

Broiling Pay close attention and this is fast and easy. Preheat the broiler; set the rack about 6 inches from the heat source. Place the bacon in a roasting pan large enough to hold it in one layer and slide it into the oven. Check after 2 minutes; separate the slices if necessary. Continue to broil, turning occasionally, and checking every minute or two; total time will be about 10 minutes.

Omelet

Makes 2 servings • **Time:** 10 minutes

Master this technique and you'll never be without a quick breakfast, lunch, or supper again. The butter (or oil, if you prefer) is an integral part of the flavor of this creation; don't skimp unless you must.

> 2 tablespoons plus 1 teaspoon butter (you can use less with a non-stick pan, or substitute extra-virgin olive oil)
>
> 4 or 5 eggs
>
> 2 tablespoons milk or cream
>
> Salt and freshly ground black pepper to taste

1　Place the 2 tablespoons butter in a medium-to-large skillet, preferably non-stick, and turn the heat to medium-high. Beat together the eggs and milk or cream, just until blended; add salt and pepper to taste.

2　When the butter melts, swirl it around the pan until its foam subsides, then pour in the egg mixture. Cook undisturbed for about 30 seconds, then use a fork or thin-bladed spatula to push the edges of the eggs toward the center. As you do this, tip the pan to allow the uncooked eggs in the center to reach the perimeter.

3　Repeat until the omelet is still moist but no longer runny, a total of about 3 minutes. If you prefer, you can even stop cooking a little sooner, when there are still some runny eggs in the center; most of this will cook from the heat retained by the eggs, and you'll have a moister omelet.

4　Use a large spatula to fold the omelet in half or in thirds and place it on a plate. Rub the top of the omelet with the remaining teaspoon of butter and serve.

Five Ideas for Filling Omelets

Use about 1 cup of filling per omelet.

1. Any cooked and diced vegetable (leftovers are fine, whether steamed, boiled, or sautéed; rinse with boiling water before using, if necessary, to remove unwanted flavors).

2. Peeled, seeded, and diced tomatoes.

3. Minced ham, crisp-cooked bacon, sausage meat, or other chopped meat.

4. Minced fresh herbs, preferably a combination of 2 tablespoons parsley, 1 tablespoon each chervil and chives, and $1/2$ teaspoon tarragon (all chopped), but you can adjust this according to taste.

5. Minced red bell pepper, or roasted red pepper (see Marinated Roasted, Grilled, or Broiled Peppers, page 128).

Mushroom Omelet: Before cooking the omelet, sauté 1 cup minced mushrooms in 2 tablespoons butter or oil in a small skillet over medium-high heat until softened, about 10 minutes. Sprinkle with salt and pepper and finish with 1 tablespoon of cream (optional). Make the omelet, keeping the mushrooms warm. Place the mushrooms across one side of the egg mixture just before it is completely set. Fold the other side over and finish as above.

Western Omelet: More like a frittata (page 186), but nevertheless an American tradition. In Step 2, when the butter melts, add to it 2 tablespoons each minced bell pepper (preferably red), onion, and ham. Cook for 2 minutes, stirring, before adding the eggs and proceeding as above.

The Basics of Omelets

Non-stick skillets changed omelet making from a skill that needed to be developed to a virtual no-brainer. Just make sure the butter (or oil) is hot before adding the eggs, and keep the heat fairly high. It may seem at first glance that this recipe for omelets goes against the rule of cooking eggs over low heat, but when you watch an omelet cook, you realize that much of the egg mixture is protected against the heat by the thin layer of egg that is in direct contact with the bottom of the skillet. So, in a way, it too cooks gently and remains tender.

Frittata

Makes 4 servings • **Time:** About 30 minutes

The basic frittata (egg pie) is very much like the basic omelet, but even easier to master. The variations may be used singly or in combination, but they all spring from this single recipe.

2 tablespoons butter or olive oil

5 eggs

1/2 cup freshly grated Parmesan or other cheese

Salt and freshly ground black pepper to taste

Minced fresh parsley leaves for garnish

1 Preheat the oven to 350°F.

2 Place the butter or oil in a medium-to-large ovenproof skillet, preferably non-stick, and turn the heat to medium. While it's heating, beat together the eggs, cheese, salt, and pepper. When the butter melts or the oil is hot, pour the eggs into the skillet and turn the heat to medium-low. Cook, undisturbed, for about 10 minutes, or until the bottom of the frittata is firm.

3 Transfer the skillet to the oven. Bake, checking every 5 minutes or so, just until the top of the frittata is no longer runny, 10 to 20 minutes more. (To speed things up, turn on the broiler, but be very careful not to overcook.) Garnish and serve hot or at room temperature.

Vegetable Frittata: Stir about 1 cup cooked and roughly chopped broccoli, asparagus, spinach, chard, or kale into the egg mixture just before turning it into the skillet. Proceed as directed.

Onion Frittata: Before beginning, sauté about 1 cup chopped onion in 1 tablespoon butter or oil until soft but not browned, 5 to 10 minutes. Cool slightly, then stir into the egg mixture just before turning it into the skillet. Proceed as directed.

Herb Frittata: Mince about 1 cup of fresh herbs—chervil, parsley, dill, or basil should make up the bulk of them, but others such as tarragon, oregano, marjoram, or chives may be added in smaller quantities—and stir them into the egg mixture just before turning it into the skillet. Proceed as directed, garnishing with whatever fresh herb you like.

Three Additions to Frittate

The basic proportions for frittata fillings are 1 to 2 cups filling for every 5 eggs.

1. Minced salami, cooked sausage, ham, cooked or smoked fish.
2. Sautéed onion, fresh tomato, and basil.
3. Sautéed potatoes and onions.

The Basics of Frittate

The classic Italian egg pie, the frittata is an attractive dish that requires no fancy rolling or split-second timing, so it can be made perfectly on the first try. And because it incorporates a substantial amount of filling—usually vegetables or carbohydrates—into just a few eggs, the frittata elicits less guilt than an omelet for those concerned with such things. (For lower cholesterol, make a frittata with 4 egg whites and 3 whole eggs in place of the whole eggs in the recipe.)

Much of the preparation for most frittate can be done in advance; the open-faced omelets also make good use of leftovers. Finally, frittate taste just as good at room temperature as they do hot; cut them into small wedges and serve as a snack or hors d'oeuvre.

Basic Pancakes

Makes 4 to 6 servings • **Time:** 20 minutes

It's a shame pancake mixes ever gained a foothold in America, for these are so easy to make.

2 cups all-purpose flour

1 tablespoon baking powder

$1/2$ teaspoon salt

1 tablespoon sugar

1 or 2 eggs

$1^1/_2$ to 2 cups milk

2 tablespoons melted and cooled butter (optional), plus unmelted butter for cooking, or use oil

1 Preheat a griddle or large skillet over medium-low heat while you make the batter.

2 Mix together the dry ingredients. Beat the egg(s) into $1^1/_2$ cups of the milk, then stir in the 2 tablespoons melted cooled butter (if you are using it). Gently stir this into the dry ingredients, mixing only enough to moisten the flour; don't worry about a few lumps. If the batter seems thick, add a little more milk.

3 If your skillet or griddle is non-stick, you can cook the pancakes without any butter. Otherwise, use a teaspoon or two of butter or oil each time you add batter. When the butter foam subsides or the oil shimmers, ladle batter onto the griddle or skillet, making any size pancakes you like. Adjust the heat as necessary; usually, the first batch will require higher heat than subsequent batches. The idea is to brown the bottom in 2 to 4 minutes, without burning it. Flip when the pancakes are cooked on the bottom; they won't hold together well until they're ready.

4 Cook until the second side is lightly browned and serve, or hold on an ovenproof plate in a 200°F oven for up to 15 minutes.

Banana Pancakes: Really, really great, and a fine use for overripe bananas. Make any pancake batter as usual. After beginning to cook each batch, simply place a few rounds of $1/4$-inch-thick slices of banana directly onto the surface of the cooking batter; press them into each cake a little bit. Turn carefully and cook a little more slowly than you would other pancakes, but be sure to cook through.

Blueberry Pancakes: Blueberries, about 1 cup, should be the last ingredient you add. If they are fresh, pick them over and wash and drain them well before adding. If they are frozen, add them without defrosting. Cook more slowly than you would other pancakes, because they have a tendency to burn.

The Basics of Pancakes

Unlike waffles, which are delicate and fairly temperamental, you can bind almost anything with flour and egg and cook it on a griddle. Here we're talking about breakfast pancakes and the best, usually reserved for weekends, are moist, delicate creatures, made with beaten egg whites or cottage cheese—something to lighten them up. The simplest breakfast pancakes contain few ingredients, take less time to prepare than it does to preheat a griddle or skillet, and are a weekday staple. Leftover batter can be kept, covered and refrigerated, for several days.

Pancakes are best hot, and adding cold butter and maple syrup does them no good. If you think of it, melt the butter and gently warm the maple syrup (I use the microwave for both) before serving.

BREADS AND BREAKFAST

Quick and Easy Waffles

Makes 4 to 6 servings
Time: 10 minutes, plus time to bake

You need a waffle iron, but once you have one this is a great treat for breakfast or dessert. If you have the time, separate the eggs and beat the whites.

Canola or other neutral oil for brushing on waffle iron

2 cups all-purpose flour

$1/2$ teaspoon salt

2 tablespoons sugar

3 teaspoons baking powder

$1^1/2$ cups milk

2 eggs

4 tablespoons ($1/2$ stick) butter, melted and cooled

1 teaspoon vanilla extract (optional)

1 Brush the waffle iron lightly with oil and pre-heat it.

2 Combine the dry ingredients. Mix together the milk and eggs. Stir in the butter and vanilla (if you are using it). Stir the wet into the dry ingredients. If the mixture seems too thick to pour, add a little more milk.

3 Spread a ladleful or so of batter onto the waffle iron and bake until the waffle is done, usually 3 to 5 minutes, depending on your iron. Serve immediately or keep warm for a few minutes in a low oven.

Five Variations for Waffles

1. Stir 1 cup chopped (not minced) nuts, granola, or shredded sweetened or unsweetened coconut into the batter.

2. Add minced or grated orange or lemon zest, about 2 teaspoons per batch of batter.

3. Add fresh fruit such as blueberries, raspberries, or other fruit cut into $1/4$- to $1/2$-inch dice to the batter.

4. Lay two or three strips of bacon over the batter after spreading on the waffle iron and before closing the lid in any of the above recipes. The bacon will cook along with the waffles; cooking time may be a minute or two longer.

5. Serve waffles topped with ice cream, whipped cream, and/or fresh fruit.

The Basics of Waffles

A good waffle is super-crisp outside and creamy inside. To achieve this, you must use a good recipe and serve them quickly.

Some guidelines:

- The iron should be hot. Most have indicator lights. Preheat yours until the light goes off.
- The iron should be clean and lightly oiled.
- Don't underbake the waffle. After pouring (or spreading) the batter onto the iron, close the top and walk away for at least 2 minutes. Gently pull up on the top of the iron. If there is resistance, give it another minute or two longer: the waffle isn't ready. (Note: the indicator light on many waffle irons goes on when they are still a bit underdone. For a crisper waffle, wait an extra minute or so after the light has gone on.)
- Eat waffles immediately.

French Toast

Makes 4 servings • Time: 20 minutes

French toast originated as a way to use stale bread, but most people now make it with packaged white bread, which almost never gets stale, but makes decent French toast, because it absorbs so much liquid. To make this mixture eggier, use less milk.

> 2 eggs
>
> 1 cup milk
>
> Dash salt
>
> 1 tablespoon sugar (optional)
>
> 1 teaspoon vanilla extract or ground cinnamon (optional)
>
> Butter or canola or other neutral oil as needed
>
> 8 slices bread

1　Preheat a large griddle or skillet over medium-low heat while you prepare the liquid mixture.

2　Beat the eggs lightly in a broad bowl and stir in the milk, salt, and optional ingredients (if you are using them).

3　Add about 1 teaspoon of butter or oil to the griddle or skillet and, when it is hot, dip each slice of bread in turn in the batter and place it on the griddle. Cook until nicely browned on each side, turning as necessary. (You may find that you can raise the heat a bit.) Serve, or hold in a 200°F oven for up to 30 minutes.

Crispy French Toast: There are two ways to give French toast a bit of a crust: Stir ¹/₂ cup flour into the batter. Or, dip the bread in the batter, then dredge it in sweetened bread crumbs or crushed cornflakes. In either case, cook as above.

Good To Know

Oatmeal

Makes 2 servings • Time: 15 minutes

One of the simplest and good-for-you comfort foods. Buy rolled oats (not instant oatmeal) in bulk and keep them in the refrigerator or freezer; rolled oats are perishable. I like oatmeal fairly creamy, but if you prefer it thicker, use a bit less water.

> 2¹/₄ cups water
>
> Dash salt
>
> 1 cup rolled oats
>
> Butter to taste (optional)
>
> Salt, sweetener (such as maple syrup, sugar, or honey), and/or milk or cream as desired

1　Combine the water, salt, and oats in a small saucepan and turn the heat to high. When the water boils, turn the heat to low and cook, stirring, until the water is just absorbed, about 5 minutes. Add butter if desired, cover the pan, and turn off the heat.

2　Five minutes later, uncover the pan and stir. Add other ingredients as desired and serve.

Glossary

adjust seasoning: To "adjust seasoning," taste what you're cooking just before serving, and salt, pepper, or add other seasoning to suit your taste. Remember that it's always easier to add seasoning than to compensate for too much.

al dente: Pasta should be cooked until it is firm to the bite, or al dente, from the Italian phrase "to the tooth." You should taste pasta as it cooks, aiming for pasta that is tender but not mushy, firm but never hard, chewy but not crunchy. Pasta cooked al dente might seem undercooked to those of us who grew up eating mushy spaghetti and meatballs, but it will provide the optimum consistency for whatever sauce you choose. Remember, too, that pasta will cook a little from its retained heat as you drain and sauce it.

all-purpose flour: Like all white flours, this is milled from the inner part of the wheat kernel and contains neither the germ (the sprouting inner part) nor the bran (the outer coating). It's a combination of hard (high-protein, or bread) and soft (low-protein, or cake or pastry) flours, and is suitable for most purposes. Avoid bleached flour if possible.

allspice: A pungent dried seed pod from an evergreen tree, with a flavor of cinnamon, nutmeg, and cloves—hence the name. Also called Jamaican pepper (in Jamaica it's called pimento), because it looks like a big peppercorn and the best is grown on that island.

anchovies: Small, silvery fish that are usually cured with salt. Many are then tightly packed with oil in flat 2-ounce tins, but salt-cured anchovies are also available. These should be rinsed, and may need to be filleted before using.

aromatic: A vegetable, herb, or spice that gives food a lively fragrance and flavor. In classic cooking, a reference to "aromatics" most often means onion, carrot, and celery.

bacon (slab): This is bacon in a chunk—you must slice it by hand (and may want to remove the rind first). Often the only way to find top-quality bacon.

193

bake: To cook food in an oven, which supplies free-circulating dry heat. It's important to preheat the oven and to know the actual temperature, especially when baking breads or pastries. Because oven gauges are surprisingly inaccurate (electric ovens tend to be better than gas, but neither is reliable), buy an oven thermometer and use it. The term "bake" is used mostly for bread and desserts; savory food is more often "roasted," at high temperatures. Prebake or "blind bake" is to bake a crust before filling to ensure browning and crispness.

baking powder: A derivative of baking soda, baking powder is a double-action leavener, activated when it's mixed with liquid, and further stimulated when exposed to heat. Most commercial baking powders have a distinctive flavor that comes from aluminum and other additives. For a functional homemade baking powder without this odd flavor, you can combine cream of tartar with baking soda.

baking sheet: Good baking sheets (also called cookie sheets) are thick, and the best are insulated. But a careful eye during baking can compensate for cheap aluminum baking sheets. Non-stick baking sheets make life easier.

baking soda: Shorthand for sodium bicarbonate, baking soda is a good leavener in those pastries that contain acid, which stimulates a chemical reaction that produces gas—making your baked good rise. Use baking soda freely whenever you're baking with buttermilk, sour cream, or yogurt. If there is little to no acid in your recipe, you should use baking powder, which already has acid in it.

baking (pizza) stone: It's best to bake pizza and bread directly on a hot surface, and a baking stone gives you just that. It preheats while your oven does so your pizzas cook more evenly and your bread crusts are crisper. Just leave it on the bottom rack of your oven; you may need to replace it every few years.

balsamic vinegar: Real *aceto balsamico* is made only in the area around Modena, Italy, from the juice of white Trebbiano grapes, and gets its dark color and intense flavor from aging in barrels of various woods and graduating sizes. High-quality balsamic vinegars are aged 10 years or more and can be quite expensive. But the cheap, mass-produced, commonly found versions are not as good as sherry vinegar, which is relatively inexpensive. Medium-quality balsamic vinegar, aged 3 years or so and costing about $10 a bottle, is a luxury that's worth it—use it by the teaspoonful and it will last for a while.

barbecue: Don't confuse barbecuing with grilling. Grilling is food cooked over high, direct heat; barbecuing is a long, slow method, usually involving indirect cooking with smoke.

basmati rice: This aromatic long-grain rice has a perfumy, nut-like flavor and aroma. The kernels are incomparably long and slender. White basmati rice is most common, but you can also find brown (whole-grain) basmati rice at most health food stores.

baste: To spoon, brush, or drizzle food with butter, sauce, pan juice or other liquid as it cooks. Although it does add flavor to the exterior of food, basting's ability to keep food moist is largely overrated. Use a bulb baster if you have one, but a spoon or brush will do.

batter: A semi-liquid mixture made of flour, a leavening agent (such as eggs or baking powder), and a liquid. Batter can be spooned or poured; dough is thicker and most often molded by hand.

beat: To mix ingredients rapidly until they are well blended.

beef fillet (filet mignon): This tender but expensive boneless cut of meat comes from the small end of the tenderloin. It should be cooked quickly by grilling or sautéing. It should be sauced, too, because it is among the least flavorful pieces of meat.

bell peppers: Also known as sweet peppers, bell peppers are "mature" when they turn bright green, but they are not yet ripe; their flavor is sharp, even acrid at this point. The same peppers picked a week or two later will have turned red, yellow, or orange, and their flavor will have mellowed considerably. Yellow and orange peppers are the most mellow, but they're usually expensive, so red is the common first choice. Avoid green if you have other options. (Note that purple peppers are just green ones in disguise.)

boil: The term not only means heating liquid until bubbles break the surface, but applies to cooking food in boiling liquid. Temperatures can be controlled not only by raising and lowering the heat of the burner, but by partially covering the pot. Actual boiling—with bubbles rapidly appearing—is useful for pasta, potatoes, and many vegetables. Most food is cooked at a simmer—a few bubbles breaking the surface, not rapidly.

braise: To cook food, first by browning it in a little fat, then by adding liquid to the pan, covering it, and finishing the cooking over moist, low heat. The browning step is optional; although it most definitely adds flavor, it's an additional step that won't make or break the dish.

bread crumbs: There are two kinds of bread crumbs: fresh and dry. They should not be used interchangeably. Fresh crumbs can be made in a food processor or blender. Dried bread crumbs are lightly browned and may be plain or flavored. They can be bought or made from good-quality stale bread.

broil: To cook food directly under the heat source, with the aim of producing a crisp crust while cooking the interior to the desired degree of doneness. (Grilling is identical to broiling, except the food is above the heat source.) Generally, the best foods to broil are less than 1 inch thick; the thicker the food, the greater distance it should be from the heat source.

broth: Closely related to stock, this is the basis of almost all soups. It is made by cooking vegetables, meat, or fish in water, then straining and defatting the resulting stock. Broth is widely available in stores (stock less so), if not homemade.

brown: To cook food quickly in order to "brown" the outside, while keeping the interior moist. Browning is usually done in a hot skillet on top of the stove, but a very hot oven, broiler, or grill will also work well.

brown sugar: Brown sugar is simply white sugar combined with molasses. Dark brown sugar has lots of molasses; light brown sugar contains less. To re-create brown sugar, add 2 tablespoons molasses to 1 cup white sugar.

butter: Butter is generally labeled either salted or sweet (unsalted); salt is incorporated largely as a preservative and can be added anytime.

buttermilk: Once upon a time this was the milk remaining in the churn after the butter had been removed. Today, all commercial buttermilk is produced by adding a culture to whole or skimmed milk, which gives it the thicker texture and slightly tangy flavor associated with buttermilk.

caramelize: To slowly dissolve sugar (granulated or brown) in water, then heat the resulting syrup until it turns caramel-brown. Caramelized sugar is sometimes called burnt sugar.

casserole: A casserole may be any deep, oven-proof vessel, usually used to cook food slowly. Dutch ovens are similar. It also describes the food made in the cooking dish.

cheesecloth: Essentially cotton gauze that doesn't fall apart when it gets wet and won't flavor the food it touches. Especially useful for straining liquids when you want to remove even the tiny particles that flow through a fine strainer.

chile powder: Chile powder may be ground-up chiles, or it's a seasoning mixture of garlic, onion, cumin, oregano, coriander, cloves, and/or other spices.

chipotle chile: Smoked, dried jalapeños with a distinctive flavor, usually very hot. When dried, soak before using. Also sold canned in sauce (called adobo).

chocolate: Unsweetened chocolate, also sold as bitter or baking chocolate, is simply unadulterated chocolate. Bittersweet, semisweet, extra-bittersweet, and sweet cooking chocolates result from the addition of cocoa butter, sugar, vanilla, and chocolate liquor (bittersweet contains at least 35 percent chocolate liquor; semisweet and sweet contain between 15 and 30 percent). Although bittersweet and semisweet chocolate can be interchanged in some recipes, stick to the recipe's suggestion for best result.

chop: To cut food into pieces, ranging in size from $1/4$ to $1/2$ inch or so (finely chopped) to somewhat larger than that (coarsely or roughly chopped). Very fine chopping is called mincing.

cider vinegar: Fruity vinegar made from fermented apple cider.

cocoa powder: From the cocoa bean, cocoa powder provides the basis for hot chocolate and is used in many baked goods. Dutch cocoa is cocoa that has been treated with alkali, which makes the cocoa more soluble and neutralizes its natural acidity.

compote: Fresh and/or dried fruit cooked slowly in a sugar-water mixture (sugar syrup). Served warm or refrigerated and served cold.

compound butter: Butter creamed with herbs, spices, garlic, wine, or whatever you wish. Perfect for finishing sauces or jazzing up just about any grilled or broiled food.

confectioners' sugar: This powdered sugar is best in those recipes that will not be cooked at all, such as frostings, because it dissolves better than regular granulated sugar; it's also good sprinkled on top of baked goods.

core: To remove the center or core of a fruit. The core might be woody and tough, as in apples, or contain small seeds, as in tomatoes. Use a paring knife or apple corer.

cornstarch: This is one of the most useful thickening agents in the kitchen, with twice the power of flour. Mix it with a small amount of cold water or other liquid before stirring it into other foods.

cream: To beat an ingredient, usually a fat such as butter or margarine, alone or with sugar until softened and well blended.

cream of tartar: An acidic, fine white powder that can be used, along with sodium bicarbonate, to make baking powder.

croutons: Nothing more than crisped bits or whole slices of bread. They may be dried in the oven with no seasonings at all, or cooked in oil or butter, with or without garlic and/or herbs.

curry powder: Widely used in Indian cooking, curry powder is actually a blend of up to twenty spices; tumeric gives it its characteristic yellow color. Curry powder quickly loses its pungency, so store it, airtight, for no longer than 2 months.

custard: Like pudding, custard is a thick, creamy mixture of milk, sugar, and flavorings. Custard is thickened with eggs, pudding with cornstarch or flour. Remove custard from the oven while the center is still slightly wobbly; once it appears set, it's almost always overcooked.

cutlet: A tender, thin, boneless cut of meat; it could be part of a chicken or turkey breast, or veal, lamb, or pork, usually taken from the leg.

dash: An approximate term of measurement for seasoning meaning little more than a sprinkle of the specified ingredient, as in "a dash of salt." Start with a tiny amount, and add more until the flavor of the dish suits your tastes.

deep fry: To cook food in hot fat deep enough to cover the food being fried. The fat should be around 350° to 375°F: if it's not hot enough, too much fat will be absorbed, but if it's too hot, the food will burn. (A frying thermometer or electric deep-fryer will help regulate.) Use plenty of oil; dry the food well with paper towels before deep frying; and add the food in small increments to keep the temperature from dropping too much.

deglaze: A quick and easy way to make a reduction sauce. After sautéing meat or other food, remove it from the pan and add a small amount of liquid to the flavorful bits left in the pan; heat and stir until the liquid is reduced to the desired consistency. You can deglaze with water, lemon juice, vinegar, wine, stock, juice, cream, or a combination.

dice: To cut food into small ($\frac{1}{8}$ to $\frac{1}{4}$ inch) cubes of equal size.

double boiler: A duo of pots used to warm or cook heat-sensitive foods, like custards and chocolate. The lower pot holds water, which heats the ingredients in the upper pot that sits inside it. You may need a double boiler arrangement at some point, but the chances are good you can rig one up by setting one pot on top of another; the fit need not be perfect.

dough: Dough is a mixture of flour, liquid, and usually a leavening agent (such as eggs or yeast), which is stiff but pliable. The primary difference between dough and batter is the consistency: Dough is thicker and must be molded by hand, while batter is semiliquid, thus spooned or poured.

dredge: To lightly coat food for frying, usually with flour, cornmeal, or bread crumbs.

dry-sauté: Dry-sautéing, or pan-grilling as it is also called, is cooking food over high heat with no oil at all. Non-stick pans make this possible. You can also dry-sauté sturdy food with even surfaces (such as steaks) in a well-seasoned cast-iron skillet.

Dutch oven: This big sturdy pot with a tightly fitting lid is used for moist cooking, such as braising or stewing. A 6- to 8-quart Dutch oven—or covered casserole of the same size—is a near-necessity for most cooks.

emulsion: A mixture of two or more liquids that don't easily combine, such as oil and vinegar. Should you decide to emulsify vinaigrette (it isn't crucial, but it does have nice texture), you can use a food processor or blender to make an emulsion that's stable for hours. You can also whisk the oil, vinegar, and seasonings, or shake them vigorously in a jar to create a short-lived but perfectly acceptable emulsion.

fillet: A boneless piece of fish; can also be used to describe meat or chicken.

fold: To incorporate a light, fluffy mixture, such as beaten egg white, into a heavier mixture by gently lifting from underneath with a rubber spatula, spoon, or hand.

food processor: The most important electric tool in the kitchen, a food processor can grate massive amounts of almost anything in seconds; make bread and pie dough in an instant; grind meat; and puree and slice vegetables. Small ones are valuable, but a large model that can handle at least 6 cups of batter or dough is best.

garnish: You can garnish for appearance, flavor, or both. A sprig of parsley next to a sautéed chicken breast does little. A small handful of parsley sprinkled over that same meat adds great flavor and lends color contrast. Garnishes are often optional.

gelatin: This thickening agent (made from pure protein) is odorless, tasteless, and colorless, but when dissolved in hot water and then cooled, it forms a jelly that thickens whatever food it's been added to.

granulated sugar: Basic, refined "white sugar," for daily use and most baking.

grate: To reduce firm or hard food to small particles or shreds in a food processor or by rubbing it against a grater. Graters come in several shapes and sizes; a small, handheld device will do for grating Parmesan onto pasta; for grating potatoes and the like, you need a food processor or a sturdy box grater.

gravy: Gravy is simply a sauce made from meat juices. It's usually diluted with water, milk, wine, or stock, and thickened with flour or cornstarch.

grill: To cook on a rack over direct heat. Unlike barbecuing, grilling creates a seared crust. Almost any food that can be broiled can also be grilled.

grind: To use a food processor, chopper, grinder, or mortar and pestle to break solid food down into small pieces. Food can be ground coarsely, finely, or somewhere in-between.

hoisin sauce: Brownish-red, sweet and spicy sauce, made from soybeans, garlic, chile pepper, and assorted spices. Can be thought of as Chinese ketchup, although it's usually added to stir-fries during the last couple of minutes of cooking. Sold in cans or jars; store in a tightly sealed jar in the fridge.

Hollandaise sauce: Rich, creamy, emulsified sauce similar to mayonnaise but made with butter instead of oil and always served hot. Very lemony.

hull: To remove the outer covering, or pull out the stem and leafy top portion, of berries, especially strawberries.

infuse: To extract flavor from an ingredient, such as herbs or tea leaves, by slowly steeping in a hot liquid.

julienne: To cut solid food, usually vegetables, into slender strips of equal length. The thin strips are also called matchsticks.

knead: To mix pliable dough (usually bread dough) with your hands, electric mixer, or food processor in order to develop gluten, which makes dough elastic.

kosher salt: Coarse-grained salt that is easy to handle; keep a container near the stove and use it while you cook.

lard: Pork fat, rendered and clarified, with a firm texture and good flavor. Lard has fallen out of favor, but is great in pie crusts and good for frying (especially beans).

leavening agent: An ingredient that causes dough or batter to rise, lightening its texture and increasing its volume, such as beaten eggs or egg whites, baking powder, baking soda, and yeast.

liqueur: Sweet alcoholic beverages flavored with fruits, herbs, or spices, usually served after dinner. Some, such as Amaretto and Grand Marnier, are useful as flavorings in desserts.

mandoline: The original food processor, and still highly useful, the mandoline is the easiest way to cut thin slices of vegetables.

margarine: Vegetable oil made hard through a process called hydrogenation, margarine tastes lousy and is bad for you. Note that "shortening" is essentially white margarine. Stick with oil and butter as your primary cooking, baking, and eating fats; even lard is preferable to margarine.

marinate: To soak meat, vegetables, or fish in seasoned liquid. Adds flavor but, contrary to conventional "wisdom," does little to tenderize.

mash: To crush a food, such as avocados or cooked potatoes or beans, into a smooth mixture.

mesclun: A word used to describe a mixture of a dozen or more wild and cultivated greens, herbs, and edible flowers. Unless you're a gardener, you have no choice about what is included in a mesclun mix, but a good one will contain greens of various textures and flavors—including sweet, spicy, and bitter greens, and at least a smattering of herbs. Relatively speaking, it costs a fortune, but a $1/2$ pound will serve four.

mince: To cut solid food into very fine pieces.

olive oil: There are two kinds of olive oil worth buying. The best is extra-virgin oil, which comes from the first, cold pressing of olives, and ranges from reasonably priced to very expensive. "Pure" olive oil is also decent—it may be extra-virgin oils that didn't make the grade, or, more often, oils extracted from the pulp left after making extra-virgin oils. Olive oil is the only truly all-purpose oil.

paprika: Ground dried red peppers, may be hot or sweet, and best when Hungarian in origin.

parboil/blanch: To parboil, or blanch, you partially cook food, usually vegetables, in boiling water to cover. This method keeps vegetables bright, while partially tenderizing them (see Precooked Vegetables in Butter or Oil, page 118, for details).

paring knife: Thin, sharp knife with a 3- to 4-inch blade. Essential kitchen tool.

Parmesan: Made from cow's milk, this nutty-sweet dry cheese is the best for grating (and good for eating out of hand). Parmigiano-Reggiano is the true Parmesan; everything else is a copy.

peanut oil: This flavorful oil borders on all-purpose. Its flavor, though distinctive, is not overpowering, and it is a great oil for cooking (especially highly spiced foods and Asian dishes in which olive oil is out of place), as well as for the occasional salad dressing. Also use it for sautéing and all stir-frying.

pectin: Found naturally in fruits and vegetables, gelatin-like pectin is used as a thickener in jellies and jams. Available in liquid and dry forms.

pimentos: A name used for roasted red peppers that have been canned or bottled in liquid. Look for brands without preservatives.

pinch: A very small amount, so-called because it can be held between the thumb tip and the forefinger.

pine nuts: Also pignoli nuts, these small, pellet-shaped nuts from the pine cone have a wonderfully sweet, rich flavor. The Southwestern pignons are similar.

pizza peel: A flat, broad sheet of wood or metal with a handle, also called a baker's peel. Allows you to slide breads and pizzas easily onto a stone.

poach: To cook by submerging food in a very gently boiling liquid.

poblano chile: Dark green, relatively mild chile known as ancho when dried.

polenta: Fluffy combination of cornmeal and water, successfully prepared by a variety of methods. Best served sauced or allowed to harden, sliced, and grilled.

porcini: Also called cèpes, these meaty, large-topped mushrooms are simply the best. Although they are most frequently sold dried, it's becoming easier to find them fresh; they're expensive but a real treat.

preserves: Fruits or vegetables, whole or chopped, simmered in a sugary syrup.

puree: To finely blend and mash a food to a smooth, lump-free consistency. You can puree foods in a blender, food processor, or food mill.

reconstitute: To bring a dried, dehydrated food back to its original consistency by adding a liquid.

red pepper flakes: The dried flakes of the red hot chile pepper.

reduce: To cook a liquid, usually a sauce or stock, over high heat, thereby decreasing its volume and intensifying its flavor.

reduction sauce: A sauce that uses as its base the pan juices that are created from stove-top cooking or oven-roasting meat, fish, poultry, or vegetables. Reduction sauces can be made easily and quickly.

render: To cook a food over low heat until it releases its fat.

roast: This form of cooking uses indirect, dry, and usually high heat. Roasting should crisp up the exterior of foods while allowing the interior to cook relatively slowly. Liquids that result from roasting make great sauces.

roasting pan: Purchase an 8 × 12- or 9 × 13-inch metal or ceramic pan, which will come in handy for broiling meat, roasting chicken, making macaroni and cheese, and even baking breads or brownies. Stay away from uncoated aluminum.

saffron: Fragrant, thread-like, hand-picked stigmas from the crocus. Adds super color and good mild but bitter flavor to many dishes. Highly expensive.

salad spinner: A manual tool that is wonderfully helpful in draining excess moisture from freshly washed greens. Good investment.

salmon: One of the most popular finfish, rich, oily (it's beneficial oil), and highly flavorful. Easy to cook—in any number of ways (salmon can be poached, steamed, grilled, or broiled).There are many varieties to choose from, and purchasing salmon can be very confusing. Many markets sell "Norwegian" salmon as if it were a distinct species; but it is actually Atlantic salmon (and Atlantic salmon is now grown in the Pacific Northwest, northern Europe, Chile, and any other place where there is cold, protected seawater). There are five species of wild Pacific salmon: king (or Chinook) and sockeye, which are leaner than Atlantic salmon, and equally as flavorful; coho (silver); chum (keta); and pink (which is usually canned).

sauté: French for "jump." Refers to cooking food in a hot pan with some amount of fat until nicely browned. Best for thin cuts.

striped bass: Firm-textured fish with meaty, pearly flesh. When wild, striped bass are highly flavorful. Now being farm-raised in California. Can be substituted in recipes that call for cod or other milder fish, and some stronger fish, too. Easy to grill.

superfine sugar: This finely granulated sugar is good in meringues and cold drinks; it dissolves quickly and easily.

swordfish: Highly popular fish, wonderful on the grill. When buying, look for bright flesh with tight swirls; should smell good. Skin is inedible.

Tabasco: A brand-name hot sauce that is essentially chile peppers combined with salt and vinegar.

tahini: Creamy paste of toasted sesame seeds, originally from the Middle East. Best in hummus or use as a substitute for sesame paste with Asian noodle dishes.

toss: To quickly mix together ingredients, usually for a salad or pasta dish, with a large spoon and fork.

tuna: An excellent steak fish (and the most popular canned fish), with tender, flaky, and highly flavorful flesh; the best substitute for a good steak, especially when cooked rare.

Yellowfin is most common; bluefin, an endangered species, is best, but not widely available.

vanilla: Vanilla comes in two forms: vanilla beans, long thin pods that are the fruit of an orchid plant native to Mexico, and vanilla extract, which is made by processing vanilla beans in an alcohol-water solution. There are times when the subtle flavor of whole vanilla beans can have a profound effect on a recipe; in most cases, good quality vanilla extract is perfect. Make sure the extract you buy contains alcohol and vanilla only, and not vanillin, an artificial ingredient made from wood. The label should say "pure vanilla extract"—avoid labels that say "imitation vanilla flavor" or some variation.

vinaigrette: Simply acid and oil, combined; every other addition is up for grabs. The acid may be freshly squeezed citrus juice, usually lemon or lime, or vinegar—the best you can find. The acidic ingredient is the most basic flavor of a vinaigrette, so it should be delicious. Oil can add to a vinaigrette or it may be nothing more than a carrier of other flavors. (For more about vinaigrettes, see page 3).

whip: To beat rapidly, by hand or with a whisk or electric mixer, to add air and increase volume. Egg whites or cream are common ingredients that are whipped.

whisk: This metal utensil has a series of looped wires that make lumps disappear as if by magic. You need at least one medium-sized stiff one for keeping sauces smooth, but if you beat cream, egg whites, and so on electronically, you may not need more than that.

whole wheat flour: White flour has had the germ and the bran removed; whole wheat flour contains both. It is nutritionally superior and has a stronger flavor that not everyone likes. The ground germ contains oil, which can grow rancid and bitter, so buy only as much as you plan to use in the following month or so. Store whole wheat flour in the freezer, if you have room (you need not defrost before using).

wine vinegar: Wine vinegar can be made from either red or white wine. It may be made by the traditional "Orleans method"—that is aging in barrels. But most reasonably priced wine vinegar is made by more efficient methods; it can be quite decent as long as it contains only wine. Good raspberry, tarragon, or other flavored vinegars usually begin with high-quality wine vinegar.

yeast: A living organism that generates gas as a byproduct of its consumption of carbohydrates. Combine yeast, liquid, and flour, and you get bubbles, which are in turn trapped by the flour-liquid mixture, causing the dough to rise.

zest: The outermost colored peel of lemons, oranges, and other citrus fruits. Employing a special utensil called a zester is the easiest way to remove it but not the only way. You can use a vegetable peeler or paring knife to remove the peel in long ribbons. Since this inevitably brings part of the bitter white pith with it, to do a perfect job you should then lie the strips down on a cutting board and scrape the white part off with a paring knife.

Index

Note: *Italicized* page references indicate illustrations.

A

Aioli, 7
Apple(s)
  baked, 140
  basics of, 141
  fruit crisp, 146
  peeling and coring, *140*
  pie, 152–53
    additions to, 153
    traditional (double crust), 152
  pork chops with, 90
  sautéed, 144
Appliances and electric gadgets, x
Asian noodles, basics of, 33
Asian sauce, 62
Asparagus
  basics of, 121
  preparing, *120*
  roasted, broiled, or grilled, 120

B

Bacon
  basics of, 183
  corn bread, 179
Baked apples, 140
  additions to, 140
Baked beans, 114
  vegetarian, 114
Baked croutons, 13

Baked macaroni and cheese, 25
Baked potatoes, 130
Baked sweet potatoes, 131
Baking dishes, about, viii
Baking powder biscuits, 174
Banana(s)
  basics of, 144
  -nut muffins, 177
  pancakes, 189
  sautéed, 144
  summer fruit compote, 145
Basic grilled or broiled lamb chops, 94
Basic roast duck, 78
Basic roast turkey breast, on the
    bone, 76
Basil
  chicken cutlets, with tomato
    and, 58
  tomato, and mozzarella salad, 5
Béchamel sauce, 31
Bean(s), 101, 108–16
  about, 101, 111
  baked, 114
    vegetarian, 114
  basics of buying and preparing, 109
  black
    and rice, Spanish-style, 115
    soup, 15
  chili con carne, 113

  chili non carne, 113
  classic, 108
    additions to, 109
  faster, 108
  Hoppin' John, 116
  lexicon, 111
  pressure-cooked, 110
  and rice, southern, 116
  soups, additions to, 14
  white
    lamb shanks with, 97
    soup, 14
    Tuscan-style, 112
Beef
  burger, classic, 84
  cuts, *83*
    basics of, 83
  meatballs, 28
  meat loaf, 100
  pot roast, 88–89
  prime rib, 86–87
  roast, basics of, 87
  sauerbraten, 89
  steak
    broiled, 80
    grilled, American-style, 80
    grilled porterhouse (T-bone), 80
  stew, classic, 82
  and vegetable soup, 10

Berry (ies). *See specific types of berries*
  basics of, 149
  fruit cobbler, 147
  pies (single crust), 148
  summer fruit compote, 145
Best and simplest green salad, 2
Best From Scratch recipes
  Baked Croutons, 13
  Béchamel Sauce, 31
  Dark Chocolate Glaze, 168
  Easy Tomato Sauce, 27
  Flaky Pie Crust, 150–51
  Mayonnaise, 7
  My Favorite Bread Stuffing, 75
  Pizza Dough, 172–73
  Prebaked Flaky Pie Crust, 151
  Quickest Chicken Stock, 17
  Reduction Sauce or Pan Gravy, 62
  Traditional Cranberry Sauce, 75
  Vanilla Butter Cream Frosting,
    168
  Vinaigrette, 3
Biscuits
  baking powder, 174
  cheese, 174
  drop ("emergency"), 17
  yogurt of buttermilk, 174
Black beans. *See* Beans
Blackberry
  basics of, 149
  pie, 148
Blanching, basic, xiv
Blueberry
  basics of, 149
  muffins, 177
  pancakes, 189
  pie (single crust), 148
Boiled, steamed, or microwaved
    Spinach, 134
Boiled or steamed lobster, 54
Boiling, xiv
Boneless prime rib, 86
Boule, shaping, *170*
Bowls, about, viii
Braising, basic, xiii
Bran muffins, 177

Bread(s), 169–79
  biscuits, yogurt or buttermilk, 174
  corn, 178–79
  muffins, 176–77
  pizza, 172
  pizza dough, 172
  strawberry shortcakes, 175
  yeast, 170
Bread crumbs
  flavored, broiled cod or other
    thick white fillets with, 40
  in meatballs, 28
  in meat loaf, 100
  in sautéed chicken cutlet dishes, 60
Bread stuffing, my favorite, 75
Breakfast dishes, 169, 180–92. *See
  also* Bread dishes
  egg dishes. *See* Eggs
  French toast, 192
  frittate, 186–87
  oatmeal, 192
  omelet, 184–85
  pancakes, 188–89
  waffles, 190–91
Broccoli
  basics of, 123
  simmered, steamed, or
    microwaved, 122
  stir-fried chicken with, 68–69
Broiled cod or other thick white
    fillets, 40
  with white wine and herbs, 41
Broiled flatfish or other thin white
    fillets, 36
  with garlic-parsley sauce, 37
Broiled steak, 80
Broiling, basics of, xi–xii
Brownies, 162
Burger(s)
  basics of, 85
  classic, 84
  flavoring, 84
Butter
  precooked grains with, 107
  precooked vegetables in, 118
  quick-braised carrots with, 124

sage, and Parmesan, pasta with, 24
sauce, mussels with, 52
Buttermilk biscuits, 174

C
Cabbage, coring and shredding, *9*
Caesar salad, 4
Cake(s), 157, 162–68. *See also*
    Cookies; Cupcakes; Frosting
  about, 157
  basics of, 164
  brownies, 162
  coffee, quick, 164
  layer, chocolate, 167
  layer, golden, 166
  lemon squares, Gabrielle's, 163
  pound, 165
Carrots
  basics of, 124
  dicing, *124*
  quick-braised, with butter, 124
  red snapper or other fillets in
    packages with zucchini and, 39
  roasted root vegetables, 138
Cauliflower
  basics of, 123
  stir-fried chicken with, 68–69
Cheese. *See also specific types of
    cheese*
  biscuits, 174
  and macaroni, baked, 25
  and pasta, basics of, 24
Chicken
  breasts, boneless, basics of, 59
  cutlets, grilled or broiled, 58
    grilled or broiled, in sweet
      soy marinade (chicken
      teriyaki), 58
    grilled or broiled, with basil
      and tomato, 58
  cutlets, sautéed, 60
    basics of, 61
    extra-crisp, 60
    fried, 64–65
      chile-spiced, 65
  Parmigiana, 61

parts
  basics of, 67
  roast, with herbs and olive
    oil, 66
  roast, 66, 70–71. *See* Roast
    chicken
  soups, 16
  stir-fried
    additions to, 69
    with broccoli or cauliflower,
      68–69
  stock, quickest, 17
  teriyaki, 58
Chile-spiced fried chicken, 65
Chili con carne, 113
Chili non carne, 113
Chinese noodles, stir-fried, with
  vegetables, 32
Chocolate butter cream frosting, 168
Chocolate chip cookies, classic, 158
Chocolate cupcakes, 167
Chocolate glaze, dark, 168
Chocolate layer cake, 167
Chunky cookies, 158
Clams
  basics of, 51
  shucking, *50*
  steamed, 50
Classic American potato salad, 6
  additions to, 6
Classic beans, 108
  additions to, 109
Classic beef stew, 82
Classic burger, 84
Classic chocolate chip cookies, 158
Classic lasagne dishes, 30
Classic muffins, 176
Cobbler, fruit, 147
Classic risotto, 105
Cod, broiled, 40
  with flavored bread crumbs, 40
  with white wine and herbs, 41
Coffee cake, quick, 164
Cold noodles with sesame or peanut
  sauce, 34
Coleslaw, spicy, 8

Compote
  with dried fruits, easy, 145
  summer fruit, 145
Cookies, 157–63
  about, 157
  brownies, 162
  chocolate chip, classic, 158
  chunky, 158
  lemon squares, Gabrielle's, 163
  oatmeal, 159
  peanut butter, 161
  refrigerator (rolled), 160
  rolled, lighter, 161
Cooking, what to know before you
    begin, v–xiv
  equipment, vi–x
  ingredients, vi
  recipes, vi
  time, v
Coriander seeds, roast leg of lamb
  with garlic and, 98
Corn (fresh)
  basics of, 125
  preparing, 125
  steamed, 125
Corn bread, 178
  additions to, 179
  bacon, 179
  lighter, richer, 179
Crab cakes, 56
Cranberry
  jelly, very firm, 75
  muffins, 177
  sauce
    traditional, 75
    very firm, 75
Cream, mussels with, 53
Creamed spinach, 134
Cream of broccoli (or any vegetable)
  soup, 12
Crisp, fruit, 146
Crispy French toast, 192
Croutons, baked, 13
Crust. *See* Pie crust
Cupcakes
  chocolate, 167
  golden, 166

Custard pie, 156
Cutting boards, about, ix

D
Dark chocolate glaze, 168
Deep-frying, basics of, xiii
Dough, pizza, 172–73
Drop ("emergency") biscuits, 174
Duck, roast, basic, 78
Dutch apple pie, 152

E
Easy compote with dried fruits, 145
Easy tomato sauce, 27
Egg(s). *See also* Frittate; Omelet
  basics of, 181
  fried, 182
  hard-boiled, 181
  scrambled
    additions to, 180
    weekday morning, 180
Eggplant
  basics of, 137
  sautéed, 137
"Emergency" biscuits, 174
Equipment, basic, about, vi–x
Extra-crisp chicken cutlets, 60

F
Fast-cooked short- or medium-grain
    rice, 103
Faster beans, 108
Fastest yeast bread, 170
Fettuccine "Alfredo", 24
Fish, 35–56. *See also specific types
  of fish*
  about, 35
  basics of
    fish steaks, 43
    thick white fish fillets, 41
    thin white fish fillets, 37
  clams, steamed, 50
  cod, broiled, 40–41
  crab cakes, 56
  fish fillets, broiled, ideas for, 36
  fish fillets, pin bones, removing, *44*

Fish (cont.)
  fish fillets, thick white
    broiled, 40
    broiled, with flavored bread
      crumbs, 40
    with white wine and herbs, 41
  fish fillets, thin white
    broiled, 36
    in packages, 39
    in packages with carrots and
      zucchini, 39
    sautéed, 38
  fish fillets, white
    broiled, with garlic-parsley
      sauce, 37
    sautéed, with soy sauce, 38
  fish steaks
    grilled, 42
    grilled, herb-rubbed, 42
    grilled or broiled, ideas for, 42
  flatfish. See Flatfish
  lobster, boiled or steamed, 54–55
  mussels, steamed, 52–53
  red snapper in packages, 39
  salmon fillets. See Salmon
  shrimp. See Shrimp
  swordfish, grilled, 42
  tuna, grilled, 42
Flaky pie crust, 150–51
Flatfish
  broiled, 36
    with garlic-parsley sauce, 37
  sautéed, 38
    with soy sauce, 38
Free-form tart with fruit, 154
French fries, 133
  flavorings for, 133
French toast, 192
  crispy, 192
Fried chicken, 64–65
  chile-spiced, 65
Fried eggs, 182
Frittata (-e), 186
  additions to, 187
  basics of, 187
  herb, 187

onion, 186
vegetable, 186
Frosting
  chocolate butter cream, 168
  dark chocolate glaze, 168
  vanilla butter cream, 168
Fruits. See also specific types of fruit
  cobbler, 147
  compote, summer, 145
  crisp, 146
  desserts, 139–47, 154
  dried, easy compote with, 145
  free-form tart with, 154

G
Gabrielle's lemon squares, 163
Garlic
  mayonnaise (aioli), 7
  mincing and peeling, 126
  and oil, linguine with, 20
  precooked grains with, 107
  roast leg of lamb with coriander
    seeds and, 98
  roast pork with rosemary and, 93
  sautéed mushrooms with, 126
Gazpacho, red, 18
Glaze, dark chocolate, 168
Golden cupcakes, 166
Golden layer cake, 166
Good To Know recipes
  Baked Macaroni and Cheese, 25
  Baked Sweet Potatoes, 131
  Basic Roast Turkey Breast, on the
    Bone, 76
  Black Bean Soup, 15
  Chocolate Layer Cake, 167
  Cold Noodles with Sesame or
    Peanut Sauce, 34
  Easy Compote with Dried Fruits,
    145
  Fruit Cobbler, 147
  Gabrielle's Lemon Squares, 163
  Herb-Roasted Boneless Turkey
    Breast, 77
  Oatmeal, 192
  Oatmeal Cookies, 159

Precooked Grains with Butter or
  Oil, 107
Pressure-Cooked Beans, 110
Pumpkin Pie, 156
Quick and Easy Waffles, 190
Red Snapper or Other Fillets in
  Packages, 39
Sautéed Eggplant, 137
Southern Beans and Rice, 116
Spicy Grilled or Broiled Shrimp, 49
Strawberry Shortcakes, 175
Grains, 101–16
  about, 101
  bean dishes. See Beans
  cooking, basics of, 106
  precooked
    with butter or oil, 107
    with garlic, onions, or
      mushrooms, 107
  rice dishes. See Rice
  simple precooked, 106
Gravy
  pan, 62
  roast turkey and, without
    stuffing, 72–73
Greek salad, simple, 2
Greens, dark leafy, basics of, 135
Grilled or broiled chicken cutlets, 58
  in sweet soy marinade (chicken
    teriyaki), 58
  with basil and tomato, 58
Grilled porterhouse (T-bone)
  steak, 80
Grilled skewered lamb chunks, 96
Grilled steak, American-style, 80
Grilled swordfish, tuna, salmon, or
  other steaks, 42
Grilling, basics of, xi–xii

H
Hard-boiled eggs, 181
Heat, basics of, xi
Herb(s)
  broiled cod or other thick white
    fillets with white wine and, 41
  fresh, linguine with, 20

frittata, 187
roast chicken parts with olive oil
and, 66
-roasted boneless turkey breast, 77
-rubbed grilled swordfish, tuna,
or other steaks, 42
Hoppin' John, 116

J

Jelly, cranberry, very firm, 75
Julienne cuts, making, 119

K

Knives, about, vii

L

Lamb
basics of, 95
chops, basic grilled or broiled, 94
chunks, grilled skewered, 96
cuts, 94
leg of
basics of, 99
carving, 99
roast, 98
roast, with garlic and coriander
seeds, 98
in meat loaf, 100
shanks with white beans, 97
Lasagne, classic
Bolognese-style, 30
Italian-American-style, 30
Leaner meatballs, 28
Lemon, sautéed medallions of pork
with parsley and, 92
Lemon squares, Gabrielle's, 163
Lighter, richer corn bread, 179
Lighter rolled cookies, 161
Linguine
with fresh herbs, 20
with fresh tomato sauce and
Parmesan, 26
with garlic and oil, 20
Liquid, cooking in, basics of,
xiii–xiv

Lobster(s)
basics of, 55
boiled or steamed, 54
how to eat, 55
Long-grain rice, 102

M

Macaroni and cheese, baked, 25
Marinade, sweet soy, grilled or
broiled chicken cutlets in, 58
Marinated roasted, grilled, or
broiled peppers, 128
Mashed potatoes, 132
Mayonnaise, 7
garlic, 7
Meat, 79–100. See also specific types
of meat
about, 79
beef dishes. See Beef
chili con carne, 113
lamb dishes. See Lamb
meatballs
leaner, 28
spaghetti and, 28
meat loaf, 100
pork dishes. See Pork
stir-fried noodles with, 33
sauce, pasta with, 29
Microwaved broccoli, 122
Microwaved spinach, 134
Minestrone, 10
Moors and Christian, 115
Mozzarella
in chicken Parmigiana, 61
tomato, and basil salad, 5
Muffins
banana-nut, 177
blueberry, 177
bran, 177
classic, 176
cranberry, 177
savory, 177
spice, 177
Mushroom(s)
basics of, 127
omelet, 185

precooked grains with, 107
sauce, 62
sautéed, with garlic, 126
Mussels
basics of, 53
with butter sauce, 52
with cream, 53
debearding, 52
steamed, 52
Mustard, pork chops with, 90
My favorite bread stuffing, 75

N

Noodles. See also Linguine; Pasta;
Spaghetti
Asian, basics of, 33
Chinese, stir-fried, with
vegetables, 32
cold, with sesame or peanut
sauce, 34
stir-fried, with stir-fried
vegetables, 33

O

Oatmeal, 192
Oatmeal cookies, 159
Omelet, 184
basics of, 185
filling, 184
mushroom, 185
western, 185
Onion(s)
frittata, 186
pilaf with raisins, pine nuts,
and, 104
precooked grains with, 107
preparing, 11

P

Packages, red snapper or other fillets
in, 39
Pancakes, 188
banana, 189
basics of, 189
blueberry, 189
Pan gravy, 62

Pan-grilled salmon fillets, 44
    with sesame oil drizzle, 44
Pan-grilled steak, 81
Pans, about, vii–viii
Parboiling, basic, xiv
Parmesan. *See also* Cheese; Pasta
    butter, and sage, pasta with, 24
    linguine with fresh tomato sauce
        and, 26
Parmigiana, chicken, 61
Parsley, sautéed medallions of pork
    with lemon and, 92
Pasta, 19–34. *See also* Linguine;
    Noodles; Spaghetti
    about, 19, 21
    with pesto, 22
    basics of cooking, 21
    with butter, sage, and
        Parmesan, 24
    and cheese, basics of, 24
    lasagne, 30–31
    macaroni and cheese, baked, 25
    with meat sauce, 29
    with minimalist pesto, 22
    with pesto with butter, 22
Pastry pans, about, viii
Peanut butter cookies, 161
Peanut sauce, cold noodles with, 34
Pears
    basics of, 143
    poached in red wine, 142
Peppers
    basics of, 129
    marinated roasted, grilled, or
        broiled, 128
    preparing, *128*
Pesto
    pasta with, 22
    basics of, 23
    with butter, pasta with, 22
    minimalist, pasta with, 22
Pie, 139, 148–56
    apple, traditional, 152–53
    berry, 148
    blackberry, 148
    blueberry, 148

crust
    flaky, 150–51
    fluting, *153*
    prebaked flaky, 151
    sweetened enriched, 151
    custard, 156
    Dutch apple, 152
    pumpkin, 156
    raspberry, 148
    shell for a two-crust pie, 151
    strawberry, 148
    tart, free-form, with fruit, 154
Pilaf, rice, 104
    with onions, raisins, and pine
        nuts, 104
Pin bones, removing, *44*
Pine nuts, pilaf with onions, raisins,
    and, 104
Pink tomato sauce, 27
Pizza, 172
    dough, 172–73
    shaping, *173*
Poaching, basic, xiv
Pork. *See also* Bacon
    basics of, 91
    chops
        with apples, 90
        with mustard, 90
        sautéed, 90
    cuts, *91*
    meatballs, 28
    in meat loaf, 100
    medallions of, sautéed, with
        lemon and parsley, 92
    roast, with garlic and rosemary, 93
Porterhouse steak, grilled, 80
Pot roast, 88–89
    basics of, 89
    vinegar-marinated, 89
Potato(es)
    baked, 130
    basics of, 130
    French fries, 133
    mashed, 132
    roasted root vegetables, 138
    salad, classic American, 6

sweet
    baked, 131
    basics of, 131
Poultry, 57–78
    about, 57
    chicken cutlets. *See* Chicken
        cutlets
    chicken, roast. *See* Roast chicken
    duck, roast, 78
    timing chart for roasting large
        birds, 73
    turkey, roast, 72–77
Pound cake, 165
Prebaked flaky pie crust, 151
Precooked grains, 107
Precooked vegetables in butter or
    oil, 118
Pressure-cooked beans, 110
Pressure cookers, basics of, x, 110
Prime rib
    boneless, 86
    for a big crowd, 86
    roast, 86
Pumpkin pie, 156
Puttanesca sauce, 27

Q
Quick and easy waffles, 190
Quick-braised carrots with butter,
    124
Quick coffee cake, 164
Quickest chicken stock, 17

R
Raisins, pilaf with onions, pine
    nuts, and, 104
Raspberry
    basics of, 149
    pie, 148
Real tartar sauce, 7
Red gazpacho, 18
Red snapper or other fillets in
    packages, 39
Reduction sauce, 62
    basics of, 63
Refrigerator (rolled) cookies, 160

Rib roast, carving, *87*
Rice
  basics of, 103
  long-grain, 102
    and beans, southern, 116
    chicken soup with, 16
  pilaf, 104
    black beans and, Spanish-style,
      115
  risotto, 105
  short- or medium-grain, 102
    fast-cooked, 103
Risotto, classic, 105
Roast beef, basics of, 87
Roast chicken
  basics of, 71
  carving, *71*
  parts with herbs and olive oil, 66
  simple, 70
  ways to flavor, 70
Roast duck, basic, 78
Roasted, broiled, or grilled
    asparagus, 120
Roasted root vegetables, 138
Roasting pans, about, viii
Roast leg of lamb, 98
  with garlic and coriander seeds, 98
Roast pork with garlic and
    rosemary, 93
Roast turkey
  breast, basic, on the bone, 76
  and gravy, without stuffing, 72–73
  with stuffing, 73
  timing chart for, 73
Rolled cookies, 160–61
Root vegetables, roasted, 138
Rosemary, roast pork with garlic
    and, 93
Round loaf, shaping, *170*

S

Sage, butter, and Parmesan, pasta
    with, 24
Salad(s), 1–9
  about, 1
  Caesar, 4

coleslaw, spicy, 8
  Greek, 2
  green, best and simplest, 2
  potato, classic American, 6
  tomato, mozzarella, and basil, 5
  vegetable, basics of, 5
Salmon
  basics of, 45
  fillets, pan-grilled, 44
    with sesame oil drizzle, 44
  steaks, grilled, 42
Sauce(s)
  Asian, 62
  béchamel, 31
  butter, mussels with, 52
  cranberry, 75
  garlic-parsley, broiled flatfish
    or other white fillets
    with, 37
  meat, pasta with, 29
  mushroom, 62
  Puttanesca, 27
  reduction, 62–63
  sesame or peanut, cold noodles
    with, 34
  soy, sautéed flatfish or other white
    fillets with, 38
  tartar, real, 7
  tomato. *See* Tomato sauce
Saucepans and pots, about, viii
Sauerbraten, 89
Sautéed apples, 144
Sautéed bananas, 144
Sautéed chicken cutlets, 60
Sautéed eggplant, 137
Sautéed flatfish or other white
    fillets, 38
Sautéed medallions of pork with
    lemon and parsley, 92
Sautéed mushrooms with garlic,
    126
Sautéed pork chops, 90
Sautéed summer squash or zucchini,
    135
Sautéing, basics of, xii
Sauté pans, about, vii

Savory muffins, 177
Sesame oil drizzle, pan-grilled
    salmon fillets with, 44
Sesame sauce, cold noodles
    with, 34
Shell, pie, for a two-crust pie,
    151
Short- or medium-grain rice, 102
Shortcakes, strawberry, 175
Shrimp
  basics of, 47
  cocktail, 46
  my way, 48
  preparing, *46*
  "scampi", 48
  spicy grilled or broiled, 49
  stir-fried noodles with, 33
Simmered, steamed, or microwaved
    Broccoli, 122
Simmering, basic, xiv
Simple Greek salad, 2
Simple precooked grains, 106
Simple roast chicken, 70
Skewered lamb chunks, grilled, 96
Skillets, about, vii
Soup(s), 1, 10–18. *See also* Stew
  about, 1
  beef and vegetable, 10
  black bean, 15
  chicken
    additions to, 16
    with rice or noodles, 16
    stock, 17
    thick, with rice or noodles, 16
  cream of broccoli, 12
  gazpacho, red, 18
  minestrone, 10
  stock, chicken, 17
  vegetable, additions to, 11
  white bean, 14
Southern beans and rice, 116
Soy marinade, chicken cutlets
    in, 58
Soy sauce, sautéed flatfish or other
    white fillets with, 38
Spaghetti and meatballs, 28

Spice muffins, 177
Spicy coleslaw, 8
Spicy grilled or broiled shrimp, 49
Spinach
    basics of, 135
    boiled, steamed, or microwaved, 134
    creamed, 134
    simply cooked, toppings for, 134
Squash, summer
    basics of, 135
    sautéed, 135
Steak. *See* Beef; Fish steak
Steamed clams, 50
Steamed corn, 125
Steamed mussels, 52
Steaming, basic, xiv
Stew, beef, classic, 82
Stewing, basic, xiii
Stir-fried chicken. *See* Chicken
Stir-fried chinese noodles with vegetables, 32
Stir-fried noodles with meat or shrimp, 33
Stir-fried noodles with stir-fried vegetables, 33
Stir-frying, basics of, xii–xiii
Stock, chicken, quickest, 17
Strawberry (-ies)
    basics of, 149
    pie, 148
    shortcakes, 175
Stuffing
    bread, my favorite, 75
    roast turkey and gravy without, 72–73
    roast turkey with, 73
Summer fruit compote, 145
Summer squash. *See* Squash
Sweetened enriched pie crust, 151
Swordfish steaks, grilled, 42
    herb-rubbed, 42

T
Tart(s)
    basics of, 155
    with fruit, free-form, 154
Tartar sauce, real, 7
T-bone steak, 80
Techniques, basic, about, x–xiv
Teriyaki, chicken, 58
Thick chicken soup, 16
Timing chart for roasting turkey and other large birds, 73
Tomato(es)
    chicken cutlets, with basil and, 58
    mozzarella, and basil salad, 5
    preparing, *26*
    sauce
        easy, 27
        fresh, and Parmesan, linguine with, 26
        with herbs, 27
        pink, 27
Traditional apple pie (double crust), 152
Traditional cranberry sauce, 75
Tuna steaks, grilled, 42
    herb-rubbed, 42
Turkey
    breast
        boneless, herb-roasted, 77
        roast, basic, on the bone, 76
    carving, *74*
    roast, 72–73, 76. *See* Roast turkey
    timing chart for roasting, 73

U
Utensils, ix

V
Vanilla butter cream frosting, 168
Veal. *See* Meat loaf; Spaghetti and meatballs
Vegetable(s), 117–38. *See also* *specific types of vegetables*
    about, 117

and beef soup, 10
basics of buying, 119
frittata, 186
making julienne cuts, *119*
precooked, in butter or oil, 118
root, roasted, 138
soups, additions to, 11
stir-fried, stir-fried noodles with, 33
Vegetarian baked beans, 114
Very firm cranberry sauce or cranberry jelly, 75
Vinaigrette, 3
    basics of, 3
Vinegar-marinated pot roast (sauerbraten), 89

W
Waffles
    basics of, 191
    quick and easy, 190
    variations for, 190
Weekday morning scrambled eggs, 180
Western omelet, 185
White beans. *See* Beans
Wine
    red, pears poached in, 142
    white, broiled cod or other thick white fillets with herbs and, 41

Y
Yeast bread
    basics of, 171
    fastest, 170
Yogurt or buttermilk biscuits, 174

Z
Zucchini
    basics of, 135
    red snapper or other fillets in packages with carrots and, 39
    sautéed, 135

Doneness Temperatures

Use an instant-read thermometer for the best possible accuracy; always measure with the probe in the thickest part of the meat, not touching any bone (ideally, measure in more than one place). When you gain experience in cooking, you'll be able to judge doneness by look and feel.

Beef
125°F = Rare
130–135°F = Medium-rare
135–140°F = Medium
140–150°F = Medium-well
155°F + = Well-done

Pork
137°F = Temperature at which trichinosis
   is killed
150°F = slightly pink but moist
160°F = Well-done (and probably dry)

Chicken
160°F = Breast is done
165°F = Thigh is done

Lamb
125°F = Very rare
130°F = Rare
135°F = Medium-rare
140°F = Medium
150°F = Medium-well
160°F + = Well-done

USDA–Recommended Internal Temperatures

The recommended internal temperatures given in this book for meats and poultry are based on producing the best-tasting food, and are in line with traditional levels of doneness. The United States Department of Agriculture (USDA), however, generally recommends higher temperatures, which reduces the potential danger of contracting illness caused by bacteria.

Beef, Veal, and Lamb
Ground meat (hamburger, etc.) 160°F

Roasts, Steaks, and Chops
145°F = Medium-rare
160°F = Medium
170°F = Well-done

Pork (all cuts including ground)
160°F = Medium
170°F = Well-done

Poultry
Ground chicken and turkey: 165°F
Whole chicken and turkey: 180°F
Stuffing: 165°F
Poultry Breasts: 170°F
Poultry Thighs: Cook until juices run clear
Egg Dishes: 160°F